Empathy Fatigue

Dr. Mark A. Stebnicki is a professor and director of the graduate program in rehabilitation counseling at East Carolina University. He holds a doctoral degree in rehabilitation counseling and is a licensed professional counselor (LPC) in North Carolina. He has national certifications as a certified rehabilitation counselor (CRC) and certified case manager (CCM); he is also certified by the Washington, DC-based crisis response team, the National Organization for Victim Assistance (NOVA). Dr. Stebnicki is also a Level III Reiki Master practitioner and has training in shamanism. He has over 18 years experience working with the psychosocial and mental health needs of adolescents and adults with acquired chronic health conditions.

Dr. Stebnicki is an active teacher, researcher, and practitioner who has written over 23 articles in peer-reviewed journals, has written two other books, and has presented regionally, state-wide, and nationally at well over 60 seminars, workshops, and conferences on topics that range from empathy fatigue, youth violence, and traumatic stress to the psychosocial aspects of adults with chronic illnesses and disabilities.

He served on the crisis response team for the Westside Middle School shootings in Jonesboro, AR (March 24, 1998), and has done many stress debriefings with private companies, schools, and government employees after incidents of workplace violence, hurricanes, tornadoes, and floods. He consulted with former President Bill Clinton's staff on addressing the students of Columbine High School after their critical incident (April 20, 1999). His youth violence program, the Identification, Early Intervention, Prevention, and Preparation (IEPP) Program, was awarded national recognition by the American Counseling Association (ACA) Foundation (2001) for its vision and excellence in the area of youth violence prevention.

Empathy Fatigue

Healing the Mind, Body, and Spirit of Professional Counselors

MARK A. STEBNICKI, PhD, LPC, CRC, CCM

SPRINGER PUBLISHING COMPANY

NEW YORK

Springer Publishing Company, LLC
11 West 42nd Street
New York, NY 10036
www.springerpub.com

Acquisitions Editor: Philip Laughlin
Production Editor: Julia Rosen
Cover design: Joanne E. Honigman
Composition: Apex Publishing, LLC

08 09 10 11/ 5 4 3 2 1

Library of Congress Cataloging-in-Publication Data

Stebnicki, Mark A.
   Empathy fatigue : healing the mind, body, and spirit of professional counselors / Mark A. Stebnicki.
       p. cm.
   Includes bibliographical references and index.
   ISBN 978–0–8261–1544-7 (alk. paper)
   1. Counselors—Job stress.   2. Counselors—Mental health.
3. Empathy.   I. Title.
   BF636.64.S74 2008
   158'.3—dc22
                                    2008009539

Printed in the United States of America by Bang Printing.

Contents

Introduction

To say that we are in the midst of a paradigm shift in the counseling and allied helping professions is clearly an understatement when it comes to dealing with the extraordinarily stressful and traumatic events that have taken place globally. Catastrophic events have accelerated worldwide within the last seven years. In America, the horrific terrorist attacks of Tuesday, September 11, 2001, and Hurricane Katrina, which took place on August 29, 2005, left emotional, physical, spiritual, and environmental scars upon our minds, bodies, and souls. The desolation left in the aftermath has created a sort of historical trauma among Westerners that seems to have prompted a consciousness shift within the counseling field and other helping professions. Fires, floods, drought, and school shootings require our complete attention to the survivors of such events. As professionals, we are constantly in a state of disaster preparedness and mental health disaster response. As a consequence, we are emotionally, socially, physically, spiritually, and vocationally exhausted. I would propose that many of us are experiencing "empathy fatigue."

Our empathy fatigue has been extended on a global basis. This is evidenced by the cataclysmic event that took place on December 26, 2004, when a tsunami and an earthquake, registering 9.0 off the west coast of Northern Sumatra, injured or claimed the lives of millions of people. How easily we forget about this distressing event affecting countries such as Sri Lanka, India, Indonesia, Malaysia, Thailand, and many others. Where did all the disaster volunteers, angels, and earthly saints that descended upon these countries go? Did they have to retreat to their homes for the sake of their own emotional, physical, and spiritual well-being? Who has taken their place? The ensuing wars in Afghanistan, Iraq, and the Middle East are also constant reminders of how fragile our physical safety, mental health, and overall well-being can be. For many, planet earth does not appear to be a safe place to live in, because of the multitude of critical events.

These scenarios of enormous loss of human life, psychological grief, physical pain, and spiritual suffering are replayed on the nightly news, by quick-release television and Hollywood-style movies, in the print media, and over the Internet. The world has become much smaller through the use of satellite television, video cellular phones, and Internet technology. The disaster scenarios that we view on the global media stage add another dimension of reality. In real time, we can watch tragedies unfold in our own backyard and as they happen globally.

Such extraordinarily stressful and traumatic events affect a wide range of members of the population, who require specialists able to work with children and adolescents, college students, middle-aged and older adults, and others who have been victimized in their past. Interestingly, I have found that clients or consumers of outpatient mental health services do not seem to be as severely affected on a daily basis by world events. This may be because they are already consumed by their internal and external environment of intense personal distress.

New clients and consumers of mental health, rehabilitation, and allied health services, who are secondary survivors of extraordinary stressful and traumatic events, seem to be emerging. These include but are not limited to spouses, children, and family members that have a loved one serving in Iraq and Afghanistan; soldiers who have come home injured; and a new population of survivors of sexual abuse perpetrated by online predators. The fact that some of our political and church leaders, who purportedly are defined by their high moral character and ethical behavior, are among the perpetrators is extremely confusing to children and difficult to discuss with them. Is there anyone we can trust?

Despite the fact that most Americans are far from the epicenter of such critical incidents, many are affected at some level of consciousness. This new, intense level of anxiety and traumatic stress affects those who work in school systems, government social services, hospitals and medical centers, faith-based programs, volunteer and professional rescue organizations, and a host of other organizations and institutions. We seem to be in a constant state of disaster preparedness, emergency response, and disaster relief.

So how do we come out of the darkness and into the light to facilitate emotional, social, physical, psychological, spiritual, and occupational healing strategies that can heal our soul wound experience? The existential question, *Why do bad things happen to good people?* requires a skilled professional who can process and facilitate the meaning of such events and bring people's lives back into balance.

Counselors and other helping professionals are profoundly affected by the individuals, groups, families, and systems they serve. Many have been close to the epicenter of extraordinarily stressful and traumatic events themselves. Understanding this new form of professional fatigue is essential, because for some professionals, the occupation itself can be mentally, physically, and spiritually debilitating. The epidemiological significance of empathy fatigue is far-reaching for professional helpers, organizations, institutions, and the individual clients/consumers we serve.

While medical professionals, police officers, and rescue workers all prepare for physical rescue in the multitude of disaster scenarios, counselors and other mental health professionals are called on to provide mental health rescue. Today, many counselors and other human service professionals are required to have training in the various models of crisis intervention. These include but are not limited to workers associated with the Disaster Mental Health response of the American Red Cross (ARC), critical incident stress debriefing (CISD), critical incident stress management (CISM), the National Organization for Victims' Assistance (NOVA) Group Crisis response, and acute traumatic stress management (ATSM). Crisis response teams are formed by various governmental agencies such as Homeland Security and Environmental Protection, computer and internet security specialists, the commercial airline industry, public school and higher education personnel, private companies, faith-based and charitable organizations, and various other groups and organizations.

The literature in counseling and psychology suggests that many mental health practitioners and other helping professionals are affected by the same persistent or transient physical, mental, and psychological symptoms as their clients; many clients have been at or near the epicenter of critical incidents. We need to be open to the idea that preparing our minds, bodies, and spirits is of paramount importance to meet the intense challenges of the 21st century. This should be a principal concern for practitioners, counselor educators, clinical supervisors, and those in the allied helping professions.

This book was inspired by my own experience of empathy fatigue, an expression I coined around 1998. During March 1998, I worked and lived in Jonesboro, AR, and served on the crisis response team for the Westside Middle School shootings, where four students and one teacher were killed and 15 others were injured by 11- and 13-year-old shooters. Since this time I have been trained in various crisis response models and have provided stress debriefings and group crisis response to persons employed in state and county government, private companies, day care centers and schools, and to persons in the media, survivors of brutal crimes, and individuals who have been at the epicenter of hurricanes, floods, and tornadoes.

As a counselor educator, researcher, and practitioner I have found that there appears to be an emotional, social, psychological, mental, physical, spiritual, and vocational cost to providing counseling and stress debriefings to individuals who have been at the epicenter of some of the most horrific human-made and natural catastrophic events imaginable. I have observed empathy fatigue in my colleagues for many years. These professionals treat persons with substance abuse, sexual and physical abuse, and mood, anxiety, and stress-related disorders. Some work in career and vocational settings. Others are nurses, allied health professionals, school teachers, and case managers who work with children and adults with mental and physical disabilities. Very few of these individuals deal with mental health crises or disaster response, yet they have acquired what I refer to as acute and/or chronic empathy fatigue. They follow their chosen careers in person-centered environments with an aura of compassion and a good heart. Basically, they are skilled helpers who are empathetic and are required to facilitate attachments with others. As a consequence, empathy fatigue appears to be a natural artifact of working in "high touch" or person-centered environments.

There is a growing interest in psychology, counseling, and related fields in preventing the professional fatigue syndromes that go by various terms, such as empathy or compassion fatigue, burnout, and counselor impairment. These syndromes will be described throughout this book. In order to facilitate the reader's understanding of these concepts, Part I of *Empathy Fatigue* provides the reader with a unique in-depth analysis of the construct of empathy fatigue and describes this phenomenon from a mind, body, and spiritual perspective. Part I also discusses the phenomenon of working close to the epicenter of critical incidents and how it impacts the overall wellness of both younger and older helping professionals. The research is clear that cumulative occupational or job stress, even outside the psychology and counseling professions, can lead to higher levels of impaired functioning, including depression, anxiety, and substance abuse disorders. Accordingly, it is important, in order to lessen empathy fatigue, that we make ordinary sense out of the non-ordinary stressful and traumatic events that have taken place in our clients' lives.

Part II of *Empathy Fatigue* calls for an integral approach to healing the professional's empathy fatigue. Fundamental to the emotional, physical, and spiritual well-being of preprofessional and professional counselors are self-care strategies that promote resiliency for the prevention of empathy fatigue. Minimizing or ignoring the personal negative countertransference associated with extraordinary and traumatic stressors has a physical, emotional, spiritual, and psychological cost.

Part III of *Empathy Fatigue* offers guidelines for counselor educators and clinical supervisors, enabling them to identify the emotional, physical, and mental exhaustion that occurs early on in the chosen career. Clinical supervision is critical because of the cumulative and long-term nature of the stress and anxiety that impact the client-counselor relationship and may result in an empathy fatigue reaction. The collective wisdom of indigenous cultures throughout the world has much to offer to 21st-century healers. Thus, this section presents the foundational Eastern and Western philosophies of healing the wounded soul. This section also offers guidelines and activities for an integral approach to paying attention to the mind, body, and spirit while working in "high touch" person-centered environments.

As is described throughout this book, empathy fatigue results from a state of mental, emotional, social, physical, spiritual, and occupational exhaustion that occurs as counselors' own wounds are continually revisited by their clients' life stories of chronic illness, disability, trauma, grief, loss, and extraordinarily stressful events. This type of "fatigue reaction" and its consequences are recognized as "counselor impairment" by the American Counseling Association's Taskforce on Counselor Wellness and Impairment. The American Psychological Association (APA) has also been proactive in self-care practices for "impaired psychologists," and it established a task force in 1986 to address such issues. The American Medical Association (AMA) recognizes a similar condition called "physician impairment," defined basically as a physical, mental, and behavioral disorder that hinders the physician's ability to safely treat patients. The nursing profession for years has called this compassion fatigue. Regardless of the term used, there appears to be a mind, body, and spiritual cost to both the individual and the profession.

The unique approach communicated throughout *Empathy Fatigue* is the emphasis on promoting self-care approaches for the wounded healer. Overall, this book honors the collective wisdom of indigenous cultural practices and philosophical beliefs with regard to healing the healer's mind, body, and spirit.

PART I

1

A Theoretical Framework for Understanding Empathy Fatigue: Analyzing the Critical Pathways

In traditional Native American teaching, it is said that each time you heal someone you give away a piece of yourself until at some point, you will require healing. The journey to become an Indian doctor, or medicine man/woman, requires an understanding that the healer at some point in time will become wounded and require healing (Tafoya & Kouris, 2003). As in the Native American culture, many professional counselors in the West also encounter a wounded healer type of experience. I refer to this phenomenon as empathy fatigue. It results from a state of psychological, emotional, mental, physical, spiritual, and occupational exhaustion that occurs as the counselors' own wounds are continually revisited by their clients' life stories of chronic illness, disability, trauma, grief, and loss (Stebnicki, 1999, 2000, 2001, 2007a). Similar observations and measurements of professional impairment and fatigue have been noted in the nursing, psychology, counseling, and mental health literature (e.g., as compassion fatigue, secondary traumatic stress, burnout, vicarious traumatization). For example, compassion fatigue, first introduced to the nursing literature by Joinson (1992) and then expanded by Figley (1995), Stamm (1995), and others in psychology, suggests that therapists who deal with survivors of extraordinarily stressful and traumatic events are more prone to a compassion or secondary stress type of reaction as a result of feeling compassion and empathy toward others' pain and suffering. Consequently,

3

"vicarious traumatization" (McCann & Pearlman, 1989) is experienced by therapists when they become deeply emotionally involved in their client's traumatic stories.

IMPAIRED PROFESSIONALS: A CONCERN FOR PERSON-CENTERED DISCIPLINES

Professional associations in the person-centered professions have recently expressed a concern to identify and prevent professional fatigue reactions. This is because of the significant negative impact of working with professionals who have acute and chronic mental and physical health conditions that may compromise or even pose harm to the clients/consumers receiving services. These professional fatigue reactions and their consequences have been recognized as "counselor impairment" by the American Counseling Association's Taskforce on Counselor Wellness and Impairment (American Counseling Association [ACA], 2003). The American Medical Association (American Medical Association [AMA], 2004) recognizes a similar condition, termed "physician impairment" and defined basically as a physical, mental, and behavioral disorder that hinders the physician's ability to safely treat patients. The American Psychological Association (APA) is also concerned about impaired psychologists and has created the Advisory Committee on Colleague Assistance (ACCA) to address such issues (American Psychological Association [APA], 2007).

The nursing profession is quite familiar with professional impairment and fatigue syndromes, given the intense level of psychological and physical health care that its members provide. The nursing literature has referred to this experience as "compassion fatigue." In fact, the American Nurses Association (ANA, 2007) has addressed this concern in its code of ethics and has provided resources designed to reduce the effects of professional fatigue syndromes, much as many other professional associations have done. Regardless of the definition used in the counseling, psychology, and medical fields, the mental, emotional, social, physical, spiritual, and occupational cost of professional fatigue syndromes is enormous to the profession and to consumers of services.

The Dalai Lama (1999) has observed that those in the caring professions, such as counselors, do in fact experience a fatigue reaction. His Holiness proposes that counselors are sometimes exhausted by their duties because of constant exposure to the suffering of others, which can induce feelings of helplessness and despair. During a presentation, the Dalai Lama (see Berger, 2006) stated that "empathy is really what we are describing when we talk about compassion fatigue and... it is the simple compassion a person experiences when they want to see another person free from suffering" (p. 1).

Counseling is a "high touch profession" (Naisbitt, 1984), in which there are multiple potential hazards that can exacerbate one's personal and professional difficulties (Skovholt, Grier, & Hanson, 2001). Members of the high touch community of professionals should be aware that "constant empathy, interpersonal sensitivity, and one-way caring... can take tremendous effort, and the relationship with the client, while perhaps collaborative, is not reciprocal" (Skovholt et al., 2001, p. 170). Thus, life for professional counselors can be extremely difficult at times because they must have a high level of critical awareness of their client's thoughts, feelings, and experiences. Additionally, evaluating client success is sometimes a problematic process because outcomes are not immediately apparent. Such evaluation involves a complex interplay in the client-counselor working relationship. Thus, it is incumbent upon the professional to develop realistic expectations of client success and balance clients' psychological, social, emotional, physical, spiritual, and occupational well-being against the professional's ability to remain in his or her chosen profession.

EMPATHY FATIGUE: A CONSEQUENCE OF MULTIPLE CLIENT STORIES

Clearly, counselor empathy is essential within the healing process. It sometimes requires the professional helper to respond to and even experience vicariously the client's pain and suffering. However, after attending, listening, and responding to multiple client stories with intense emotional themes, professional helpers may experience an empathy fatigue reaction. Despite the professional helper's best efforts to reduce the level of intensity of the client's emotional pain and suffering, an empathy fatigue experience may emerge. It may be experienced by many well-intentioned helping professionals as an ambiguous sense of loss, grief, or stress, and helpers may react to their own intense level of emotions. Accordingly, when clients express feelings of pain, confusion, shock, trauma, distress, or other significant emotions, these can sometimes be transferred or projected onto the professional helpers' psyches. For counselors, having an understanding and awareness of their own empathy fatigue buttons can help them gain closure with regard to their own, maybe confusing, emotions. From a content analysis of well over 100 studies on professional counselor impairments such as burnout and compassion fatigue (Jones, 2007), the following conclusions were reached concerning the characteristics of professionals who are affected by counselor fatigue syndromes:

- Professional counselors who primarily engage in crisis counseling for a living tend to burn out at much higher levels than those that have just a general mental health caseload (involving, e.g., anxiety and mood disorders, substance abuse, marriage counseling).
- Race, gender, and professional certification and licensure (e.g., LPC, CRC, Licensed Clinical Social Worker [LCSW]) are not correlated with level of burnout. Most professional helpers are affected by professional fatigue syndromes regardless of the counseling specialty.
- Higher client/consumer satisfaction is positively correlated with lower counselor burnout. Counselors who have established a stronger rapport with their clients/consumers also have a stronger working alliance.
- When counselors reported higher levels of ego development and a sense of personal accomplishment, lower levels of burnout were noted.
- Counselor supervision was found to be a key element in counselor satisfaction and lower levels of professional impairment. In other words, when counselors reported that they received good supervision and had a positive supervision experience, they felt supported and their level of burnout was significantly less than for those that did not receive supervision or feel supported in their work environment.

KEY CONCEPTUAL AND THEORETICAL TENETS OF EMPATHY FATIGUE

There is a constellation of professional fatigue reactions. The labels that are given to the various fatigue syndromes (e.g., burnout, compassion fatigue, secondary traumatic stress, vicarious traumatization) vary depending upon the researcher and the discipline. Despite the perceived theoretical and conceptual differences that will be described later, those who approach their work empathically with their client/consumer appear to be profoundly affected by their client's story of loss, grief, daily stress, anxiety, depression, and traumatic stress. This should be of paramount concern for professional counselors, counselor educators, and supervisors so that they may identify and prevent empathy fatigue reactions. Such a life's work requires that we prepare our mind, body, and spirit to grow and develop in ways that help us to become more resilient in working with individuals at intense levels of interpersonal functioning.

Most counselors trained in counselor education programs in the West have been trained in the foundational person-centered skills of empathy as a therapeutic strategy to communicate understanding and respect and establish client rapport, so that they may advance toward a therapeutic working alliance and use more complex counseling theories and strategies. Thus, person-centered approaches, such as client-focused empathy, as well as many other counseling theories and strategies, have typically been integrated into the foundational training of counselors. Despite the fact that most professional counselors describe their philosophy, theory, and approach to counseling as eclectic, the nature of the counseling relationship requires a below-the-surface level of intense and compassionate listening. This requires the counselor to be deeply empathically involved with clients' critical life stories.

Depending on their developmental level of experience and other personality attributes, counselors may be at low, moderate, or high risk for empathy fatigue. This of course is related to multiple characteristics and variables relating to the individual. Despite the varied characteristics and professional identities of counselors, a majority of individuals chose their profession because of its humanistic nature. Thus, many counselors may have a natural intuitive ability to be compassionate and empathic. As a result of the cumulative effects of empathic and compassionate attending, listening, and responding, counselors many times will experience parallel emotions that are almost as deep as their clients' intense feelings of loss, grief, pain, trauma, or suffering. These feelings can be triggered by a counselor's perception of stress and they range along a continuum of empathic stress from minimal to very intense levels.

The client's disclosure of intense personal emotions can result in some degree of countertransference or secondary traumatic stress (STS) for the counselor (see Figley, 1995). However, this may or may not be experienced as a rapid onset or acute reaction of empathy fatigue, because individuals do not turn on their physiological and emotional stress responses in exactly the same manner. It is suspected that professional helpers who do not engage in crisis response or facilitate stress debriefing groups may also experience empathy fatigue due to both the cumulative and the intense nature of their work setting, as well as the types of clients, consumers, or patients they serve.

Despite the subjective self-reporting nature of empathy fatigue and the painstaking, ongoing efforts required in scale development to measure such fatigue syndromes, at the end of the counselor's day, the physical, emotional, psychological, and spiritual costs of working with clients/consumers at intense interpersonal levels is quite evident to self and others. At a minimum, the professional helper's stress level has increased significantly. This should be a major concern for the counseling profession, because it is well documented by stress researchers that the physiological and psychological costs of acute and cumulative stress can have adverse consequences on the mind, body, and spirit of the individual. Accordingly, the key conceptual and theoretical tenets of empathy fatigue (EF) are as follows:

- EF is viewed as an impairment that can occur developmentally early in one's professional career due to an interaction of variables that include but are not limited to (a) personality traits; (b) general coping resources; (c) counselor age and developmental factors; (d) opportunities to build resiliency; (e) organizational and other environmental supports; and (f) the interrelationship between the individual's mind, body, and spiritual development.
- EF many times goes unrecognized or ignored by the individual and the individual's professional environment. This is because the EF reaction for many counselors is thought to be (a) an unconscious process, (b) an expected or anticipated emotion after dealing with clients who have extraordinary stressful and traumatic issues, and (c) a professional obligation of the therapist. Consequently, many counselors do not verbally communicate their experience of empathy fatigue to their colleagues. Doing so may signal that they are impaired professionals. This could potentially jeopardize their standing in their professional setting.
- Counselors who are significantly impaired are not practicing as competent and ethical professionals. Impaired professionals may not be providing services in the best interests of their clients/consumers. The inability to control or cope with personal stress, adversity, psychological dysfunction, and/or excessive maladaptive

emotional reactions interferes with the client/consumer's welfare. Accordingly, the various codes of ethics in counseling and psychology address specific ethical standards related to counselor impairment. These standards have the explicit intention of consumer protection. However, there is much work to be done to clearly define "counselor impairment." Outside of the obvious impairments (e.g., the counselor has a drug or alcohol relapse or a mental health disorder resurfaces), impaired counselor behaviors may be open to interpretation based on the counseling setting, client population, and many other factors. The questions become (a) how do we measure counselor impairment? and (b) at what point in the therapeutic relationship does the counselor become impaired or constitute a risk to the client/consumers? Because counselor impairment syndromes many times may be invisible and range on a continuum from "no impairment" to "significantly impaired," there appears to be some ambiguity with regard to the construct of compassion or empathy fatigue and counselor burnout. Despite the fact that there are real ethical dilemmas in clinical settings, the disciplines of counseling and psychology have struggled to address issues related to impaired professionals.

■ EF has both acute onset and cumulative emotional, physical, and spiritual reactions that are unique to each individual. Accordingly, an EF reaction does not follow a predictable linear path from healthy to unhealthy functioning. Rather, there are degrees of professional impairment and competency, and evaluating such behaviors can be problematic. Also EF does not exclusively follow the pattern of job burnout or countertransference. There are multiple intervening variables that are unaccounted for. Many professionals are affected by EF and they tend to move back and forth along a continuum of feeling from "affected very little" to "affected significantly" by this experience.

■ The unhealthy symptoms and unethical behaviors of counselors experiencing EF can often be recognized by others in the professional environment; whereas the professionals themselves may not recognize the acute or cumulative symptoms. Eventually, professionals experience daily reminders that their minds, bodies, and spirits are out of balance and that their mental health and well-being has been compromised. Accordingly, different forms of supervision (i.e., group, individual, peer) are critical to the counselor's mental, physical, and spiritual well-being. Thus, clinical supervision can serve impaired professionals in a supportive and facilitative manner, as opposed to a punitive role. A fully functioning professional is required to facilitate competent and ethical therapeutic interactions.

■ It is not necessarily the nature of the client's stress, trauma, loss, or grief issues that creates a sense of EF among professional counselors. Rather, it is the counselor's perception of a particular client and critical incident that determines the response. This depends on multiple interacting variables. Thus, counselors have their own emotional (empathy fatigue) buttons that can trigger this experience.

CRITICAL PATHWAYS TO EMPATHY FATIGUE

Based on a comprehensive review of material on professional fatigue syndromes and counselor impairment, the following analysis of critical pathways is provided to the reader. Accordingly, in analyzing the critical pathways that result in the phenomenon of empathy fatigue, these are the present author's contentions:

1   Most counselors trained in counselor education programs in the West have acquired the foundational person-centered skills of empathy to establish client rapport and develop a therapeutic working alliance. Those professionals that facilitate therapy with a high level of empathy are more significantly affected by EF.

2   Despite the fact that most professional counselors describe their philosophy, theory, and approach as eclectic, the nature of the counseling relationship requires a below-the-surface person-centered level of intense and compassionate listening, requiring counselors to be deeply empathically involved with their clients' critical life stories.

3   As a result of empathic and compassionate relationships, counselors many times will have parallel emotions that are nearly as intense as their clients' feelings of loss, grief, pain, trauma, or suffering, and these feelings range along a continuum from "affected very little" to "affected significantly."

4   Depending on their developmental level of experience, work setting, and empathic states and traits, counselors may be at low, moderate, or high risk of empathy fatigue.

5   Clients' intense emotional issues have acute, chronic, and delayed onsets for counselors, resulting in a fatigue reaction of the professional's mind, body, and spirit.

6   The counselor's experience of empathy fatigue is very similar to a stress response, which is a complex, cumulative interaction of the person's mind, body, spirit, and environment. The EF response may or may not be related to serving clients who have been through extraordinarily stressful and traumatic events. The significantly impaired phase of EF, which may last weeks, months, or years, results in a total professional burnout in which the individual is emotionally, psychologically, physically, spiritually, and occupationally depleted. As a result of this experience of depletion, the professional will actively avoid exposure to the aversive triggers of EF.

SUMMARY OF CRITICAL PATHWAYS

Overall, it is hypothesized that the cumulative effects of multiple client sessions throughout the week may lead to a deterioration of the counselor's resiliency or coping abilities for dealing with client caseloads that range along a continuum from "daily hassles" and stress to extraordinarily stressful and traumatic issues. Although it is recognized that the client's traumatic story can negatively impact counselor emotions immediately, the acute nature of extraordinarily stressful and traumatic events many times turns into a chronic and persistent mental and physical health condition for the client. Accordingly, the professional who is a highly compassionate individual and facilitates therapeutic interactions in a highly empathic manner is at high risk for experiencing the parallel mental, physical, and spiritual exhaustion related to the client's experiences.

According to this hypothesis, professional counselors who experience empathy fatigue appear to have a diminished capacity to listen and respond empathically to their client's stories, which may or may not contain various themes of acute or traumatic stress. There appear to be multiple variables interacting with the counselor's experience of empathy fatigue. For example, some professionals find it difficult to work with children and adolescents with life-threatening chronic illnesses and disabilities. Conversely, other counselors may thrive in such therapeutic interactions within the pediatric rehabilitation setting.

In light of these key conceptual tenets, professional helpers who experience empathy fatigue are at risk for acquiring feelings of stress, grief, loss, detachment, anxiety, and/or depression, which culminate in professional burnout. They often feel that their therapeutic interactions with a client have very little meaning and purpose in their client's overall life. Thus, in summary:

- The cumulative effects of multiple client/consumer sessions throughout the week may lead to a deterioration of the counselor's resiliency or coping abilities.
- Empathy fatigue is a highly individualized process because not all counselors have the same caseloads, work in the same settings, or respond to work-related stress in the same manner.
- Empathy fatigue has both acute and delayed onset reactions that range along a continuum from dealing with clients/consumers who report daily hassles and stress to dealing with those who have experienced extraordinarily stressful and traumatic events.
- Counselors are at the epicenter of their client/consumer stories, they are captive to the client/consumer's toxic emotions, negative vibrations, disharmony, and blocked flows of energy, which occur moment-to-moment within the sessions.
- Counselors are bound ethically to act in beneficent ways: (a) to assist their clients/consumers to reach optimal levels of functioning; (b) to be present throughout the session and respond empathically; (c) when appropriate, to challenge their client/consumer's pattern of dysfunctional thinking, feeling, and behaving; and (d) to act in many other intentional ways to cultivate a holistic plan of optimal functioning.
- The communication (verbal and nonverbal) that is exchanged between clients and counselors during therapeutic interactions becomes integrated through the counselor's thoughts and emotions, which become associated with a physiological reaction. Consequently, some specific or universal meaning is construed regarding the counselor's felt sense of self and what the counselor is experiencing during client interactions. Bringing meaning to this relationship may be an existential or spiritual pursuit for some counselors. Accordingly, clinical supervision early in one's career and ongoing peer supervision are critical for maintaining personal growth, for development as a counselor, and for the protection of clients/consumers from impaired professionals.

CONCLUDING REMARKS

As professional counselors engage in therapeutic interactions, this may predispose them to an empathy fatigue reaction that ranges along a continuum from low or moderate to high. There are also multiple other risk factors, as identified in Stebnicki's (2000) Empathy Fatigue Risk-Factor Functional Assessment, which will be discussed in chapter 10 in part III. Multiple client stories can result in the depletion of the professional counselor's empathic energies, resulting in empathy fatigue.

2

Comparing and Contrasting Professional Fatigue Syndromes

Understanding the epidemiology of the helping professions' new anxiety and traumatic stress-related condition requires a shift in thinking about professional fatigue syndromes in general. First, we should be open to the idea that such fatigue conditions do in fact exist among different helping professionals. Since counselors may experience some type of professional fatigue or counselor impairment, they may distance themselves from friends, family, and colleagues. At times, counselors may feel that they have experienced something more than just a "bad day at the office" and that no one can possibly understand the extraordinary stress and secondary trauma they have been exposed to. Accordingly, I make some important distinctions between empathy fatigue (EF) and other fatigue syndromes in a revision of my previous position on the topic (see Stebnicki, 2000, 2007a). I theorize as follows:

1   EF, as opposed to other fatigue syndromes (e.g., compassion fatigue, burnout, vicarious traumatization) is experienced by professional counselors who primarily use person-centered and empathy-focused interactions to build rapport with their clients so they can achieve a therapeutic working alliance.
2   EF has acute, cumulative, and delayed onset reactions that are associated with client stories that may or may not be trauma

15

related. Thus, EF results from the cumulative effects of multiple client sessions that contain themes ranging from daily hassles, stress, anxiety, depression, and addictions to other unhealthy and negative emotions.

3 The cumulative affects of multiple client sessions throughout the week may lead to a deterioration of the counselor's resiliency or coping abilities for dealing with client caseloads that range along a continuum from daily hassles and stress to extraordinarily stressful and traumatic issues.

4 The professional counselor who facilitates therapy using higher levels of empathy (as measured by valid and reliable empathy scales) will be more affected by empathy fatigue than counselors who exhibit lower levels of empathic concern.

Overall, empathy fatigue results from a state of psychological, emotional, mental, physical, spiritual, and occupational exhaustion that occurs as counselors' own wounds are continually revisited by their client's life stories of chronic illness, disability, trauma, grief, and loss.

The labels that are given to the phenomenon of the professional fatigue syndromes (e.g., compassion fatigue, burnout, secondary traumatic stress, vicarious traumatization) vary depending upon the researcher and the discipline. Despite the conceptual differences, there appears to be one critical factor common to the different helping professions and disciplines. Primarily, the helping professionals who approach their work empathically with their client/consumer appear to be profoundly affected by their client's story of loss, grief, daily stress, anxiety, depression, and traumatic stress. Such a life's work requires that we prepare our mind, body, and spirit to grow and develop in ways that help us to become more resilient in working at such intense levels of interpersonal functioning.

Regardless of the constructs described by researchers with regard to the various fatigue syndromes, the constellation of professional fatigue experiences may be best described anecdotally by various counseling professionals. For professionals as for clients and consumers of mental health services, having a diagnostic category can create fear and anxiety or it can be liberating. There may be some solace in knowing that others in the counseling profession experience similar types of physical, emotional, and spiritual fatigue. At a minimum, it would be beneficial for professional counselors, counselor supervisors, and counselor educators to identify and prevent such professional fatigue syndromes. Thus, the following distinctions are made between empathy fatigue and other types of counselor impairment and fatigue syndromes.

COUNTERTRANSFERENCE

Countertransference was first discussed within psychoanalytic theory and has been discussed in the general counseling literature for many decades. Freud first described this concept in 1910 as a reflection of the counselor's unresolved internal conflicts that encompasses thoughts, feelings, and emotions that are related directly to specific client issues. Thus, to manage classical (Freudian) countertransference, the therapist must possess healthy emotions, while maintaining a balance of counselor empathy so as not to overidentify with the client's unhealthy emotions (Salston & Figley, 2003). Rogers (1961) suggests that as a result of "negative countertransference," counselors may exhibit reduced feelings of warmth, acceptance, respect, or positive regard for their clients. Emotionally intense relationships can easily blur the boundaries between the therapist's personal conflicts and those of the client, which may eventually hinder the client's capacity to change and work through her or his extraordinarily stressful and traumatic issues.

Professional helpers who work with persons who have life-threatening chronic illnesses and disabilities are especially vulnerable to the effects of countertransference. Rando (1984) discusses this concept as it relates to caregivers of persons that have bereavement or death and dying issues. She states that dying persons touch us personally in at least three ways. They may (a) make us painfully aware of our own losses, (b) contribute to our apprehension regarding our own potential and feared losses, or (c) arouse existential anxiety in our personal death awareness. Thus, professional helpers must take care of their unfinished business, which may relate to feelings of grief, separation by death, and loss.

A more contemporary perspective on countertransference as discussed in the traumatology literature delineates the unique attributes of therapists who often experience countertransference reactions from hearing clients' stories that contain extremely violent and graphic themes. Hence, classical countertransference takes on a new meaning today, especially in trauma counseling (Baranowsky, 2002; Danieli, 1996; Salston & Figley, 2003). In traumatic-specific-transference (TST; Wilson, 2001) and countertransference, there is an unconscious absorption of the trauma survivor's story by the professional counselor. As a result, the client's traumatic story involves a type of symbolic or parallel experience for the counselor. Since empathy is a helpful form of intense listening that should be facilitated by the trauma counselor (Jackson, 1992), the helper unconsciously makes him- or herself available to the absorption of the client's traumatic story (Figley, 2002b). In dealing with the challenging aspects of either classical or trauma-specific countertransference, the therapist must possess a healthy personality and character structure in order to manage the anxiety associated with clients who have issues of traumatic stress (Hayes, Gelso, Van Wagoner, & Diemer, 1991).

There is however a "shadow side" to frequent empathy with others. For instance, counselors who are unaware of their own unresolved personal issues tend to experience increased levels of countertransference, which may manifest as empathy fatigue reactions. Thus, an empathy fatigue reaction may be much like the experience of countertransference, where the counselor has intense feelings of being overwhelmed by listening to multiple client stories of loss, grief, stress, or trauma. Many therapists who communicate deep levels of empathy will occasionally experience an overidentification with their clients' issues (Gelso & Hayes, 1998). Consequently, after repeated client stories of stress and trauma, professionals may dissociate and distance themselves from their clients' overwhelming feelings of loss, grief, and helplessness.

Managing the natural response of countertransference requires more than just awareness, knowledge of the topic, or the acquisition of a specific set of skills to manage this unconscious process. It is suspected that this process is a function of a unique blend of personality characteristics and other counselor attributes (Hayes et al., 1991). It requires some deeper level of insight to integrate the client's traumatic experience into the counselor's own personal and existential understanding of life.

THE EXPERIENCE OF PROFESSIONAL BURNOUT

The literature on burnout is quite extensive. There are well over 1,100 articles and over 100 books on this topic in the Psychological Abstracts database alone (Figley, 1995). Burnout, a word first coined by Freudenberger (1974), has been described as a state of physical, emotional, and mental exhaustion in which individuals who are "burned out" have negative feelings about themselves, the other professionals with whom they work, and the clients whom they serve (Maslach, 1982, 2003; Pines & Aronson, 1988). The theoretical aspects of burnout were first discussed by psychologists in the occupational stress literature as it related to human service and mental health professionals. Burnout is considered a specific type of job stress that results from prolonged social and interpersonal interactions between the helper and the recipient (Maslach, 2003). Without the appropriate level of organizational support and internal hardiness, the human service professional is at risk for acquiring this unique type of psychological strain.

The hallmark of the burnout syndrome is a negative shift in the way professionals view people they serve (Maslach, 1982, 2003). As a consequence, professional helpers may respond to their clients with less compassion, genuineness, or unconditional positive regard. There tends to be a progressive loss of physical energy, a loss of the sense of idealism about their job, and a dearth of feelings of personal accomplishment. Pines and Aronson (1988) identified three basic characteristics within the role and function of the professional helper that may contribute to the experience of burnout: (a) the work they perform is emotionally draining, (b) they are characteristically sensitive to the people they serve, and (c) they typically facilitate a person-centered orientation.

One of the most widely used measures of workplace burnout is the Maslach Burnout Inventory (MBI; Maslach & Jackson, 1981, 1986). Jenkins and Baird (2002) assert that the MBI is the most widely accepted and best validated measure of burnout. The MBI is multidimensional and contains three subscales that have been identified during the scale development process. These three factors include emotional exhaustion (EE; feelings of being emotionally overextended), depersonalization (DP; an impersonal response style to clients), and reduced personal accomplishment (PA; the loss of feelings of competence and success resulting from job stress).

Maslach (2003) recently revisited some of her earlier theoretical constructs about the phenomenon of burnout. She found strong support for first assessing and measuring the situational sources of job-related stress and the interpersonal stressors or demands that are placed on the professional. Traditionally, researchers on burnout tended to overanalyze the personality characteristics and other attributes of the individual concerned. However, this may only be a small piece of the puzzle. Maslach (2003) suggests that when there has been no immediate change in the individual's work environment, then the person concerned tends to view him- or herself as the cause of the occupational stress. As a consequence, the individual internalizes this belief into her or his cognitive schema (e.g., there must be something wrong with me, I am too incompetent to handle this type of work, I should be able to handle my caseload). Historically, researchers have identified job-related stress and the interpersonal demands of the work environment as explanations for burnout. Thus, personality characteristics were the early rationale used to explain the experience of burnout.

Despite the fact that personality continues to be a factor in assessing and predicting the severity and degree of burnout, Maslach (2003) suggests that the phenomenon of burnout varies widely in terms of the types or groups of individuals that are most affected. For instance, there are sociocultural, career development, and other issues that need to be addressed in regard to interpreting the individual's experience of burnout.

There appear to be some similarities between empathy fatigue and burnout. First, it is recognized that burnout is a cumulative condition that results in physical, emotional, and mental exhaustion. As a consequence, people who are considered burned out become overly involved emotionally in their work, overextend themselves by juggling too many projects all at once, and feel overwhelmed by the emotional demands imposed by other people in their work environment. The experience of empathy fatigue, I believe, is also cumulative in nature. The professional counselor is required to be actively engaged empathically with the client/consumer's issues. In other words, to establish a therapeutic relationship with others and to achieve a working alliance, the counselor should be genuine, possess unconditional positive regard for the other person, exhibit an intense posture of verbal and nonverbal attending and listening, and respond to the client's emotional experience. Consequently, counselors can become overwhelmed by their client/consumer's emotional life story as they are called upon to assist in problem-solving a variety of life issues in a solution-focused manner. Given the multiple client issues and professional demands, it is not surprising that the emotional exhaustion observed in burnout plays a central role in the experience of empathy fatigue.

COMPASSION FATIGUE

Compassion fatigue (CF) is an evolving construct within the field of traumatology and is inextricably linked to both posttraumatic stress disorder (PTSD) and secondary traumatic stress (STS), which will be discussed below. The terms CF, compassion stress (CS), and STS are used synonymously because there tends to be a parallel experience between CF, CS, STS, and PTSD (Salston & Figley, 2003). The term CF was first discussed in the literature as it related to the burnout that nurses experience when working in high stress situations with those who are traumatized (see Joinson, 1992). Charles Figley (1995, 2002b) has written extensively on this topic. He suggests that professionals who work with others in crisis can also be traumatized by being exposed to the client's intense story of traumatic experience. The primary difference is that the client (known as the primary survivor) is the individual exposed to the traumatic event. However, there is a "cost to caring" in Figley's model, as the professional helper (referred to as a secondary survivor) can acquire a reaction very similar to that of the client's posttraumatic stress experience. Figley (1995) suggests that "those who have enormous capacity for feeling and expressing empathy tend to be more at risk of compassion stress" (p. 1) or compassion fatigue.

The research in CF was first developed through hundreds of case studies of therapists who have worked with those who have been traumatized by some critical life event. Anecdotally, these therapists have described a unique kind of stressor through which they have acquired symptoms of frequent sadness, depression, sleeplessness, generalized anxiety, and other forms of emotional pain and suffering that are directly related to their trauma counseling practice. Many professionals tend to avoid these CF symptoms, resulting in a diminished capacity for empathy and compassion for others that they serve. CF not only affects the professional helper but also the helper's family, friends, and colleagues, who may also become secondary survivors of the critical incident. Consequently, there appears to be a "contagion effect" transmitted to the professional's support system (Figley, 1993).

The experience of CF is thought to transcend the cumulative, emotional, mental, and physical exhaustion that is typically associated with organizational burnout. This is because CF is considered to be more acute in nature while burnout is cumulative in its effects. Additionally, burnout has been described as more of a general psychological stressor associated with working with difficult clients having complex issues (Trippany, White Kress, & Allen Wilcoxon, 2004).

More recently, Figley (2002b) has suggested that CF is just one form of burnout. Not all agree, however. Other researchers (Jenkins & Baird, 2002; Schauben & Frazier, 1995) have suggested that burnout is more related to the "chronic tedium of the workplace" rather than to exposure to clients who have been traumatized. Accordingly, the construct of empathy fatigue (EF) is both the same as and different from burnout or CF. Similarities to EF include the physical energy depletion and emotional exhaustion factors that are observed in burnout and CF. However, it is hypothesized within the theoretical constructs of EF that some preprofessional personality characteristics may predispose the individual to the depletion of the mind, body, and spiritual energy needed to pursue a career in the counseling profession. Additionally it is hypothesized that professional counselors who report having the experience of EF do not necessarily work with clients/consumers who have traumatic issues. Rather, these professionals deal with persons who are trying to cope with daily hassles (e.g., school or relationship issues), significant life stressors (e.g., divorce or legal issues), and life-adjustment issues (e.g., loss of a job, geographic relocation).

SECONDARY TRAUMATIC STRESS

Professionals working with clients/consumers who are closest to the epicenter of a critical incident are indeed secondary survivors of the traumatic event. For many professional helpers, the physical, psychological, emotional, and psychosocial symptoms are very real and tend to mirror the symptoms of the traumatized person (primary survivor). Figley (1993, 1995) and his colleagues have done extensive research in this area and refer to this phenomenon as secondary traumatic stress (STS). Figley suggests that the symptoms of STS are nearly identical to those of PTSD. The experience of STS is acquired by the helper as a natural consequence of knowing about a traumatizing event. This exposure results in a special type of compassion stress that professionals experience because they are compelled to help the traumatized individual(s).

Figley (1995) has advocated for the inclusion of STS as a diagnostic category in the *Diagnostic and Statistical Manual of Mental Disorders* (American Psychiatric Association [APA], *DSM–IV–TR*, 2000). He further contends that PTSD should be renamed "Primary PTSD," because the same set of symptoms appears in those who are caregivers for the traumatized. Accordingly, professional helpers who are deeply involved with traumatized individuals tend to acquire an experience parallel to that of primary survivors, many of whom are diagnosed with acute stress disorder and then PTSD (30 days later if the symptoms persist). In Figley's model, the term "secondary traumatic stress disorder" (STSD) is used to characterize this experience. The only difference between PTSD and STSD is that the client experiences the traumatizing event at first hand while the professional helper experiences it through therapeutic interactions with the traumatized client. Figley believes that it is the unconscious attunement to the absorption of the traumatized victim's stresses and traumas that leads to this type of trauma-specific countertransference experience.

More recently, Figley (2002b) has delineated more clearly his conceptualization of PTSD and STSD:

> Compassion fatigue is a more user-friendly term for secondary traumatic stress disorder, which is nearly identical to PTSD, except that it applies to those emotionally affected by the trauma of another (usually a client or family member). Compassion fatigue is related to the cognitive schema of the therapist (social and interpersonal perceptions or morale). (p. 3)

COMPARING AND CONTRASTING EMPATHY WITH COMPASSION FATIGUE

Despite the fact that Figley recognizes empathy as a major resource for trauma workers (Figley 2002a), I would like to make a basic distinction between empathy and compassion fatigue. I contend that empathy fatigue is a condition acquired by those professionals who first and foremost are perceived by self and/or others as facilitating therapeutic interactions in an empathic manner. Second, these professionals may or may not be exposed to clients that have extraordinary stressful or traumatic issues to deal with. Rather, empathy fatigue can be acquired by professionals who approach their work empathically and deal with a variety of clients/consumers who have been exposed to everything from daily hassles (e.g., school, work, relationship problems) and life adjustments (e.g., divorce, job loss, major grief) to traumatic stress-related issues (e.g., exposure to death, rape, homicide).

Professionals who have obtained their graduate-level training in nationally accredited counselor training programs (i.e., Council for Accreditation of Counseling and Related Educational Programs [CACREP] and Council on Rehabilitation Education [CORE]-accredited counselor training programs) may be more at risk for empathy fatigue because the concept and practice of empathy is inherent in various parts of the curriculum. This is the point at which supervisees typically first acquire the basic and advanced skills of attending, listening, paraphrasing, questioning, summarizing, and responding empathically to their clients' stories. These stories may or may not contain themes of extraordinarily stressful and traumatic events; especially during the supervisees' first clinical experiences (i.e., practicum and internship). Accordingly, counselors who approach their work compassionately use the skills of empathy as a tool or resource to establish a client rapport and build the therapeutic working alliance. More importantly, this is where many preprofessionals begin to recognize that their empathy fatigue buttons are being pushed. Depending upon the competence of the supervisee's clinical supervisor, the supervisee may or may not understand this as a countertransference experience.

In Figley's (2002b) conceptualization of CF, he suggests that "empathy is the vehicle whereby helpers make themselves open to absorption of traumatic information" (p. 20). Again, I contend that empathy fatigue can be acquired by professionals who work in areas other than trauma counseling. Both acting in a compassionate manner and using the skills of empathy appear to predispose the therapist to the absorption of the client's stressors. If a counselor is acting compassionately and using the skills of empathy on a daily/weekly basis, then the counselor may become fatigued by the cumulative effects of multiple client stories that may or may not contain themes of extraordinarily stressful and traumatic events. Thus, for some counselors, empathy fatigue is a cumulative process, while others may experience it more rapidly as in CF.

I also contend that counselors who facilitate therapeutic interactions in a highly empathic and intuitive state may experience empathy fatigue more easily. Likewise, persons who are perceived by themselves and others as highly empathic may be more prone to an empathy fatigue reaction. Thus, empathy may be a personality state or trait of some professional counselors, and some may be more affected because empathy is part of their personality structure.

It is possible that many counselors have personalities that overidentify with their client's issues, resulting in a negative form of countertransference. Consequently, professionals who do not have the awareness and capacity to monitor this maladaptive response or do not receive competent clinical supervision may be repeating the pattern of having their empathy fatigue buttons pushed. These professionals may experience empathy fatigue on a daily/weekly basis and thus it becomes a more deeply rooted trait or state in their cognitions, schemas, emotional brain, physiology, and spirit.

Overall, CF is viewed as more acute in nature, resulting from the experience of counselors who deal mostly with clients who have traumatic stress issues. On the other hand, EF results from dealing with clients who have a variety of nontraumatic issues. The cumulative effects interact with the counselor's mind, body, and spirit, and professionals who exhibit higher levels of empathy during therapeutic interactions tend to be more predisposed to this particular fatigue experience. This process may begin with a personality structure characterized as possessing high levels of both compassion and empathy. However, having to be empathically available to clients/consumers on a daily/weekly basis has an emotional, physical, and spiritual cost. The theoretical framework for empathy fatigue will be discussed in greater detail at various points in this book in order to provide better clarity.

VICARIOUS TRAUMATIZATION

The term vicarious traumatization (VT; McCann & Pearlman, 1989, 1990a, 1990b; Pearlman & Saakvitne, 1995) has been used widely to describe professional counselors' complex traumatic reactions resulting from cumulative exposure to primary survivors' traumatic events. Vicarious victimization (McCann & Pearlman, 1990b) and contact victimization (Courtois, 1988) have been used in the literature to describe similar reactions. However, VT is a unique concept because it presumes a developmental and constructivist model of personality in which meaning and relationship are integral to the human experience (Pearlman & Saakvitne, 1995). The developmental and constructivist model is an interpersonal theory that explains the impact of trauma on the counselor's psychological development, adaptation, and identity. As a result of this traumatic exposure, there appear to be profound changes in the cognitive schemas of the counselor's identity, memory, and belief system. It is this intense empathic engagement with the client's traumatic issues that appears to transform the therapist's inner psychic experience and results in the experience of VT. The psychological symptoms are reported to include depression, despair, cynicism; alienation from friends, colleagues, and family; premature job changes; and a multitude of other psychological and physical symptoms that are similar to those of the primary trauma survivor (Pearlman & Saakvitne, 1995).

The differences between VT and the other fatigue syndromes previously mentioned are not always clear in the literature (Figley, 1995;

Trippany et al., 2004). For example, VT is not always associated with the counselor's reaction to her or his own past traumatic experiences. The experience of VT appears to be mostly associated with the counselor's here-and-now experience when counseling the traumatized. It appears there may be some overlap with STS, since the VT experience can be emotionally, interpersonally, and physically debilitating to the professional helper. Overall, within the framework of recognizing, assessing, and treating professional fatigue syndromes such as VT, we see a profound personal cost to the therapist who is empathically engaged in counseling those who have been traumatized.

LOADING

The literature addressing the phenomenon of loading is sparse. Eisner (1995), who describes this experience, states that loading occurs when the professional takes on another person's psychic pain. Eisner's discussion of this phenomenon is not limited to the therapist's shared pain, which may result in a tremendous energy drain. Rather, this experience has been observed when two individuals are emotionally tied to one another (e.g., spouses, family, friends). Further, loading can be experienced where each takes on the "load" of the other's stressful, traumatic, or critical life-changing event. Loading can occur when the "ill person" appears to transmit or project his or her pain, suffering, and negative moods to the other person, who may or may not be a professional helper. Loading is particularly familiar to those in the helping professions who work with persons experiencing issues of loss, grief, death, and dying.

CONCLUDING STATEMENT

The overall effect of listening to multiple client stories of stress, anxiety, depression, trauma, grief, and loss appears to a depletion of the counselor's interpersonal effectiveness, creating an experience of mental, physical, cognitive, and spiritual fatigue. Depending upon the counselor's work setting and the type of clients served, this experience can have both acute and cumulative consequences.

A point that is of paramount importance to the construct of EF is that this experience may be either a chronic or an acute negative reaction in a variety of counseling interactions. Consideration should be given to the possibility that an EF reaction for some professionals is a "counselor trait" as opposed to a "counselor state." Hence, the cumulative effects of the professional counselor's EF experience may lead to a chronic and persistent mental health condition that may, in fact, manifest as a chronic malaise or transient condition that parallels that of the client. As the counselor's dysthymic mood lingers, it may go unrecognized by self and/or others. Overall, each professional will react to different levels of fatigue. In the case of EF, this reaction ranges along a continuum from low or moderate to high levels of fatigue.

There are various assessment instruments that measure counselor impairment and professional fatigue. However, some researchers have viewed self-report measures of counselor impairment and professional fatigue as subjective and artificial in nature. Self-report instruments tend to qualitatively measure the individual's unique experience of specific feelings and emotions. Additionally, this type of measurement relies on the personal, subjective experience of the professional counselor who qualitatively assesses the client's sense of personal distress, anxiety, or depression.

Regardless of how the different professional fatigue syndromes are measured, at the end of the day, the professional will require self-care strategies to continue in the chosen profession as a competent and ethical counselor. The counselor's cumulative exposure to multiple client stories, regardless of the degree of intensity, seems to interact with the counselor's mind, body, and spirit, resulting in a type of loss or detachment from the self. As we will see in chapter 4, the meaning of empathy changes depending upon who is observing such a trait or state.

3 Empathy as a Way of Being

A BRIEF HISTORY OF EMPATHY

The conceptual underpinnings of empathy can be traced back to a time long before its modern application in research and practice as described by Carl Rogers (1902–1987), who published his seminal work, *Client-Centered Therapy*, in 1951. According to Barrett-Lennard (1981), the beginning of the modern use of the word and concept of empathy was identified by R. L. Katz (1963). Katz noted that the nonclinical use of empathy was first conceptualized in 1897 by Theodore Lipps (1851–1914). Jackson's (1992) research into the origins of the foundational aspects of the theory and practice of empathy indicates that these can in fact be traced to Theodore Lipps and his concept of *Einfühlung*. Lipps used the German term *Einfühlung* to refer to the process of becoming totally absorbed in an external object, or projecting oneself into an aesthetic object such as a form of art. Later, Lipps and a colleague, Robert Vischer (1847–1933), suggested that *Einfühlung* is a particular emotion that can manifest as one's appreciation for the feelings and attitudes of another person. Sigmund Freud referred to Lipps's concept of *Einfühlung* in his *Jokes and Their Relation to the Unconscious* in 1905. Although Freud did not infer the clinical application of this concept, he suggested that this emotion produced a feeling of projecting oneself into the psychological state of another person.

By 1909, the expression "empathy" became the accepted translation of *Einfühlung* in Western psychoanalytic theory at the suggestion of Edward B. Titchener (1867–1927). Barrett-Lennard (1981) suggests that as E. B. Titchener introduced the word empathy as the English equivalent of *Einfühlung*, its meaning and usage advanced in theory. The concept of empathy advanced significantly into experimental and clinical practice during the 1940s and 1950s through the separate, often unacknowledged, scholarly work of Roy Schafer (1922–present), Heinz Kohut (1913–1981), and Ralph R. Greenson (1911–1979).

One of the other early pioneers of empathy was Alfred Adler (1931), who simply stated that if we are genuinely interested in the other person then "we must be able to see with his eyes and listen with his ears" (p. 172). Barrett-Lennard (1981) suggests that empathy was not brought to prominence in counseling theory and practice until the work of such thinkers as Rogers and Katz. These individuals made the primary point that empathy was a process of "feeling into" the other person in a deeply responsive way and that one must experience this awareness. Today, most research studies concerned with the clinical application of empathy have accepted, incorporated, and credited Carl Rogers's client-centered therapy (e.g., empathic attending, listening, understanding, responding) as the primary contribution to the 20th and 21st century of this therapeutic facilitative approach.

EMPATHY AS METACOMMUNICATION

Throughout the history of the helping professions, the most fundamental approach to communicating with others has been rooted in compassion or empathy. Empathy has been discussed in the counseling and psychology literature as a skill that can be both developed and learned if facilitated by a competent professional (Barone, Hutchings, Kimmel, Traub, Cooper, & Marshall, 2005). Empathy as a way of being (Rogers, 1980) is also a form of communication that involves attending, listening, observing, understanding, and responding to the concerns of others with a deep respect and genuineness. In fact, much of what we communicate to one another is done nonverbally. Empathy involves being aware of the other's metacommunication through eye contact, body language, silence, tone of voice, gestures, facial expressions, physical space, and many other methods. Empathic communication cannot be understated in the helping relationship. It is a tool to build the foundation for a trusting, genuine, and therapeutic relationship. Its intention is to build a strong working alliance with others.

The concept of empathy is often misunderstood; it becomes confused with sympathy. Sympathy, as an emotional reaction to another person's life event, is essentially stating: "I'm sorry this has happened to you." Conversely, empathy communicates verbally and nonverbally to others by affirming: "I'm sorry this has happened to you; it has to be very difficult for you; what can I do to help?" Accordingly, empathy requires the professional helper to be an active participant during therapeutic interactions and to be deeply involved with others in a powerful way.

If we expect our clients to develop the capacity to understand, express their thoughts openly, honestly, and directly, resolve problems on their own, and make good decisions in life, then a high level of empathic communication must be at the foundation of the therapeutic alliance. It is vital that helping professionals model this deep level of awareness, understanding, and responding during person-centered interactions. Accordingly, to be a competent and effective communicator, it is essential that professional helpers (a) hold positive beliefs about themselves as well as their clients, (b) have a healthy self-concept, (c) embrace and express values that respect other people and cultures, (d) are able to fully listen to and understand others, and (e) possess the skills of empathy. If the skills of empathy are not present within person-centered interactions, there will likely be very little respect, understanding, or compassion communicated to the individuals we are trying to help. Otherwise, there is a risk that the therapist will respond with an attitude of indifference, apathy, and overall lack of concern for others.

EMPATHY AS THERAPEUTIC LEVERAGE

Despite numerous problems of research design in the study of empathy, the core conditions of empathy as it relates to positive therapeutic outcomes have been enthusiastically supported in most studies conducted between 1960 and 1989 (Duan & Hill, 1996; Patterson, 1984). Paying attention to and sensing the other person's wants and needs constitute the focal point of any client-centered relationship. Attending, listening, and responding to others in such a way that they know they have been understood and heard is perhaps one of the oldest and most powerful tools for understanding the human experience and others' worldviews (Corey & Corey, 2003; Egan, 2002; Young, 1998). Skilled helpers such as professional counselors use empathy to build the foundation of a trusting relationship for the purpose of establishing an effective working alliance with others. Thus, empathy can be used as therapeutic leverage.

Carl Rogers (1957), psychologist and founder of the person-center therapy movement, introduced the concept of empathy as a *necessary and sufficient condition* for therapeutic change to occur. He hypothesized that there are core conditions that apply to all psychotherapy: (a) counselor congruence or genuineness within the therapeutic relationship, (b) an unconditional positive regard for the client, (c) the ability of the counselor to empathize with the client in this relationship, (d) communication of empathy, and (e) the expression of unconditional positive regard toward the client. Rogers (1980) talked passionately about empathy and empathic listening as "a way of being." He was known as a deeply intuitive man and provided a description of empathy:

> It means entering the private perceptual world of the other and becoming thoroughly at home in it. It involves being sensitive, moment by moment, to the changing felt meanings which flow in this other person, to the fear or rage or tenderness or confusion or whatever that he or she is experiencing. It means temporarily living in the other's life, moving about in it delicately without making judgments. (p. 142)

The richness of using basic and advanced level empathy is that it builds a relationship that is open and honest. If facilitated appropriately, empathy can build the client's self-awareness, be an impetus for personal growth and change, and spark new ways of thinking and learning. Equally important is the fact that if we are more open and honest in modeling our own emotions with clients, the better we are able to communicate and show them that we are also human. The intentional and conscious use of empathy during client-counselor sessions appears to be integral to the helper's way of being with the client both verbally and nonverbally.

Empathy involves more than just observing, attending, listening, and responding to another person with unconditional positive regard. Egan (1998) suggests that "although many individuals may feel empathy towards others, the truth is that few know how to put it into words. Empathy as a communication of understanding of the other remains an improbable event in everyday life" (p. 83). Many in the counseling field suggest that possessing the skills of empathy is a prerequisite for becoming a competent helper. The use of empathy is a person-centered approach used as a means of increasing practitioners' interpersonal effectiveness and enhancing outcomes with their clients (Corey & Corey, 1998; Egan, 1998, 2002; Ivey & Ivey, 1999; Truax & Carkhuff, 1967). However, there is a cost to being truly empathetic with our clients in this interpersonal exchange of personal feelings and emotions.

THE SHADOW SIDE OF EMPATHY

There appears to be a "shadow side" of empathy (Egan, 1998) as the helper enters the client's world deeply enough to understand issues that may be related to extraordinarily stressful and traumatic events. Some of the client's experiences, content, and emotions may become distorted as the counselor organizes issues into his or her own schema and world-view. Because of the heavy reliance in counseling and education on the basic and advanced skills of empathy, it is paramount that cultivating the practice and application of empathic communication with skilled helpers should be accomplished in a culturally competent manner.

Empathy is not simply responding to what the other person feels, for we can never really totally understand and sense another's pain and suffering. The underlying premise of acting empathically is that our compassion for another human being moves us so deeply that we instinctually have a desire to help that individual. However, communicating empathically obviously has limitations with some individuals in certain settings. This is especially relevant if the individual has to be confronted about negative and high risk-taking behaviors (e.g., adolescent substance abuse, conduct disorders, borderline personality disorders). Despite the shadow side of empathy, we can continue to facilitate therapeutic inter-actions in a compassionate manner. We can do so by understanding the individual's personality and behavioral traits, the sociocultural environ-ment in which that individual may be forced to exist, and the realities of the individual's external struggles and the barriers she or he may en-counter (e.g., severe physical or mental disabilities, racial/ethnic preju-dices, job discrimination). If our compassion is our true motivation to help others, then we can act compassionately using the skills of empathy. Despite the fact that we can never totally experience the other person's grief, pain, or loss, it is critical that we form an understanding and a working definition of the individual's unique emotional experiences as it relates to that individual's life.

CULTURAL ASPECTS OF EMPATHY

Empathy has been discussed in the counseling and psychology literature for the last 125 years and has been conceptualized as a skill that can be both developed and learned if facilitated properly (Barone et al., 2005). Empathy has a rich history, being at the foundation of most theoretical orientations within counselor education programs. However, the concept of empathy has brought new meaning to its theoretical and practical use in cross-cultural counseling settings. For instance, cultural empathy (Ivey & Ivey, 1999; Ridley & Lingle, 1996), empathic multicultural awareness (Junn, Morton, & Yee, 1995), cultural role taking (Scott & Borodovsky, 1990), ethnotherapeutic empathy (Parson, 1993), and ethnocultural empathy (Wang, Davidson, Yakushko, Bielstein Savoy, Tan, & Bleier, 2003) have all been used interchangeably to delineate various constructs of cultural empathy. There is little doubt that in the past 10 years or so, multicultural counseling issues have been at the forefront of the counseling profession. This is because of the changing demographics in the United States, where, population projections indicate, by the year 2015, racial and ethnic minorities will comprise one-third of all Americans (U.S. Census Bureau, 2000). Thus, sometime between 2030 and 2050, racial and ethnic minorities will become the majority population in the United States (Sue, 1996).

With regard to the term "cultural specific empathy," as used by some multicultural counseling theorists (Ponterotto & Bensesch, 1988; Ridley, 1995; Ridley, Mendoza, & Kanitz, 1994), empathy is seen as a skill that is pancultural or universal. If empathy can be facilitated in a culturally sensitive manner, it should help strengthen the therapeutic relationship (Ibrahim, 1991). Ridley (1995) suggests that cultural empathy has two dimensions: understanding and communication. Understanding requires that the counselor try and synthesize the idiographic meaning of the client's stories, and then respond with the accurate meaning of what the client has communicated to the counselor. Accordingly, all therapy can be culturally contextualized and a positive therapeutic outcome can be enhanced by the skills of a culturally competent counselor.

Some authors have criticized traditional counseling approaches that place a heavy reliance on empathic communication that is not culturally sensitive (Freeman, 1993; Hamilton Usher, 1989; Pedersen, 2000; Sue & Sue, 1990). If the expectations of therapy are that clients should disclose emotions at a deep level during a session, then stepping inside the private world of the culturally different client may be perceived as being too intrusive or offensive. Lee and Richardson (1991) suggest that if the discipline of multicultural counseling is to have any therapeutic value in the counseling relationship, then we must go beyond training counselors in broad conceptualizations and develop more than just cultural awareness and knowledge. Having an understanding of different cultures will not by itself allow us to develop competent practitioners who can apply the skills of cultural empathy. It will require strategies and approaches that are culturally specific and relevant so as to help build a strong trusting relationship and form a therapeutic alliance.

Ridley and Lingle's (1996) model of cultural empathy defines this construct as a "learned ability" that is interpersonally focused and has many dimensions. This model proposes that there are three processes underlying cultural empathy: (a) cognitive process (cultural perspective-taking and differentiating self from others); (b) affective process (vicarious feelings and empathy expression of concern for others); and (c) communicative process (probing for insight, expression of accurate understanding).

Corey and Corey (1998) suggest that a self-assessment and exploration of both compassion and empathy are important for beginning level counselors so that they may become aware of their clients' needs from different cultural backgrounds and respond with care, concern, and understanding. Lazarus (1999) views compassion as a double-edged sword, however. He suggests that having too much compassion toward another person can impair our ability to help others. He further states that "we must learn how to distance ourselves emotionally from the emotional significance of their suffering, so it does not overwhelm us" (p. 246). There are others who feel compassion has been left out of training programs in Western psychology, counseling, and medical education (Goleman, 2003). This may be because different ideologies and religious beliefs are attached to the meaning of the word. However, competent and ethical counselors should consistently evaluate the impact that their belief system has on the client-counselor session and the ways in which interventions that use empathy and compassion might be perceived by their clients (Corey & Corey, 1998; Egan, 1998; Ivey & Ivey, 1999).

Compassion, as opposed to empathy or sympathy, as described by the Dalai Lama (see Goleman, 2003) is a quality "that needs to be naturally drawn from within one's own inner resources" (p. 245). His Holiness places paramount importance on promoting the values of compassion, loving kindness, and altruism as significant human qualities to cultivate at a very early age. Despite the fact that compassion is a highly desirable and healthy human emotion, it does not appear to be a skill that we can teach in traditional counselor education programs in the same way that we train counselors in the skills of empathy. Intentional acts of compassion, if approached in a culturally sensitive manner, appear to be unquestionably desirable human attributes that can potentially strengthen the client-counselor therapeutic relationship.

CONCLUDING REMARKS

Throughout the history of the helping profession, compassion and empathy have been the wellsprings of establishing a rapport, building a relationship, and achieving optimal levels of therapeutic functioning with clients/consumers. If we could measure compassion and empathy as facilitated by highly developed professionals, then perhaps counselor educators and supervisors could train preprofessionals in how to model such therapeutic interactions with clients/consumers. However, measuring therapeutic interactions using empathy and compassion as the dependent variable can become quite challenging for researchers. The amount, level, degree, and quality of empathy expressed within therapeutic interactions will vary depending upon the observer, the professional, and the client/consumer. In considering the interchange of emotions during therapeutic interactions, it may be useful to examine how empathy and compassion are experienced by the counselor, client, and outside observer(s). Thus, chapter 4 will investigate such interactions and offer counselor educators and supervisors, researchers, and helping professionals the theories and conceptual models that measure empathy as (a) a personal trait, (b) a situation-specific event, (c) a cognitive-affective state, and (d) a general tool of the therapist for the purpose of facilitating a high level of empathy and compassion.

4

Theoretical Empathy Fatigue: Measuring Fatigue Reactions of the Mind, Body, and Spirit

Measurement of the counselor's experience of fatigue from a holistic mind-body-spirit perspective is rarely discussed in the counseling and psychology literature. Self-report instruments that measure burnout (MBI; Maslach & Jackson, 1981, 1986) and compassion fatigue (CFST or CSF; Figley, 1995; Figley & Stamm, 1996) and the revised compassion fatigue scale, the Professional Quality of Life Scale (ProQOL; Stamm, 2005), have primarily yielded subscales that measure: (a) compassion satisfaction, (b) burnout, and (c) compassion fatigue or secondary traumatic stress. However, the multidimensionality of empathy fatigue requires a discussion of various other psychometric instruments that measure both empathy and fatigue from a mind, body, and spiritual perspective within a cultural context. In a holistic sense, measuring the constellation of professional fatigue syndromes requires an understanding of multiple issues. These relate to the counselor's cultural worldview, personality traits, age and developmental level of competence, physical health and wellness, environment or setting of employment, external supports, and coping and resiliency skills, as well as other relevant factors.

Because empathy is used (a) as therapeutic leverage for rapport-building with clients, (b) for strengthening the client-counselor relationship, and (c) for improving client outcomes, then it should be of interest to researchers to measure such variables within the therapeutic setting.

Most importantly, measuring the construct of empathy can assist other researchers in developing screening and functional assessment instruments to deal with the constellation of professional fatigue syndromes and issues related to counselor impairment. Ultimately, the goal should be to develop prevention strategies and self-care approaches.

MEASURING EMPATHY

Empathy is a unique and complex area of study within the expanding discipline of counseling and psychology. It is a multidimensional construct because of the way it is operationally defined in the literature as well as the philosophical and theoretical differences posed within the profession itself. Thus, measuring empathy and empathy fatigue can become quite challenging for some researchers. Many have suggested that empathy is qualitatively distinct from other emotions experienced and expressed by the therapist (e.g., compassion, sympathy). This is because there are multiple variables that mediate a therapeutic relationship between the giver and receiver of empathy. Perceptual differences in the amount, level, degree, and quality of empathy expressed within the client-counselor session also seem to vary. Thus, perceptions of empathy are dependent upon who is measuring or rating the experience: the professional counselor (self-ratings of empathic competence), the client/consumer (client ratings of the counselor), or the counselor educator/clinical supervisor (expert observer ratings).

Considering the interchange of emotions during therapy it would be useful to investigate how empathy is experienced by the counselor, client, and outside observer(s). It is in the experience of feeling empathically fatigued that the research falls short. Knowledge concerning the emotional, physical, and spiritual cost of being empathic in a session would provide an understanding of why some practitioners may be unconsciously reluctant to see or purposely avoid clients who have stories of stress, trauma, grief, and loss.

Defining the Phenomenon

Through most of the 1960s, the counseling and psychotherapy literature confirmed Rogers's views and definition of empathy as a necessary and sufficient condition that should be facilitated during therapeutic interactions (see Carkhuff, 1969; Truax, 1963). Greenberg, Watson, Elliott, and Bohart

(2001) suggest that the clearest operational definition of Rogerian-style empathy includes Barrett-Lennard's (1981) delineation of the three components and perspectives of measuring empathy: (a) the therapist's experience ("empathic resonance"), (b) the observer's view ("expressive empathy"), and (c) the client's experience ("received empathy"). As a result of studying empathy from these three perspectives, instruments were developed so that this facilitative approach could be observed and measured.

Other theories and models in the literature that have conceptualized empathy for the purpose of measurement (Duan & Hill, 1996) have characterized empathy as (a) a personality trait, (b) a situation-specific event, (c) a cognitive-affective state, or (d) a general tool of the helper. Empathy has also been commonly defined as a vicarious response to a stimulus or an emphasis on the emotional aspects of a relationship (Scotland, 1969), a motivational state of the individual helper (Duan, 2000), and a cognitive phenomenon with a focus on the intellectual processes of forming an accurate perception of others (Dymond, 1949; Kerr & Speroff, 1954, as cited in Davis, 1983).

Despite the disagreements in the literature on the definition and experience of empathy, Davis, Mitchell, Hall, Lothert, Snapp, and Meyer (1999) suggest that there is general agreement in two areas: (a) the domain of empathy includes both cognitive and affective dimensions; and (b) affective dimensions encompass a variety of important emotional responses by the professional to the individual (i.e., client/consumer) who is distressed by a significant life event. There is a plethora of evidence in the research regarding the role and value of empathy in therapeutic settings. However, most studies have focused on the elements of the therapeutic alliance between the counselor and client, or the core conditions that are facilitated by the counselor within the counseling relationship (Feller & Cottone, 2003).

Empathy as a Trait or State

In personality theory, the construct of empathy has been widely studied from both trait and state levels. The preponderance of studies of individual differences in empathic styles of communication suggest that empathy is a personality trait. However, more contemporary research has analyzed empathy from both trait and state levels, measuring the interaction effects that exist between daily psychological states of functioning, moods, and specific daily events. Nezlek, Feist, Wilson, and Plesko (2001) note that few studies have measured the variability of empathy as expressed by the individual (nonprofessional) on a day-to-day basis. This group of researchers in a well-designed study assessed the daily psychological state of empathy of a group of introductory psychology students and evaluated how it covaried with state mood and the positive and negative events that occurred in conjunction with the person's state of empathy.

Based on the data, it was suggested that students adjusted their day-to-day empathic response based on more positive interactions with thers rather than negative interactions. How empathic a person perceived him- or herself to be on a particular day was a function of individual personality traits and states. It was suggested that generally people tend to feel and express the same affective states that others are experiencing and expressing. In other words, there is an emotional contagion that affects how empathy is expressed person to person. This is confirmed by other studies that have shown that people likely feel what others around them are feeling and therefore are more likely to empathize with them.

There are few studies that have claimed to actually measure the degree, level, or quality of empathy that is expressed within the client-counselor relationship. This is primarily because empathy may be both qualitatively and quantitatively different from other approaches. Thus, gaining an understanding of the correlates of empathy may provide others with insight into the multidimensional characteristics of the theoretical aspects of empathy fatigue. Ultimately this should serve as a research agenda for those interested in developing prevention approaches for impaired counselors.

Implications for Empathy Fatigue

These findings may be helpful in explaining the professional helper's response and experience of empathy fatigue during therapeutic interactions. For instance, if the professional counselor is perceived to possess an empathic state or trait during a session (by an outside observer and self-reporting) and the client is expressing a negative feeling and/or mood, then perhaps this may be enough of a vicarious experience for the professional to express reduced levels of empathy. This is confirmed by other studies that have shown that people (nonprofessionals) experience greater levels of empathy in response to positive events rather than negative ones. Perhaps the implications for the study of empathy fatigue are that (a) people in general possess and express a wide range of emotions and moods on a daily basis regardless of their occupation; (b) empathy is both a personality trait and state that most people possess; (c) persons just beginning their career in the counseling and psychology profession need to learn how to facilitate appropriate levels of empathy and self-monitor how they transition between empathic states and traits; and (d) all professionals need to be aware of when their empathic states and traits are being strained, exhausted, or fatigued during therapeutic interactions.

Instruments that Measure Empathic Emotion

Over the years, analysis of different scales purporting to measure empathy has continually suggested that empathy is a multidimensional construct (Batson, Fultz, & Schoenrade, 1987; Davis et al., 1999; Greenberg et al., 2001). The interested reader who would like to review the validity and reliability of each instrument should consult the references that follow. Discussion of these instruments will be presented for the three main types of empathy measures: (a) observer-rated empathy or ratings by expert judges such as counselor educators or clinical supervisors (i.e., the Hogan Empathy Scale, for which see Hogan, 1969; the Accurate Empathy Scale, for which see Truax & Carkhuff, 1967); (b) client ratings of empathy as expressed by the counselor (i.e., the Helpee Stimulus Expression, for which see Carkhuff, 1969; the Barrett-Lennard Relationship Inventory, for which see Barrett-Lennard, 1962); and (c) therapist or self-rating scales of empathy (i.e., the Empathy Construct Rating Scale, for which see LaMonica, 1981; the Barrett-Lennard Relationship Inventory, for which see Barrett-Lennard, 1981).

A fourth group or "fourth force" that is currently being proposed in the multicultural counseling literature is the Scale of Ethnocultural Empathy (SEE; Wang et al., 2003). According to Wang and his associates, the SEE is the only instrument developed that measures ethnocultural empathy. The SEE was developed using the general Western principles and theories of empathy, multiculturalism, and culture specific empathy. In terms of measuring cultural specific empathy, Wang and his associates hypothesize that ethnocultural empathy is composed of the following traits of counselors: (a) intellectual empathy (e.g., the ability to understand a culturally different person's thinking and/or feelings); (b) empathic emotions (e.g., the attention that one gives to the other's feelings and emotions); and (c) communication or expression of ethnoculturally empathic thoughts and feelings toward culturally different individuals and groups. It is further hypothesized that these traits can be developed over time and that the counselor has the ability to know and understand another person's inner cultural experiences and feelings. This hypothesis is confirmed by Ridley and Lingle's (1996) model of cultural empathy, which suggests that empathy is a "learned ability" (Wang et al.).

MEASURING EMPATHY BY EXPERT OBSERVER, CLIENT, AND THERAPIST RATINGS

The most accurate depictions of the level, quality, and degree of empathy expressed by the counselor during therapy are those observations that involve a triad of raters, primarily the client, counselor, and expert rater. However, few studies have utilized the triad of observer-rated empathy in their design. Additionally, the intercorrelations between the different empathy measures have been weak (Greenberg et al., 2001). Despite the lack of consistency in outcome measures in empathy research (Patterson, 1984) a description of the key findings will be highlighted and discussed separately according to the three common types of measures (expert observer-rated, client-rated, and therapist-rated empathy). The discussion of these findings is based on various authors' meta-analyses of studies related to this topic (e.g., Batson et al., 1987; Batson et al., 1996; Davis, 1983; Davis et al., 1999; Duan, 2000; Gould, 1990; Greenberg et al., 2001; Wang et al., 2003). It is important to note that these studies do not assert causality between empathy and positive therapy outcomes. However, there are important variables to consider in therapeutic relationships using empathy that may contribute to an understanding and a hypothesis about how professional counselors may become emotionally fatigued in this process.

Expert Observer-Rated Empathy

The expert observer-rating scales, for example, as developed by Truax (1967), primarily have used expert observers (e.g., trained peer raters, expert raters/counselor educators, clinical supervisors) to view and rate therapists' level of attending, listening, and responding to their clients' feelings, experiences, and content, as well as therapeutic interactions that may detract from model responses. Despite Truax and Carkhuff's (1967) argument that empathy is above all determined by the therapist, other studies indicate that therapists' level of empathy varies as a function of client characteristics. This tends to be consistent with the multicultural counseling literature.

Developmental aspects of counselors in training may also be a relevant factor with regard to rating the level, quality, and degree of empathy expressed by the professional or preprofessional counselor. However, it is interesting to note that some studies have shown a negative correlation between the therapist's level of professional counseling experience and empathy ratings. In other words, it was found that the counselor's level of experience (i.e., number of years in the profession) and the theoretical orientation facilitated in the session did not correlate highly with the counselor's ability to express empathy. Thus, the client-counselor relationship that is established during the first few sessions, not the level of experience or theoretical orientation of the professional, appears to be one of the best predictors or determinants of a strong therapeutic relationship.

To further accentuate this point in our discussion of expert observer ratings, the literature is clear that clients who felt understood by their counselor reported a more positive therapeutic experience (e.g., higher satisfaction with counseling services provided). These ratings were not dependent on the counselor's age or level of experience. Counselors who had higher empathy ratings as observed by an outside expert tended to form a stronger therapeutic alliance with their clients. Overall, expert raters found that counselors who were rated high in empathic ability had clients in therapy for a longer period of time and their clients did not terminate therapy prematurely.

Client/Consumer-Rated Empathy

One of the most widely used client-rated measures of counselor empathy is the Barrett-Lennard Relationship Inventory (BLRI; Barrett-Lennard, 1962, as cited in Greenberg et al., 2001). As Rogers (1957) hypothesized, clients who perceive their therapists as facilitating positive regard, empathy, and congruence during the session demonstrate a more positive outcome. In fact, Barrett-Lennard (1981) and Gurman (1977) concluded that clients' perceptions of their counselor's level of empathy predicted the outcome better than the expert observer or counselor's rating of the level of empathy expressed during the session. Thus, when the client's feelings are being understood, it appears to carry significant weight in measuring the level of empathy expressed by counselors. Because empathy contributes to facilitating client understanding, involvement, and openness, there is also a greater likelihood that the client will self-disclose more frequently in a session and with deeper emotion. Overall, client-rated empathy predicted therapeutic outcome best, followed by observer-rated and then therapist-rated empathy.

Therapist-Rated Empathy

Interestingly, therapist-rated empathy neither predicts therapeutic outcome nor correlates with how clients perceive the level of empathy expressed in the session. The counselor may "feel good" about a client session afterward because of a particular intervention or some other therapeutic approach that has been utilized. However, this does not correlate well with the way the client/consumer perceives the overall level of empathy expressed by the counselor during the session. Greenberg et al. (2001) suggest that "truly empathic therapists do not parrot clients' words back or reflect only the content of those words; instead, they understand overall goals as well as moment-to-moment experiences, both explicit and implicit" (p. 383).

MEASURING FATIGUE FROM A PHYSIOLOGICAL AND PSYCHOSOCIAL PERSPECTIVE

Fatigue is one of the most common complaints (Gentile, Delaroziere, Favre, Sambuc, & San Marco, 2003; Knobel et al., 2003; Prince & Jones, 2001) after headache pain (Evans, 2007) in medical practice settings and plays a prominent role in both chronic mental and chronic physical health conditions. Clearly, there appears to be a mind-body connection between empathy (an emotionally and psychologically based experience) and physical fatigue (a physiological state of limited functioning), which may trigger chronic physical (e.g., multiple sclerosis [MS], rheumatoid arthritic pain conditions) and mental health conditions (e.g., depression, general anxiety disorder).

Measuring the experience of fatigue from a biopsychosocial perspective has gained much support over the last decade (Michielsen, DeVries, Van Heck, Van de Vijver, & Sijtsma, 2004). Historically, a discussion of fatigue required an understanding of the underlying physiological and psychological processes (see Hueting & Sarphati, 1966). However, measuring such a construct appeared "unmanageable" and fatigue was discussed in the literature primarily as a physical experience. Accordingly, prior to the 1990s, fatigue was seen as a unidimensional construct (Michielsen et al., 2004). Since the 1990s there has been an abundance of studies to measure fatigue. This may have been due to the growing body of research on chronic health conditions such as chronic fatigue syndrome (CFS; Alberts, Vercoulen, & Bleijenberg, 2001).

Today, fatigue is viewed as a multidimensional construct and is frequently included within the subscales of other, broader measures, such as the Emotional Exhaustion subscale in burnout questionnaires (e.g., MBI; Maslach & Jackson, 1996) and the Energy and Fatigue subscale of the World Health Organization's Quality of Life assessment instrument (WHOQOL-100; WHOQOL, 1998), and is incorporated into different subscales of depression inventories (e.g., the Beck Depression Inventory, BDI; Beck, Ward, Mendelson, Mock, & Erbaugh, 1961) in which there are items that ask about individuals' sleep patterns, physical fatigue, and ability to perform physical functions.

It is recognized by researchers that as a result of general mental and physical fatigue, there is a reduction in one's general activity, motivation for tasks, and situation-specific types of fatigue experiences (Gentile et al., 2003; Knobel et al., 2003; Schwid, Covington, Segal, & Goodman, 2002). Despite the fact that the research on fatigue could be enhanced by a more rigorous definition and improved research designs (Schwid et al., 2002), there are typically an underlying disease process, a chronic physical or mental health condition, and specific behaviors that precipitate fatigue and interact with the individual's biological, physiological, and psychosocial experience of fatigue.

With regard to measuring this phenomenon as a biological, physiological, and psychosocial experience, few questionnaires have been developed for individuals who express chronic fatigue outside the patient population or health care institution. Much of the research that has been done in this area is with cancer patients and those suffering from chronic illnesses (e.g., MS). One particular scale developed for use with hospital patients and in nonhospital settings in community-based healthy populations is the Fatigue Scale (FS; Chalder et al., 1993).

A newer, 10-item fatigue measure, the Fatigue Assessment Scale (FAS; Michielsen et al., 2004), has been constructed and is said to possess promising psychometric qualities. In the FAS, four separate dimensions of fatigue were measured in a nonpatient, healthy Dutch population: (a) subjective experience of fatigue, (b) reduced concentration, (c) reduced motivation, and (d) reduced physical activity. The interested reader will want to consult the research design and psychometric properties of the FAS (Michielsen et al.) as well as other instruments that use the same and similar subscales to measure general fatigue. Some of these instruments and the accompanying instrument review and validation studies include the following: (a) the Multidimensional Fatigue Inventory (MFI 20), developed by a Dutch scientist, E.M.A. Smets, then translated into English (see Gentile et al., 2003); (b) the European Organization for Research and Treatment of Cancer Quality of Life Core Questionnaire (EORTC QLQ-C30; see Knobel et al., 2003); (c) the Health-Related Quality of Life scale (HRQL; see Prince & Jones, 2001); (d) the Fatigue Severity Scale (FSS; see Schwid et al., 2002); or (e) the Multidimensional Fatigue Symptom Inventory (MFSI; see Stein, Jacobsen, Blanchard, & Thors, 2004). Overall, we are just now beginning to understand the multidimensional relationships and mind-body nature of the individual's experience of fatigue.

MEASURING SPIRITUAL FATIGUE

A comprehensive review of spirituality and the measurement of the experience of "spiritual fatigue" goes beyond the scope of this chapter. This section will focus on measuring the spiritual dimension and its importance when dealing with the counselor's experience of empathy fatigue as it relates to mind, body, and spiritual fatigue. One of the first uses of the concept of spiritual fatigue in writing may have been in a religious and scientific work from 1889, written by R. Holt Hutton and edited by his niece Elizabeth M. Roscoe (see Holt Hutton & Roscoe, 1901). Holt Hutton and Roscoe eventually published this work in 1901 and suggested that "A generation of which the most impressive characteristic is its spiritual fatigue will never be truly Christian till it can husband its energy better" (p. 19). A review of the text suggests that the meaning of this statement is based in Christian conservatism and the concerns expressed are related to moral deficiencies and skepticism about various religious practices at the end of the nineteenth century.

Much of the literature during this time had a specific focus on religious or faith-based spiritual practices. Some of the mid-20th-century literature that went beyond the boundaries of the faith-based expression of spiritual fatigue was related to existential phenomenology and its philosophical underpinnings in psychology, theology, and the evolving spiritual beliefs of humankind (e.g., Tillich, 1952). During this time, psychologists, philosophers, and theologians felt it important (and healthy) to question the meaning of faith and the human emotions related to anxiety, despair, guilt, neurosis, and meaninglessness. Thus, prior to the 1970s, less attention was given to a discussion of theory, research, and spiritual integration within the client-counselor relationship.

Faith-Based Versus Secular Counselor Fatigue

Today, the literature on spiritual fatigue is primarily faith based. Interestingly, concerns about and experiences of spiritual fatigue for the faith-based clergy and the various denominations they serve appear to be both similar to and different from those of secular professional counselors. The general differences are easily distinguishable because each discipline has its own philosophy, theories, strategies, and techniques that are facilitated during interpersonal person-centered interactions (e.g., involving Christian counselors or secular professional clinical counselors). A common thread for both secular professional counselors and faith-based counselors is that both disciplines help clients deal with mental health issues related to death, loss, grief, addictions, and the meaning of physical, psychological, existential, and spiritual existence. Thus, there appears to be a shared experience of burnout, compassion, empathy, and spiritual fatigue. Accordingly, there are shared concerns over impaired or fatigued professionals and their level of competence and effectiveness with the population they serve.

A Google search of issues related to compassion, empathy fatigue, burnout, and professional fatigue specific to the clergy and other spiritual leaders will direct the reader toward thousands of retreats, retreat centers, seminars, workshops, and various types of materials that accommodate religious professionals. The stated purpose, program objectives, and content of these renewal activities translate into renewing one's mind, body, and spirit; much like the revitalizing activities for other helping professionals.

Measuring Spiritual Wellness

Integrating the client's spiritual beliefs, values, and practices has matured tremendously in the last 25 years within the field of counseling and psychology. Today's discussion of nonfaith-based spirituality tends to be organized into subspecialties, dealing with an understanding of the client's core spiritual beliefs and values, spiritual practices, and spiritual experiences. Despite the fact that both spirituality and religiosity continue to lack clarity in definition and application, many earlier researchers (Bergin, 1988; Worthington, 1988), and psychotherapists (Assagioli,

1965; Jung, 1973) contended that spirituality is a natural part of being human. Understanding the important role of spiritual health in the counselor's experience of empathy fatigue is of paramount importance. This is confirmed by the evolving body of literature in the fields of psychology and health-related sciences suggesting that a person's spiritual health has a major positive influence on the body's immune system and may affect the ability to combat stress, chronic illness, and life-threatening disability (Cousins, 1979; Goleman, 2003; Peck, 1993; Schwartz, 1994; Siegel, 1990; Simonton, 1978; Weil, 1995).

Spirituality has also been known as a source of positive coping and resiliency. Thus, the counselor who becomes spiritually fatigued appears to experience negative consequences related to mind-body health and overall wellness. In order for empathy fatigue studies to advance in theory and develop appropriate self-care strategies, it is essential that the counseling profession should understand how to evaluate this experience for prevention practices.

Some of the most comprehensive explanations in counseling and psychology of the measurement of spiritual wellness and the theory, research, and practice behind spirituality can be found in the wheel of wellness model (Myers & Sweeney, 2005; Myers, Sweeney, & Witmer, 2000; Witmer & Sweeney, 1992) and the indivisible self model of wellness (IS-Wel; Myers & Sweeney, 2004; Sweeney & Myers, 2005). Both models suggest that spiritual wellness is a multidimensional construct that is vital to a person's overall wellness. Central to this issue is the way people integrate spiritual growth and development into their lives.

The wheel of wellness is a three-dimensional model that provides one of the most comprehensive explanations of human wellness (Myers & Sweeney, 2005). The model includes five major life tasks: (a) spirituality (the awareness of a transcendent being or force that provides a deep sense of wholeness or connectedness in the universe); (b) self-direction (the manner in which the individual regulates, disciplines, and directs the self in daily pursuits); (c) work and leisure (which provide opportunities for pleasurable experiences that are intrinsically satisfying and provide a sense of accomplishment); (d) friendship (all of one's social relationships that involve a connection with others); and (e) love (relationships that are formed on the basis of a long-term, mutual commitment and involve intimacy). Simply stated, the wheel of wellness integrates a person's emotions, sense of control, problem solving, creativity, realistic beliefs, social support, and self-care into a holistic framework designed to increase the individual's personal wellness and provide opportunities for healthy spiritual development.

CONCLUDING THOUGHTS ON MEASURING EMPATHY FATIGUE

Persons who "feel fatigued" not only have a sense that there is something physiologically wrong with them, but they also experience an emotional, behavioral, and cognitive component of their general feeling of wellness. Measuring empathy fatigue will require us to truly evaluate the global, psychosocial, somatic, affective/emotional, cognitive, behavioral, and physiological symptoms of a person who feels fatigued. Measuring empathy fatigue as it relates to the mind-body-spiritual health of the professional counselor can be used as a screening method or functional assessment device to determine the degree of professional impairment that such a person experiences. The decision as to how long to stay active in such an honorable yet sometimes perilous profession should be the responsibility of the professional counselor. Considering such a decision should also provide motivation for self-care approaches. Other responsible partners in maintaining the mind, body, and spiritual wellness of the profession include the counselor's employers, professional counseling associations, counselor education and training programs, and clinical supervisors. Part III of *Empathy Fatigue* will discuss how these entities can each be brought to the table to achieve the complex multidisciplinary approach necessary to help impaired professionals.

A major point to highlight is that measuring empathy fatigue requires openness to the idea that impaired professionals experience much more than the negative emotional consequences of helping others at intense levels of service. There is a general wellness cost to providing such therapeutic interactions. In spite of efforts by other researchers to develop a framework to measure mental, physical, and other types of general fatigue, current studies of fatigue most often assess the experience of fatigue through subjective measures such as personal interviews, questionnaires, and scaling. Some researchers regard fatigue as primarily a physiological experience with less emphasis on its psychological component. Yet, mental or emotional fatigue can be equally debilitating and reflects an important variable in the measuring of empathy fatigue. Mental or emotional fatigue can reduce an individual's psychological capacity and competence for the mental and emotional aspects of the job, thereby decreasing the capacity for expressing empathy.

5 Empathy Fatigue as the Wounded Spirit and Soul of the Helper

Clearly, the search for personal meaning in one's chronic illness, disability, or traumatic experience is an existential and spiritual pursuit (Stebnicki, 2006). Accordingly, the question *What kind of God could allow such suffering or horrific acts to take place (happen to me or in my world)?* cannot be answered using a basic empathic response. In many cultures, the most significant and meaningful questions in life are related to where we came from before birth and where we will go at the time of our death (Pedersen, 2000). Pearlman and Saakvitne (1995) suggest that the loss of meaning, connection, and hope after a traumatic event can be overwhelmingly destructive in a spiritual sense to both clients and counselors. Counselors' vicarious traumatization has a profound effect on their spiritual health. To give our whole emotional attention to another person who metaphorically asks "what happens if I say damn you God" (Arokiasamy, 1994) or "why do bad things happen to good people" (Kushner, 1980) requires a compassionate and empathic response that is both existential and spiritual in nature. Thus, for counselors, taking care of the soul or being conscious of spiritual health is critical to survival and personal and professional growth.

Spiritual connectedness is a cultural attribute and can be a form of social support that empowers individuals with chronic illnesses and disabilities to cope with their environment (Harley, Stebnicki, & Rollins,

2000). Spirituality plays a prominent role in the lives of individuals from many different cultural and ethnic backgrounds. Some authors (Pargament & Zinnbauer, 2000; Shafranske & Malony, 1996) have suggested that counselors have an ethical obligation to explore the spiritual aspects of the client's life because it is consistent with facilitating counseling approaches within a holistic and multicultural framework. Thus, to work effectively with the individual's spiritual identity and worldview, it has been suggested throughout the literature that counselor educators and supervisors need to intentionally inquire about the client's spiritual health during the supervision session (Bishop, Avila-Juarbe, & Thumme, 2003; Cashwell & Young, 2004; Polanski, 2003; Stebnicki, 2007b).

Likewise, in order to be empathic and cope with our client's existential and spiritual experience of loss and grief, we must first be comfortable with our own spiritual health, in order to avoid a wounded spirit. It also necessitates that we not feel obligated to know everything that our higher power, spirit guides, or the universe has to teach us. For some professional counselors, this ambiguity and this parallel experience of spiritual confusion and of all the existential questions reach beyond the range of ordinary human experiences and levels of consciousness. Accordingly, the client's existential and/or spiritual crisis may become the counselor's crisis, resulting in an empathy fatigue reaction.

Too often, we think about the helping profession as a one-way street in which the professional or "the expert" is all knowing, and is the only person empowered to possess all the healing resources within the counselor-client relationship. By the very nature of this relationship, there is both an ethical obligation and an assumption that the professional helper reaches out in compassion and empathy to heal the client's wounded soul. Likewise, counselors have an ethical obligation to maintain confidentiality with regard to clients' stories. The fact that many counselors cannot ethically share their client's stories with anyone outside the therapeutic environment creates a kind of shroud of secrecy that many counselors take home with them. Consequently, the compassionate and empathic helper may go home at the end of the day and withdraw or try and detach from client stories that contain themes of an intense interpersonal nature.

THE WOUNDED HEALER EXPERIENCE

The "wounded healer" is an archetypal representation that psychologist Carl Jung used to describe the dynamic that takes place between client and therapist when the therapist constantly revisits her or his own emotional and psychological wounds. The basis of this phenomenon has been explained as negative countertransference experienced by the therapist. Jung felt that a wounded healer experience could harm the therapeutic alliance within the client-counselor relationship because it leaves the therapist vulnerable not only to the therapist's own issues but also to those of the clients. The term itself is actually derived from an ancient Greek legend telling of a physician named Asclepius who had mystical powers to heal his own wounds and created a sanctuary in which to treat others (National Library of Medicine [NLM], 2007). In fact, modern medicine has symbolically adopted part of this ancient philosophy, as recognized by the caduceus (two intertwined snakes grasping a staff), which is the familiar physician's symbol of the medical profession.

Truly, multiple client stories of extraordinary stressful and traumatic events, as well as exposure to clients with chronic illness and life-threatening disabilities, often place the professional helper at risk for feeling helpless and hopeless. So the question becomes one of who pays attention to and takes care of the wounded healer. Nouwen (1972) speaks to this type of counselor experience from his concept of the "wounded healer," stating that:

> When our souls are restless, when we are driven by thousands of different and often conflicting stimuli, when we are always "over there" between people, ideas and the worries of this world, how can we possibly create the room and space where someone else can enter freely without feeling himself an unlawful intruder? Paradoxically, by withdrawing into ourselves, not out of self-pity but out of humility, we create the space for another to be himself and to come to us on his own terms. (p. 91)

G. Miller (2003) proposes that from the "wounded healer" framework, counselors bring a compassionate spirit to the client-counseling relationship. Further, the client's expectations are that counselors do not possess any psychological, emotional, or spiritual vulnerability. Thus, the counselor is seen as a role model for emotional and spiritual wellness by the client who feels wounded. However, the counselor who attempts to act as a role model may not be dealing honestly and openly with the client. Showing vulnerability as a therapist and facilitating empathic understanding suggest to our clients that we responsibly share or disclose our wounds alongside of them (G. D. Miller & Baldwin, 1987). Accordingly, counselor disclosure can appropriately be used for therapeutic leverage.

Client stories that have such themes as addictions, physical or sexual abuse, and psychological trauma can adversely affect the mind, body, and spirit of the healer, or counselor. Remembering emotions related to such painful events and re-creating an internal emotional scrapbook can be extremely painful and difficult for both clients and counselors, especially for counselors new to the helping profession.

Remembering painful and traumatic memories through storytelling is an integral part of Navajo medicine where the purpose is to help make sense of a traumatic event and to bring harmony to the mind, body, and spirit. In the Navajo culture, the person who requires healing takes part in a ceremony that includes family and friends who gather for rituals including chants, dances, and prayers. The responsibility for healing is shared by most of the community, not just by the person requiring healing and the healer. Storytelling is done through ceremonial chants and the stories are usually about the creation of the Navajo people and how all things in the universe are interconnected. Storytelling in the Navajo culture is said to be healing medicine (Tafoya & Kouris, 2003) because stories have the power to clarify one's identity, purpose, connection, and harmony with the spirit world.

While some stories are healing, others have the potential to carry multiple layers of meaning that may be interpreted and perceived by others as a myth or poison that weakens the spirit of the individual and the culture (Coulehan, 1980). Nouwen (1972), drawing on his concept of the "wounded healer," states that

> Many people suffer because of the false supposition on which they have based their lives. That supposition is that there should be no fear or loneliness, no confusion or doubt. But these sufferings can only be dealt with creatively when they are understood as wounds integral to our human condition. (p. 93)

Facilitating empathic approaches in the counseling relationship requires that we help our clients unfold the layers of their stress, grief, loss, or traumatic experiences by searching through their emotional scrapbooks. The search for the personal meaning and purpose of our client's pain and suffering may contribute to the counselor's spiritual fatigue experience. If counselors are mindful of this experience, and view this as an opportunity for nurturing personal growth and development, they will then learn resiliency strategies that can help to replenish their wounded spirits.

EMPATHY AS THE SOUL OF THE COUNSELOR: AN INDIGENOUS-CULTURAL WORLDVIEW

In many cultures, the soul is regarded as the seat of the individual's emotions, feelings, and spiritual experiences. In Jungian symbolism, the center of the person's psyche is referred to as the "self" or "soul." Many professional counselors will spend a tremendous amount of psychic energy being empathic and looking for the emotional parts of their client's soul that have been lost to incest, physical abuse, addictions, loss of a loved one, chronic illness, or psychological and physical trauma. Empathy as the soul of the counselor figures prominently in the subjective experience of understanding the whole-person experience of the "fatigued" professional. This is a significant point, because there is a parallel experience between the professional helper and the fatigue syndromes (i.e., burnout, compassion, empathy fatigue) that ultimately end up affecting the mind, body, spirit, and soul.

The transition from being a professional counselor trained in the West to being a culturally competent healer requires openness to indigenous health and healing practices. West (2005) suggests that if we truly want to experience the richness of each client's cultural healing system, then we need to honor that client's belief system. Thus, integrating traditional approaches in therapy (e.g., stress management, relaxation, visualization) with more indigenous practices with culturally different clients/consumers may offer professional helpers another dimension with which to facilitate therapeutic approaches. Developing an understanding and appreciation of this will have profound implications for practice. It should be emphasized that many indigenous healing practices may also benefit the professional helper's program of self-care practices. Accordingly, the integration of cultural practices is paramount in healing the counselor's empathy fatigue.

Healing empathy fatigue among professional counselors requires diversity of thought in prevention and intervention strategies that are holistic in nature. Part II of this book will present guidelines for integrating complementary and alternative self-care practices that are indigenous to specific cultural groups. This should offer professional counselors a rich integration and expanded menu of traditional self-care practices in managing counselor fatigue syndromes (e.g., burnout, compassion, or empathy fatigue).

From an indigenous worldview, illness within the mind, body, and spirit means there is a blocking of the flow of "good" energy. In Central

African cultures (Graham, 2005), there is a belief in a "sleeping sickness of the soul," which is exhibited in indifference to the pain and suffering of others. Addictions are just one example of how the flow of energy can be blocked and prevent us from engaging in our daily routines (e.g., job, family, relationships, exercise). Regardless of the belief system, any form of energy that is blocked can distort our perceptions and attitudes about life. This ultimately affects our minds, bodies, and spirits. It can decrease our feelings and compassion for the good work that we do for others. We can easily become out of balance with life. Thus, being open to our spirit helpers and letting the universal life energy flow can decrease the possibility that our souls will become fatigued or wounded. This is an ongoing challenge for anyone who has had the opportunity to provide service to another human being.

Beginning-level but also seasoned therapists should be open to the idea of embracing cultural differences by paying attention to indigenous health and healing approaches. This may be used as therapeutic leverage for culturally different clients. The journey to becoming a professional helper requires personal and professional growth experiences that may not be provided by the typical workshop on counselor burnout. Thus, developing one's mind, body, and spirit requires openness to the idea that we must grow along with the persons we serve.

EMPATHY AND THE THIRD-EYE CHAKRA

Empathy as a trait or state of the professional counselor is not simply a counseling approach or strategy whereby the counselor grasps the meaning of the client's issues (e.g., transition from a loss), then associates this with a specific feeling (e.g., stress, depression, anxiety) and relates this to the client's overall experience (e.g., overall sense of loss and grief). Rather, it is suspected that more seasoned counselors use an empathic-intuitive connection in order to experience their client's verbal and nonverbal communication. In other words, the more established and seasoned therapist has developed a sixth sense or "third eye" for intuitiveness. Professional counselors who have engaged in multiple sessions over the years are much better than beginning-level therapists at sensing whether their client's verbal report of emotion is congruent with the client's nonverbal behaviors and cognitions, or whether their client could potentially harm him- or herself or others. Accordingly, it is suspected that more seasoned practitioners have learned over the years how to integrate their client's thoughts, feelings, and cognitions with spiritual and existential meaning and purpose. More specifically, the seasoned therapist facilitates counseling approaches using the mind, body, and spirit and integrating traditional healing approaches in Western psychotherapy with the client's culturally specific belief system.

ONE SPIRIT

Many cultures of the world believe that there is a divine spiritual energy or life force that has created order in the universe since the beginning of time. For example, in the African-centered worldview (Graham, 2005), spirituality is defined as (a) a creative life force, (b) the very essence of all things that connect human beings to others, and (c) the power that interconnects all elements of the universe: people, animals, and earthly things such as plants. Interestingly, on the other side of the world, Native or indigenous Indian tribes of North American ancestry have a very similar belief about divine spiritual energy. The Great Spirit, as referred to by most Native peoples, is the creator of all things. Likewise in this view, all things are related and interconnected to the Great Spirit; particularly the mind, body, and spirit. If one's mind is out of harmony with one's spirit then there is disharmony in all systems. Thus, One Spirit in a cultural sense suggests that the individual does not have to visit a physician to heal the body, see a counselor to heal the mind, or attend a faith-based institution to heal the spirit. The One Spirit entity is loving, compassionate, humanistic, and all knowing (noetic), and represents holistic healing at its best.

Many gifted healers and ancient sages have claimed to see the aura of this spiritual energy flowing through themselves and others as they are performing their healing rituals. As Seaward (1997) explains, this spiritual energy binds us to the source of God at all times. This connection will never be broken, because all living things emanate from this divine source. There is a sense that this universal spirit communicates and nourishes one's soul. Regardless of one's belief in a god, universal spirit, or higher power, this *chi* or *ki* continuously flows even in the wounded soul. Stress of the mind, body, and soul is felt by many in the helping profession, especially in the presence of clients who are suffering and are in pain. However, a wounded soul experience can provide us with the greatest opportunity for the growth of our soul and spirit.

CULTURALLY COMPETENT COUNSELING

Professional counselors who are particularly skilled in multicultural counseling interventions know that establishing rapport with a culturally different client is critical to achieving a good working alliance. It may mean careful attention to the client's nonverbal or covert description of disharmony in the client's mind, body, and spirit. Counselors who are skilled in multicultural counseling use their cultural intellect (i.e., knowledge and awareness of the client's cultural belief system) and their intuitive sense to understand their client's worldview. The counselor must try and understand the client holistically from a cultural perspective. This includes, but is not limited to, understanding cultural aspects of the client's (a) beliefs about good mental health and wellness, (b) psychosocial and spiritual well-being, (c) style of expressed and unexpressed emotions, (d) verbalized feelings and specific meaning behind the emotions expressed, and (e) overall experience of acculturated values. Understanding cultural differences requires cultural identity work by both the counselor and the client. Everyone has a cultural identity and is a member of an array of other cultural groups and subgroups representing such things as gender (male/female), geographic regions of the United States (southern rural/urban), age (younger/older), language (English/Spanish, or multilingual), religious/spiritual beliefs (Catholic/Protestant), as well as many other characteristics. An excellent starting point for the helping professional is to begin a journey of understanding one's own cultural beliefs and identity. The inability to understand one's own cultural beliefs and identity can create disharmony in the mind, body, and spirit. Not having such a sense of interconnectedness has its consequences in failure to understand the meaning and purpose of the life we have been given, thus creating a wounded soul experience.

Culturally competent helping professionals have learned to use the subjective experiences of culturally different individuals with whom they have come in contact, in order to learn how to skillfully build a rapport and establish a working alliance. Just as in the scientific paradigm, the counselor may make a hypothesis about the client, measure/assess the client's behaviors and weigh them against others in the norm group, focus on critical incidents associated with specific behaviors, feelings, and beliefs, and then arrive at some interpretation or hypothesis about the client/consumer. The professional's clinical judgment will either support or not support the theory created about the client's dysfunctional life patterns. However, the culturally competent professional will be attuned to the subjective experiences of the client's cultural worldview. The point is that counselors often must develop a sixth sense to search the essence of their client's mind, body, and spirit for the purpose of understanding the client holistically. This information, which is often hidden by self and others, can assist counselors in developing appropriate treatment approaches. Accordingly, preventing a wounded soul experience requires that we should be mindful of the mind, body, and spiritual cost of being empathic with others. An exploration of the meaning of our client/consumer's cultural identity and belief system is an opportune time to begin our own search of cultural identity.

CONCLUDING REMARKS

There are many rich healing traditions indigenous to various cultures around the world that are integrated in many counseling and psychotherapy practices today (Mijares, 2003; Moodley & West, 2005). In recent years, the literature has referred to these practices as complementary, alternative, or new age medicine. Professional helpers may also benefit from these practices to enrich their program of self-care, as seen in the programs offered in part III of *Empathy Fatigue*. Regardless of how modern counseling and psychology integrate the ancient wisdom of various cultural healing practices, the requirements for healing the soul or spirit center on the idea that the healer may in fact feel the suffering and pain of others (Moodley, 2005), thus taking on many of the characteristics associated with a wounded soul or empathy fatigue experience.

Today's practitioners of the healing arts must strive to restore the soul and maintain a balance of empathy and compassion so that both the client and healer can be empowered to achieve optimal levels of mind, body, and spiritual wellness. As with any treatment approach, achieving the full benefits of higher states of consciousness and optimal wellness requires good intentions and a commitment from the professional helper.

In chapter 6, we will see that empathy is not just a personality state, trait, or cultural way of being. Rather, when one expresses the emotion of empathy, it is communicated and integrated through the dynamic neural structure of the brain.

6   The Neuroscience of Empathy

The dynamic neural structure and function of the brain, as it relates to human emotions, is a complex topic that goes beyond the scope and intention of this book. However, compelling new research on the emotional mechanisms of the brain is at the forefront of understanding the mind-body effects of expressing and receiving emotions during therapeutic interactions. There are also implications for studying the brain's extraordinary powers of perception and intuitiveness within this new research paradigm. Intuitiveness and the perception of emotions in others are special gifts developed to varying degrees by professional helpers. Thus, counselors' ability to increase their level of empathic perception and of feeling a sense of self and others should provide greater opportunities for evaluating the mind, body, and spiritual characteristics of empathy fatigue.

Understanding how we think, feel, behave, and go beyond the boundaries of non-ordinary states of consciousness seems to be a natural evolutionary step for the human race, leading us to the next stage of emotional and ego development. Research into how the brain processes certain emotions appears to offer credibility to the transpersonal and metaphysical healing experiences of different indigenous and cultural practices, such as those discussed in this book. Integrating indigenous healing practices into counseling and psychotherapy transcends the boundaries of the scientific paradigm and traditional clinical psychology. Thus, having an appreciation of humanistic and transpersonal experiences as they relate to counseling and psychology has enormous cross-cultural significance (Walsh & Vaughn, 1993).

In the last two decades, the fields of science, religion, and spirituality have merged into a new dimension of cross-disciplinary collaborative research. The highly specialized fields of quantum physics, biochemistry, physiology, transpersonal psychology, and complementary medicine have shown that human consciousness is now an integral part of the divine consciousness (Seaward, 1997). The emerging field of psychoneuroimmunology, a word coined by Ader (1990) in 1981, has provided new insights into our thoughts, emotions, and physical wellness. Building upon the shoulders of giants in these highly complex specialty areas, Wilber's (1996) comprehensive work, A *Brief History of Everything*, has theoretically mapped the biological, psychological, cognitive, and spiritual development of the individual. This philosophical pilgrimage offers a unique example of how cross-disciplines can provide a clearer understanding of the complex interplay between the individual's mind, body, and spirit.

The newer integral studies in mind, body, and spiritual consciousness can assist us in our capacity for developing intuitiveness and perception of self and others. It can offer a profound new emotional state of consciousness that goes beyond the cognitive and physical realm. As Huther (2006) suggests, empathic intuitiveness and perception are the result of the individual's cumulative psychosocial development and subjective experiences of life that may help us understand the neural pathways of human compassion and consciousness. This new paradigm offers the possibilities of integrating classical studies in neuroscience with newer models of research that assimilate the individual's collective emotional development into a more comprehensive and inclusive theory.

EMOTIONS AND THE BRAIN

In the study of emotions and the brain, it is hypothesized that there are discrete, basic, and universal emotions that persons react to on a mind, body, and spiritual dimension (Bar-On & Parker, 2000; Mayne & Bonanno, 2001). Most persons have the capacity to express universal emotions (e.g., anger, love, happiness, sadness) to varying degrees and with varying levels of intensity. However, Mayne and Ramsey (2001) imply that this is only the tip of the iceberg, because expressing emotions constitutes only a measure of self-report, personal or individualized experience.

New studies report that the shared emotions and physiological arousal experienced between client and therapist contribute to our knowledge of how empathic connections are developed during psychotherapy. For example, Marci, Ham, Moran, and Orr (2007) looked at 20 client-therapist pairs, with the clients being treated for mood and anxiety disorders. The researchers specifically focused on the therapeutic relationships that were formed during psychotherapy sessions. They then took measures of the physiological reactions of both client and therapist and the client's perceived level of empathy as expressed by the therapist. They found that when high positive emotions and empathy were expressed by the therapist, then similar physiological responses were experienced by the client and therapist as measured by electrical skin conductance recordings, heart rate, voice dynamics, and body movement. Thus, it seems that a much stronger working alliance or social-emotional attachment is formed in therapy when clients perceive their therapist is communicating higher levels of empathy.

It is clear that neuroscientists and clinical and experimental psychologists measure empathy from different perspectives. From a purely dynamic physiological viewpoint, the expression of emotions has been shown to involve different body systems during therapeutic interactions. Integral studies in the mind, body, and spiritual aspects of how different emotions are experienced by an individual offers a more comprehensive understanding of this complex area of study. The mind-body neural connections within the structures of the brain are important for understanding the physical, emotional, psychological, and spiritual connection experienced in empathy fatigue. More experimental designs will be needed to measure the individual's perception of critical events (e.g., hurricanes, floods, fire, physically traumatic experiences) and the ways in which the individual's autonomic nervous system (e.g., parasympathetic and sympathetic) is activated at the time of an actual or anticipated stressful event.

Because an empathetic connection forms between client and therapist, there appears continually to be a potential for some degree of emotional and physical exhaustion to be experienced during therapeutic interactions. For instance, if the therapist experiences some degree of physiological-emotional stress during intense therapeutic interactions, this could potentially cause an acute empathy fatigue reaction. Likewise, after the professional helper is exposed to regular, prolonged periods of physiological and emotional arousal, a chronic state of empathy fatigue could result. Consequently, chronic activation of the stress response has both a physiological and an emotional cost, which can include anxiety and depressive disorders (Kabat-Zinn, 1990; Sapolsky, 1998). Because the stress response is highly individualized by perception, coping skills, capacity for resiliency, and other factors, then, theoretically, this should account for both the acute and the chronic nature of empathy fatigue. Thus, it is not surprising to note that many stress researchers believe that as much as 80% of all physical illness is caused by psychological and emotional stressors (Kabat-Zinn, 1990, 1994; Sapolsky, 1998; Selye, 1976; Weil, 1995).

DISCOVERING THE NEURAL PATHWAYS TO EMOTIONS

Kabat-Zinn (see Berger, 2006) indicates that empathy fatigue can be scientifically measured in the brain because there are specific neurological pathways to empathetic responses. The complexities of studying how emotions affect our mind, body, and spirit, require researchers to look at such problems from a multidisciplinary perspective that includes the fields of psychology, neurology, immunology, and biology. The discipline of psychoneuroimmunology (PNI) has provided a model with which researchers can study emotions and the brain. The task of PNI researchers is a difficult one because, as Sapolsky (1998) suggests, our emotions, particularly the stress response, have their own unique physiological arousal patterns of magnitude, frequency, and intensity. This is in part because people differ in how they turn on their stress mechanism and other emotional responses within the brain. Thus, emotional responses manifest in complex ways within the human neurological system because we possess different personality traits, behavioral response patterns, and motivational states (Mayne & Ramsey, 2001).

Sapolsky (1998) eloquently describes this acute physiological stress reaction that can fatigue our body. Initially, when we perceive an event to be highly stressful, our body goes into a fight or flight mode that activates our sympathetic nervous system. Our autonomic nervous system originates in the brain and reaches out into every organ, blood vessel, hormone, and gland in our body. It is important to note that this same physiological reaction is turned on even when we anticipate or believe that something bad is going to happen. Next, the hormones epinephrine and norepinephrine (the British refer to these as adrenaline and noradrenaline) are secreted in our body so that we can mobilize energy rapidly and react to a stressful or critical life event. The other half of the autonomic nervous system plays an opposing role and engages our parasympathetic system, which helps us calm down. While the sympathetic system speeds up our heart rate and blood flow, the parasympathetic system slows things down so that we are not always in a state of emergency or crisis.

Kabat-Zinn (1990) indicates that clinical studies have shown some individuals to be constantly in a state of hyperarousal. This can become a permanent way of life for some and is observed in persons with chronic and persistent anxiety-related disorders (e.g., acute stress, PTSD, Generalized Anxiety Disorder [GAD]). Many individuals internalize this physiological stress reaction and consequently never have an opportunity to store energy for when they need it for positive benefits at the cellular level. In other words, if we are constantly trying to mobilize energy, we never have the opportunity to store it so we can use it to help us achieve calm and focused states of consciousness. Overall, there is a physical and emotional cost to persistent sympathetic arousal because of the high levels of glucocorticoids released in the body. High levels of glucocorticoids constitute one of the markers for depression and anxiety disorders (Sapolsky, 1998).

Brothers (1989) points to the amygdala-cortical pathway in the brain as part of the key neural circuitry that underlies the emotions associated with the empathy response. The amygdala appears to be the specific structure of the brain that orchestrates the most intense electrical activation when we are reading, interpreting, or trying to understand the emotions of others. In fact, the amygdala is positively correlated with increases in negative affect and it consistently shows robust activation during intense emotional experiences and brain imaging studies (Feldman Barrett, Bliss Moreau, Duncan, Rauch, & Wright, 2007). Thus, over time, the counselor's inability to express a healthy and facilitative emotional response (such as empathy) based on the client's expression of feelings of stress, grief, or trauma appears to have a biological, physiological, emotional, psychological, social, and spiritual cost to the counselor. In other words, the chronic and cumulative activation of the emotional brain and the habitual repression of emotions can compromise our immune system, a system that increases our resistance to infections, chronic illness, and diseases (Pert, Dreher, & Ruff, 2005; Sapolsky, 1998; Weil, 1995).

THE EMOTIONALLY INTELLIGENT BRAIN

Awareness of one's emotions is considered to be a prerequisite for empathy and is very closely associated with measuring the emotional intelligence of children, adolescents, and adults (Bar-On & Parker, 2000; Goleman, 1995). This is an important starting point for healing empathy fatigue. However, the ability to empathize with others cannot exceed our ability to monitor our own emotional status (Lane, 2000) and may compromise our mental, physical, and spiritual health, resulting in some degree of empathy fatigue. As counselors, we should have a plethora of mind-body strategies (e.g., breathing exercises, relaxation and meditative activities, imagery, hypnotherapy, lifestyle changes) that enable us to use our mind's extraordinary capacity to positively affect the physical aspects of our body. Although we have no control over our autonomic nervous system, we do have some degree of control over our voluntary nervous system, as can be observed during a biofeedback session. Thus, we should become attuned to our thoughts, feelings, emotions, and behaviors, which are things that we have control over in life. This is central to our self-care and the care we provide to our clients.

INTUITIVENESS AND PERCEPTION AS A STATE OF CONSCIOUSNESS

Huther (2006) suggests that empathy requires a significant level of intuitiveness when perceiving and processing any type of nonverbal expression of feeling and emotion. The capacity for empathy is primarily found in those persons who possess this highly complex mechanism within the emotional part of the brain. Expressing empathy and possessing the capacity for warmth, compassion, and understanding are positive attributes and worker traits for those in the counseling and psychology professions. According to career development theorists, such people must be motivated and have an expressed or manifested interest to work therapeutically and interpersonally with others, sometimes at intense levels of interaction. A key point is that the helper must be willing to be a part of another person's emotional world; a world that may be extremely emotionally painful at times. However, it should be pointed out that the idea that only helping and human service professionals have a highly developed capacity for empathy is not necessarily accurate. When we consider all occupations, we see that counseling and psychology professionals may not necessarily possess the highest degree of empathy. It has been found that individuals in such varied occupations as those of a research scientist, design engineer, or professional book editor may possess the capacity to express empathy.

Brennan (1987), a former research scientist with NASA and currently a therapist, healer, and author, has spent a lifetime researching high sense perception (HSP) and the human energy field to try and improve the health and healing of individuals. It is evident in her writings that she and others like her who began careers outside the counseling and psychology field have a deep sense of compassion and empathy for others. Brennan explains that within the deep structures of the brain, the body's sense of time, space, consciousness, and emotions forms inseparable patterns of energy that have multiple dimensions of reality. These patterns can be seen as body auras by those who have developed the gift for this empathic-intuitive ability.

Brennan (1987) points to Albert Einstein's special theory of relativity, published in 1905, to illustrate the new look that neuroscientists have taken at the connection between one's mind, body, and spirit. She explains how Einstein confronted the thinking current in his day regarding Newtonian physics and avowed that space is not a three-dimensional entity. Rather, time and space together form a fourth dimension: hence, the space-time continuum. In other words, time is not a linear or absolute concept. Time is relative to the observer. So if two independent observers observe the same event happening at the same time, within the same general physical space, they will order the event differently in terms of when it actually occurred. This is especially true if each person moves at a different velocity relative to the observed event. As Hawking (1988) states concisely, "since the speed of light is just the distance it has traveled divided by the time it has taken, different observers would measure different speeds for the light" (p. 21). Thus, in the theory of relativity, all observers must agree on how fast light travels. They still, however, may not agree on the distance that light travels and the time it takes to travel such a distance.

The point is that Einstein's theory of relativity basically put an end to earlier ideas suggesting that time is an absolute concept. Thus, there was a major consciousness shift in our thinking and philosophy about who our ultimate Creator or Supreme Being is, where we came from, and where we are going after we die. Likewise, dissecting and measuring brain cell activity in the laboratory can no longer provide neuroscientists with answers to the question of how the human brain functions in terms of emotions (e.g., love, fear, compassion), mood (e.g., sad, excited), intelligence, or behaviors (e.g., laziness, anger). We cannot consign human beings to mere physical or biological existence. The consciousness shift on the event horizon is that there is an enormous capacity to develop our mind, body, and spirit for self-healing purposes. This integral connection is much like gravity. Gravity is an unseen form of energy that keeps us earthbound. We hardly notice gravity until we trip and fall to the ground. As quantum physicists say, "gravity is mysterious. It is a grand force permeating the life of the cosmos, but it is elusive and ethereal" (Greene, 1999, p. 61). Thus, we will require integral approaches in mind-body research, with consideration given to the existential and spiritual aspects of human beings.

This very brief discussion of the cosmos and quantum physics is a metaphor for the new paradigm shift in consciousness, transpersonality, and brain research studies. Such a discussion is required today because historically, during the second half of the 20th century, Western psychology recognized only a few states of consciousness, such as the normal waking and sleeping states (Walsh & Vaughn, 1993). Most states of consciousness were viewed as pathological and related to such conditions as being intoxicated, psychotic, or homicidal. Today, many therapists have experienced a special type of empathic awareness and intuitiveness with clients (Sollod, 2005). Although conventional psychotherapeutic approaches also emphasize the importance of focusing on understanding the client's thoughts and feelings and responding empathically, empathic intuitiveness operates at a much deeper level of consciousness and has sparked interest among mind-body researchers. Thus, we may be on the event horizon of understanding how human emotions are communicated through intentional and intuitive mind, body, and spiritual work. There are many positive aspects to understanding personal emotions at a deeper level. However, when deeper levels of compassion and empathy are experienced and communicated by the therapist, there may be a professional cost that results in an empathy fatigue reaction.

CONCLUDING REMARKS

The scientific paradigm and manifestations of transpersonal psychology and other metaphysical events should not be the subjects of disciplines that work independently of each other. Rather, blending the scientific paradigm (i.e., neuroscience) with transpersonal psychology and mysticism has been a developing area of research that has expanded within the last 20 years in psychology, theology, philosophy, and other specialty areas. When we study some time-honored healing traditions (e.g., shamanic drumming, native chants, dance, meditation, yoga), perhaps we have come full circle in our quest for understanding both ordinary and non-ordinary states of consciousness. Such indigenous practices as are facilitated by mystics, healers, and folk medicine men and women could provide models for the achievement of higher levels of intuitiveness and empathic states of consciousness for professional counselors. The synthesis of conventional counseling and psychotherapy with indigenous healing approaches can only enrich our understanding of the brain's profound capacity for deeper levels of compassion and empathy.

PART II

INTRODUCTION

Counseling and psychology are challenging fields with a prolific history of facilitating person-centered approaches to assist individuals achieve personally fulfilling, socially meaningful, and emotionally healthy lives. There is a noticeable change in the types of individuals and groups being served and the services provided by professional counselors. Today, there is an enormous need for qualified mental health professionals who can provide counseling for diverse groups of cultures and individuals who report issues ranging from daily hassles to extraordinarily stressful and traumatic events. Consequently, the professional counselor must diagnose and treat a wide range of conditions that may include anxiety, mood, and adjustment disorders, as well as substance abuse and a variety of process addictions.

A great need also exists for professional counselors who can provide critical incident interventions for situations involving school violence, workplace violence, and the multiple natural disasters that occur on our planet. Crisis response has become difficult, especially for private practitioners who work independently and are not affiliated with county, regional, or statewide crisis response and disaster mental health teams and able to use their resources and support. It is essential that professional counselors have personal and professional support from a variety of sources such as clinical supervisors, professional growth or continuing educational activities, and professional counseling associations. Assisting the wounded helper to deal with emotional, mental, physical, spiritual, and occupational exhaustion is essential to the maintenance of a balance of responsibilities that may include personal, relational, family, home, career, and wellness activities.

Traditional psychotherapy, wellness counseling, cognitive-behavioral therapy, and stress reduction techniques have been the conventional self-care approaches for those professionally fatigued or burned out. Some new ideas support integrating the healing of the wounded professional's mind, body, and spirit. Nontraditional approaches used by native Western and Eastern cultures have been underutilized in personal growth and development opportunities for professional counselors. It may be that the collective wisdom of indigenous cultural practices has something to teach us in enhancing our self-care practices.

Part II of *Empathy Fatigue* will offer professional helpers (a) information on different Western and non-Western indigenous folk-healing systems of self-care that can potentially be integrated into one's personal and cultural belief system; (b) culturally diverse guidelines and recommendations for cultivating personal wellness and resiliency approaches; and (c) principles and practices that can be utilized by clinical supervisors, counselor educators, and professional counseling associations.

The need for self-care practices has accelerated because professional counselors are working with more chronic and persistent cases in a diversity of settings. There appears to be a shift in the field from general mental health counseling to working in highly specialized areas of counseling. For instance, substance abuse counseling, marriage and family therapy, school counseling, rehabilitation counseling, play and art therapy all require specialized training, certification, and/or a counselor license to practice.

Counselors must also deal with issues related to managed care, third-party reimbursement, and the changing sociocultural and political environment. The credentialing process of the different national certifications and state professional licensing boards has created some confusion among clients/consumers. There are also misunderstandings among state legislators about the variety of professional roles, identities, responsibilities, and competencies required within the counseling field. This has created a relentless pursuit of turf protection among some professional groups. Interestingly, some of the individuals, groups, agencies, and professional associations that provide training and development to deal with conflict and crisis seem to be dealing with their own conflict and crisis. The toxic energy present in some settings appears to be systemic. It impairs the immune system of the profession's mind, body, and spirit.

There are other signs of a changing environment within the mental health system of care. We have gone from providing traditional psychotherapeutic approaches (e.g., talk therapy) for 10–15 sessions or more to short term solution-focused and motivational interviewing models of treatment (e.g., 3–6 sessions). Employee assistance programs are now the primary point for coordinating substance abuse and mental health treatment in many organizations. There is also a greater emphasis on short-term assessment, community referral to peer support groups (e.g., Alcoholics Anonymous [AA], Narcotics Anonymous [NA]), and the utilization of paraprofessional resources. Additionally, there is a greater emphasis on wellness prevention programs offered within private industry and state government.

In view of the significant changes in the mental and physical health care system, there appears to be a new social-emotional consciousness, directed toward increasing our overall health and wellness. Many consumers want to make significant life changes using various wellness approaches such as dieting, exercise, nutrition, and stress management. There is little debate concerning the critical link between one's job/career satisfaction, wellness, work-related stress, and professional burnout.

Research supports the contention that there is a much higher degree of success and achievement when wellness goals are supported and reinforced by peers, colleagues, management, and the organization as a whole. The wellness approaches that have emerged in the last 20 years are partly due to the mega health care insurance industry's research, which has documented the billions of dollars that are spent and lost each year due to employee absenteeism, employee dissatisfaction, and poor and dangerous working conditions. Consequently, we have seen a decline in both the quality and the productivity of work and an increase in work-related mental and physical stress claims (e.g., due to substance abuse and other mental health disorders, chronic lower back pain, carpel tunnel syndrome, cardiovascular disease).

It has been shown statistically that workers who have lower levels of mental and physical wellness report much greater occupational stress and are prone to more frequent incidents of worker injury. Many chronic physical and mental health stress claims require lengthy litigation. The adversarial nature of the relationship between employer and employee complicates the physical, emotional, and psychological stress and healing experienced by the individual, family members, and the organization itself.

Despite our best attempts to increase wellness for ourselves and others in our environment, workers' compensation and social security disability claims have risen significantly. Occupations that have seen a dramatic increase in employee turnover and occupational burnout include those of rescue workers, firefighters, paramedics, and police officers. The September 11, 2001, terrorist attacks on New York City and Washington, DC, the military operations in Iraq and Afghanistan, numerous natural disasters such as Hurricane Katrina in August 2005, and the southern California fires in fall 2007 all require a high degree of commitment. Clearly, people who once thought about entering the helping and human service professions may have second thoughts about them. Some may feel there is an apocalypse in the helping professions.

Within such professions, there is an ongoing need for well-qualified professionals to work with the mental health aspects of disasters and to provide social services, vocational rehabilitation, and other allied health services. There will always be a need for professionals to perform assessments, document diagnoses for third-party reimbursement, provide treatment, and coordinate services for persons with a variety of rehabilitation and mental health needs. One particular worker trait that is necessary in working successfully in the helping professions is care and compassion for humanity. It is essential to be competent and ethical in the delivery of human services. It is even more critical that the helper be motivated and possess an ongoing commitment to fulfilling the essential role of compassion and empathy in service to another human being.

The fields of counseling and psychology have studied burnout, counselor impairment, and professional fatigue syndromes for the last 15 years and confirm that these conditions do in fact exist. So we need to embrace the notion that there is an enormous emotional, mental, physical, and spiritual cost to providing services to others at intense levels of compassion and empathy. Despite our best efforts to facilitate prevention, wellness, and stress management approaches, there is much work to be done. An emphasis on approaches that integrate the mind, body, and spirit is crucial to improving self-care strategies and practices among professional helpers. It is my hope that in part II, professional counselors can begin or continue their journey of conceptualizing and identifying supports and resources for cultivating self-care practices. Ultimately, professional helpers can maximize the opportunity to feel more peace, compassion, and harmony with their personal and professional life.

7 A Call for Integral Approaches in Healing Empathy Fatigue

In the documentary film *A Time of the Sixth Sun* (Worldwide Productions, 2007) there is a discussion featuring the collective wisdom of some of the planet's tribal elders, wisdom keepers, new scientists, and spiritual teachers, who make the comment that "There's never been more information at our disposal. From ancient tribal wisdom, religious texts, myth, prophecy, new sciences, spiritual teachings, and divine guidance. In the end, we will all have to make the journey within and decide what is the truth for each of us individually." The film suggests that we have entered into a critical time of our history in which significant events around the world have come together. It is perhaps a spiritual sign of a personal and cultural transformation or shift in the planet's consciousness that relates to all aspects of our life. Assuming there is a culture shift occurring with regard to the world's spirituality, religious beliefs, cultural values, global climate changes, political ideology, and immigration of various cultural and ethnic groups in North America, world health concerns, economic collapse in some markets, and other changes in our internal and external environment, then perhaps we ought to pay attention and be mindful of the opportunities that exist at this time in our lives. As Taoism teaches us about the unity of opposites (i.e., yin-yang; with crisis comes opportunity), then perhaps integrating Western and Eastern approaches has much to offer us in terms of our self-care practices.

This chapter presents an overview of the different domains of self-care practices and healing strategies that are integral to healing the mind, body, and spirit in empathy fatigue. Managing, coping with, and preventing professional fatigue syndromes such as empathy fatigue requires that we draw from a diversity of traditional and nontraditional self-care approaches. Additionally, this chapter highlights the integration of healing strategies for the wounded soul that have been used for thousands of years by shamans and medicine men/women in many indigenous cultures for healing the mind, body, and spirit. The chapters that follow, particularly in part III, will offer specific guidelines and recommendations for integrating such indigenous or folk-medicine approaches.

The most troubling aspect of counselor impairment and fatigue syndromes such as empathy fatigue is that we separate our cognitive, emotional, physical, and spiritual well-being from ourselves. We are disconnected holistically and come to be in disharmony with our mind, body, and spirit. In fact, our personal aura looks and feels different as we try and balance our personal and professional lives. Many professional helpers rely heavily on traditional or conventional approaches in managing and coping with their own occupational, organizational, and personal stress. This is because the majority of counselor training programs use conventional psychotherapeutic, humanistic, and cognitive-behavioral approaches to train professional counselors in the diagnosis and treatment of mental health conditions.

Carl Jung appeared to have an understanding of counselor fatigue syndromes. He observed a significant need for therapists to rebalance their minds, bodies, and spirits after spending countless hours in psychotherapy sessions with their clients. He was inspired by the belief that humans are spiritual beings, not just biological, instinctual, or behavioral organisms. He explored manifestations of the soul and the process of transforming the mind, body, and spirit into a greater awareness of the self to increase one's purpose in life. Jung was obviously well versed in analytical, critical, rational, and linear human thinking. Later, his work developed into metaphor, symbols, and intuition using the conscious and unconscious mind to communicate between these two worlds. As a result of the client tapping into his/her wealth of content, feeling, and experience, guided by a competent psychotherapist, monumental leaps were made in psychotherapeutic techniques that facilitated rich insight into and awareness of the mind, body, and spirit. In Jung's worldview, regaining psychic equilibrium appears to be paramount in healing one's mind, body, and spirit. Although Jung may have discovered the evolutionary experiences of the individual's collective consciousness and advanced the development of deep personal insight and awareness, the personal quest and hunger for soul-searching and self-discovery have been present for thousands of years prior to the development of psychotherapeutic techniques.

Native healers, mystics, and shamans talked about soul-searching and self-discovery for thousands of years. They facilitated transcendental approaches to the mind, body, and spirit through meditation, journeying, drumming, sweat lodge ceremonies, and hundreds of other rituals. The key therapeutic value was that healing was done one on one and within the social group. Facilitating such practices was the responsibility of everyone within the tribe. Each person contributed to the personal wholeness and harmony of the other members' minds, bodies, and spirits. In Western counseling and psychology, such experiences are discussed in terms of transpersonal or metaphysical occurrences and are facilitated through individual or group therapy sessions. However, indigenous cultures viewed such healing practices differently. Healing the mind, body, and spirit also took place outside of the healing rituals and ceremonies. This experience took place in all aspects of life by harmonious connection, moment by moment, to the great divine spirit. In contrast, Western psychotherapy tries to achieve this same experience through a one-hour client-counselor or group therapy session. Although many therapeutic communities try to facilitate health and wellness activities, the clients/consumers go home at the end of the day or after 30 days of rehabilitation treatment.

The collective wisdom of Western counseling, psychology, theology, and philosophy should not be disregarded in favor of indigenous healing approaches. Rather, the subjective metaphysical and spiritual experiences of old-world cultures can help bridge the gap between Western psychology and folk-medicine approaches. Cumulative insights from both old and new healing techniques will certainly provide a richer synthesis for those professionals open to reconnecting with the healing wisdom of older generations. Although some self-care practices are separated from others by hundreds and even thousands of years, their foundations and philosophies for self-healing should not be seen as independent of each other. All cultures have something to contribute to self-care and self-healing practices. At the core of working from a holistic and integrative perspective, professional counselors have much to gain by understanding the inner wisdom and self-healing potential of the mind, body, and spirit. We must learn how to integrate traditional counseling and psychotherapeutic approaches with some of the time-honored healing traditions that have been facilitated by mystics, healers, and folk-medicine men and women.

Healers past and present who have felt the extraordinary presence of the divine, seen intuitively with their third-eye chakra, or experienced a physical purification have likely sat in absolute stillness with an overwhelming sense of peace and compassion for themselves and others in the world. This may seem like a paradox for some professionals, because the wounded healer asks for answers to tough questions such as *How could life and death, joy and suffering, everlasting love and traumatic experiences exist all within the same day in the lives of my clients/consumers?* The thought is disorienting and begs for an answer from something other than another workshop on job burnout and managing stress. It calls on a divine source for our mind-body health and spiritual healing. The great spiritual leaders of the 20th century (e.g., Rev. Billy Graham, Rev. Martin Luther King, the Dalai Lama, Mother Teresa), who have prayed, meditated, and wrestled with such existential and spiritual questions, have acquired a deeper level of understanding by paying attention to the healing work of Buddha, Jesus Christ, God, the Great Spirit, Mohammed, or some other higher power. Thus, beginning or continuing a journey in healing the mind, body, and spirit requires courage and commitment.

When professional counselors help guide their clients/consumers on the path to find vocational and educational opportunities, jobs and careers, heal family and personal relationships, grieve losses, overcome addictions, or find meaning in their pain and suffering, the professional helpers must also have the courage and commitment to travel the path that is parallel to their clients' experiences. However, there is a cost to the pathfinder. Because of the uncertainty and complexity of our clients' lives, everyday helping interactions can precipitate a similar experience of acute stress, anxiety, and depression in the counselor. A wounded spirit or empathy fatigue experience is a likely result for professionals who facilitate helping interactions in an empathetic and compassionate manner.

From a historical perspective, it is suggested that the healer has experienced the same or similar pain and suffering as the person receiving the healing. Shamans and other great healers have always been able to mediate the healing process between the physical and spiritual worlds. The purpose is to create a unity between the giver and receiver of the healing. The healer facilitates such healing encounters by calling upon spirit helpers for the purpose of bringing relief from pain and suffering. Perhaps we are coming full circle, because there appears to be a shift toward the inclusion of more culturally centered philosophies and belief systems in healing the minds, bodies, and spirits of professional helpers.

COMPLEMENTARY, ALTERNATIVE, AND INTEGRAL APPROACHES

There are promising indicators in the mind-body-spirit research that some professional counseling and psychological associations, as well as other like-minded nonprofit institutes and organizations, want to advance the education and training in and the practice of complementary and alternative medicine (CAM) or integral medicine (IM) for clients/consumers and counselors who have undergone a wounded healer or counselor fatigue experience. Health care researchers suggest that approximately 75% of Americans have used CAM approaches and spent over $60 billion annually to treat chronic illnesses and disabilities and increase their overall wellness. The terms CAM and IM have been used for at least the last 30 years and are umbrella terms that represent over 600 healing modalities. Most CAM and IM approaches have been developed from the collective wisdom of ancient indigenous cultures. Health and healing approaches such as breathing, meditation, visualization, homeopathy, and body energy work have been around for thousands of years. Today many authors, organizations, and products inaccurately label these approaches as "new age" discoveries for treating mental and physical ailments. Ironically, many younger individuals considering entering the professions of counseling and psychology believe that most CAM approaches have been developed within the Western humanistic, psychoanalytic, and transpersonal psychology movement.

It is quite difficult to give recognition to any specific cultural group or spiritual or religious practice that has developed such healing approaches as breathing, meditation, visualization, or prayer. The healing technique may have arisen simultaneously within different cultural groups throughout history. Spiritual identity and peak spiritual experiences are not the special property of any one particular culture. The healing techniques were practiced in all world cultures and communicated from older to younger tribal members and some were written down. Scientifically speaking, the positive benefits of CAM or IM have not been totally validated or recognized. Folk medicine appears to have been relegated to the area of subjective findings with regard to metaphysical healing or the "placebo effect." Despite this criticism, one element that many CAM and IM modalities have in common is that they are safe and natural, have few if any side effects, and treat the person from a holistic or mind, body, and spiritual perspective. Mostly, when individuals utilize CAM or IM approaches they are empowering themselves with self-care health and healing practices.

The "worried well" and those wanting to increase their physical, mental, and spiritual well-being are particularly attracted to CAM and IM approaches. Unfortunately for some, this may be an impulsive flight into health, repeating the cycle of searching for a quick fix or quick solution to their anxiety, depression, and/or stress-related problems. For many counselors, CAM and IM approaches are attractive and novel ways to help clients who may not benefit from verbal therapies. However, a single workshop or book will not assure the competent and ethical practice of a particular alternative approach. Thus, the shift from conventional psychotherapeutic approaches to CAM and IM can be rather confusing for some helping professionals. This is primarily because it is difficult to find counselor education programs or professional workshops that can train and supervise counselors in practices such as breath work, transcendental meditation, shamanic drumming and journeying, or walking meditation using the labyrinth, as well as the hundreds of other techniques.

Today, CAM modalities are underrepresented in medical schools, counselor training, and psychology programs. Most programs offer specialized training in traditional or conventional Western models of counseling and psychotherapy. Nonetheless, there appears to be a promising shift on the horizon in counseling and psychology with the establishment of the National Center for Complementary and Alternative Medicine (NCCAM) within the National Institutes of Health (NIH). Despite the fact that the NCCAM is held to stringent scientific principles by the NIH, it continues to encourage and support good research on CAM approaches such as body energy work, herbal treatments, and a multitude of mind-body and other therapies that have a spiritual focus. Perhaps we have come full circle. We may be learning how to reconnect the mind, body, and spirit by respecting the contributions and advances that ancient cultures have made in health and healing practices.

UNINTENTIONAL RELUCTANCE TO INTEGRATE MIND, BODY, AND SPIRITUAL ASPECTS IN COUNSELING

Traditional Western models of counseling and psychotherapy continue to prevail within the core curriculum of counselor education and training programs. Despite encouraging signs from government-supported research and from funding sources that allow CAM and IM therapies, there remains reluctance by accredited counselor education and psychology programs to introduce culturally based spiritual practices and other mind-body approaches within the core curriculum or to develop a CAM/IM specialty area under the accreditation umbrella. This is clear from licensing and certification exams that are heavily reliant on content areas based on Western theories and practices in counseling and psychology. Other core content areas such as human growth and development, psychological testing, and career development theories seem to be deficient in salient aspects of multiculturalism. The multicultural counseling literature has attacked Western counseling and psychology as a monocultural science. For those entrenched in conventional Western counseling and psychotherapeutic approaches, it must feel as if the field is on the verge of an apocalypse and that our professional identities have been compromised. Likewise, for those that would like to move forward with a full agenda of multiculturally centered models of counseling and psychotherapy, it also must feel as if they face a formidable challenge.

We cannot ignore the contributions of Western psychoanalytic, behavioral, cognitive-behavioral, humanistic, solution-focused, and other therapies that have provided essential strategies and approaches for wellness and healing. The building blocks of counseling and psychology continue to provide the foundational skills of establishing client rapport through intentional interviewing skills (e.g., attending, listening, and appropriate eye contact), client assessment (e.g., administration of psychometric tests), and individualized treatment plans for clients/consumers. However, although there may be some universal approaches to establishing a relationship with others, there is still a barrier to building a working or therapeutic alliance with those who are culturally different.

The problem may stem in part from a bias toward what is perceived to be state-of-the-art empirically based research that supports or endorses specific counseling theories and techniques. Accordingly, some practitioners and agencies are entrenched in counseling theories, strategies, approaches, and programs that are institutionalized forms of treatment or state-mandated protocols for certain populations of people requiring mental health and substance abuse treatment, career counseling or occupational services, as well as many other types of counseling services. If practitioners have been trained in facilitating cognitive-behavioral therapies, facilitating step-groups such as AA/NA, and facilitating other therapies with a Eurocentric base, then it is difficult to transition to nonconventional models of counseling and psychotherapy. In reality, the boundaries appear to be prescribed based on the counselor's work setting, organizational policies, accreditation standards, competence to provide culturally sensitive therapeutic approaches, and the overall continuum of care or service delivery system, which is often protocol driven. Consequently, many professionals find a lack of meaning and purpose in what they are trying to achieve with their clients/consumers. For some, this has been a trigger for occupational burnout or empathy fatigue.

It is unfortunate that we have become an outcome-oriented profession with pressure from licensure and certification boards, third-party payers, and accrediting bodies. This sociopolitical influence does not work well when we are trying to establish healing partnerships with culturally different clients/consumers who desire more indigenous health and healing approaches. Despite the fact that the various counselor codes of ethics mandate professional counselors to possess cultural competence, empower their clients with supports and resources, and facilitate client autonomy, it would appear that prescriptive therapeutic approaches based in Western theories of counseling and psychology provides a foundation for our treatment goals and interventions. Comparing and contrasting old-world with new-world therapies, it almost appears that some indigenous folk practices would be unethical to practice because they have not met the rigors of the scientific paradigm.

If in fact modern counseling and psychology support different cultural paradigms of healing practices, should we not also be educating and training others in how to integrate spiritual practices in counseling and psychotherapy, or how to partner with cultural healers that can perform certain rituals and healing ceremonies? There appears to be a general lack of attention to our client/consumer's belief system when it comes to (a) structuring the counseling relationship, (b) developing culturally appropriate expectations for a good working alliance, (c) understanding cultural assumptions about the frequency and amount of time spent in a session, (d) awareness of spatial distance and other nonverbal communication, (e) the person's spiritual/religious beliefs, (f) engaging family members in therapy and their expectations of services to be provided, and (g) many other cultural aspects of the client's indigenous belief system.

Despite the fact that most therapists describe their counseling and treatment approaches as eclectic, most facilitate the Euro-eclectic counseling strategies and techniques as acquired through their academic training and clinical supervision. In reality, there appears to be a reluctance to try or lack of support for trying creative approaches that value indigenous healing roots. Practitioners who partner with other culturally competent healers who facilitate such nonconventional therapy as shamanic drumming, sweat lodge ceremonies, Reiki, mindfulness meditation, or walking meditations using the labyrinth appear to be stigmatized by some counselors and counselor educators because they do not fit into the mainstream concept of "eclectic" counseling practice. Thus, the term "eclectic" as it appears in counseling texts seems to function as describing one particular approach used by Western models of counseling and psychotherapy.

The reality is that most counselors trained in Western counseling theories and techniques have not had the opportunity to acquire the knowledge and skills in working with the mind, body, and spirit by partnering with indigenous folk healers. Those that do practice some of these time-honored traditions are often viewed by their colleagues as perhaps working on the fringe of the profession. Accordingly, if we do not have an interest in or the expertise to work with clients or ourselves using indigenous folk ways, then perhaps we need to expand our knowledge of community and regional resources and make appropriate referrals for ourselves and the individuals we serve. If we are resistant to the integration of folk healing practices into a program of self-care, then we will not afford ourselves the opportunities to benefit from such a rich source of healing for the purpose of bringing harmony to our mind, body, and spirit.

THE PARADOX OF MIND, BODY, AND SPIRITUAL WELL-BEING

The recent emphasis on curative lifestyles, disease prevention, and healthy aging activities in the medical news media (Weil, 1995, 2005) appears to suggest that we have a fair amount of control over our mental and physical well-being. For example, there are thousands of consumer Internet

Web sites that promote herbal supplements, botanical remedies, and behavioral health strategies for optimizing our mental and physical health. Some of the popular approaches that are endorsed include dieting, exercise, watching nutritional intake, weight loss, meditation, visualization, and stress management. This can be very confusing for many individuals who have acquired serious chronic illnesses, diseases, or disabilities. There appears to be an underlying implication that we are responsible for our own good health and that we can prevent, control, or reduce the negative effects of inactivity, poor nutritional habits, and many other negative lifestyle factors.

This is paradoxical to many individuals who do not have optimal physiological functioning but possess a strong desire to improve their mental, physical, and spiritual well-being. In fact, credible medical studies confirm the link between our DNA, biological composition, environment, and predisposition toward certain mental and physical conditions. So, how much control do we really have and what aspects of our lives can we really control? How can we possibly facilitate strategies to empower our clients/consumers to take responsibility for their mental, emotional, physical, and spiritual health if our biological composition is predetermined and we cannot escape our present environment? These questions relate directly to the meaning and purpose of our work as professional helpers. Such questions also influence our behavior and motivation to try alternative self-care approaches.

Having a sense of an internal locus of control does in fact improve our ability to maintain our mind, body, and spiritual wellness. Conventional prevention approaches (e.g., quit smoking and drinking, engage in dieting and exercising) tend to focus on making intentional changes to the physical body and transforming our cognitive-behavioral health. Knowing that we have some control over important choices within the life we are given is essential for understanding how to increase our mind, body, and spiritual health. Managing our health can be done through a variety of systems and institutions. It may take the form of (a) the medical model of treatment such as a visit to a psychiatrist or our family physician's office, or consuming a pharmaceutical product; (b) CAM or IM approaches that guide us through breathing, relaxation, meditation, or visualization experiences; (c) spiritually centered work such as attendance at religious/spiritual services, ceremonies, and rituals; (d) lifestyle or wellness approaches that may include diet, exercise, nutrition, or reduction of health risk factors; or (e) integrating, coordinating, and partnering with other mind-body-spiritual healers in activities that may be indigenous to our cultural beliefs about health and healing. Integral approaches can provide a wellspring of self-care practices.

THE MASK OF THE HEALER

Being a good therapist does not translate into being a good client. In other words, many therapists do not practice what they advise with their clients, such as CAM approaches. Therapists have difficulty with motivation and commitment as well. However, we give the erroneous impression to persons we serve that our mind, body, spiritual health, and interpersonal relationships are well balanced. We strongly communicate, verbally and nonverbally, to others that we are in total control of our emotional, physical, and spiritual well-being. However, this is the mask of the healer; a defensive and coping mechanism of sorts. When this occurs, we are at the far end of the empathy fatigue continuum. Thus, it is time to examine our motives for being in the counseling and helping professions.

It is important to communicate to our clients that our own wellness can also be a challenge. This is being genuine not only to ourselves but in the therapeutic relationships we build with our clients. While it is true that we have to be somewhat more healthy, functional, and resilient than our clients, we need to give ourselves permission to experience the shadow side of having to be empathically available at all times to our clients/consumers. Being empowered with the knowledge skills, gifts, and talents to help others at very intense levels of service on a daily basis does not protect our mind, body, and spirit from the experience of empathy fatigue. If we insulate ourselves from our clients' pain and suffering or if our emotions go unrecognized, then as a consequence, the level and quality of empathy expressed toward our clients will likely be compromised. Given the nature of working with others on a daily basis, the therapist will likely experience some degree of professional impairment or fatigue, such as negative countertransference, burnout, compassion, or empathy fatigue.

THE SOCIOCULTURAL DEMOGRAPHIC SHIFT

There appears to be a significant shift in conventional or traditional counseling and psychotherapy. This shift is prompted by population and demographic changes in the United States with the inclusion of different languages, religious and spiritual beliefs, family rituals, political ideologies, and many other indigenous traditions that have cultural significance to individuals. This is apparent in most geographic areas of the United States. As a result of this cultural shift, many professional helpers have been required to attend diversity and multicultural training workshops, learn key words and phrases in a language such as Spanish, or to enlist the help of a translator to assist in intake interviews, assessments, and the overall counseling process. The adjustment involved in this cultural shift may be less for those who have grown up in larger cities. Surveys of Chicago-area hospitals reported that they have had to deal with well over 25 different cultural-ethnic groups and languages spoken on a daily basis (Bauza, 2007; Business Wire, 2004). Some of these groups have been well established in the region at the time the first European settlers arrived in America.

People in rural areas of our country may have a more difficult adjustment to the culturally diverse groups moving into their region. This may be due to the lack of contact and experience that people in rural areas have had with those who are culturally different. However, changes in the population are evident in small downtown areas where storefront signs are seen in Spanish. As a consequence of this culturally enriching experience, many mental health professionals have had to change their role and scope of practice in providing services. The point is that the cultural shift tends to stress organizations and systems, as well as professional helpers. Individuals in the mental and physical healthcare professions may already be extended in their practice. Consequently, the cultural shift can increase their professional fatigue experience.

The implications for professional helpers are enormous. The conventional system of mental health care and treatment is already showing strain. There are infrastructural cracks in the bridge to other racial/ethnic groups. It is well known in the United States that persons from minority sociocultural backgrounds have had very limited access to traditional mental and physical health care. Research has shown that minority clients typically cannot afford good mental and physical health care and must rely on the support of local county, regional, or state government human services. Thus, they cannot take advantage of the American system of private mental and physical health care. In addition to the financial reasons for their limited access to health care, minority members encounter many professionals trained in conventional theories of counseling and psychotherapy who have difficulty forming therapeutic relationships with clients/consumers who are culturally different. Consequently, minority members frequently leave services prematurely and/or stay in therapy for shorter periods of time.

It has been well documented in the multicultural counseling literature that culturally different groups of individuals have had to rely primarily on folk medicine traditions and health and healing practices indigenous to their culture. These cultural values and beliefs are brought from their country of origin and are practiced among their own groups. Integrating indigenous practices with traditional counseling and psychological approaches is very difficult. This is primarily because little consideration has been given to integrating traditional folk-healing practices into conventional counselor education programs, clinical supervision experiences, or Western counseling and psychological services.

There is recent evidence of attempts to integrate indigenous healing practices with conventional counseling and psychotherapy. Recently, there has been a movement away from verbal therapies to facilitating the healing power of ceremonies and rituals led by persons from diverse cultural backgrounds. Integral to these culturally relevant approaches on the horizon is the therapist's warmth, compassion, and empathy. Unfortunately, therapy today may be less about the therapeutic relationship and the working alliance, and more about the exchange of information in terms of the content of the client's story and then the facilitation of brief, solution-focused therapies. The point to this discussion is that there is a cost to not understanding or showing an interest in our client's philosophy or system of health and healing. Essentially, we may lose the opportunity to integrate some indigenous healing strategies into self-care approaches for ourselves and others.

Despite the usefulness of the cultural debate in the helping professions, professional helpers have much to learn in terms of integrating ancient wisdom, indigenous folk medicine, and indigenous healing practices into a modern program of self-care practices. One example of such integration is provided by the practices and teachings of the various forms of Buddhism and Hinduism, which have influenced a large segment of the psychology and behavioral medicine movement. For the last 30 years or so, communities have been in existence in the West that practice mindfulness meditation. Body-energy and body-centered approaches such as yoga, Reiki, and tai chi have also been integrated into traditional models of counseling and psychotherapy.

We all have the possibilities for constructing our own cultural identity. Being open to the idea that demographically, life in American is changing and that we each have a culture, may choose which parts of our culture to retain, are not bound by the values of our cultural identities (e.g., person of color, disabled, male/female, religious/spiritual beliefs), and have opportunities to enrich our lives by sampling different elements of other cultures will perhaps deepen our knowledge, awareness, and skills for a diversity of self-care practices.

CONCLUDING REMARKS

This chapter has presented an overview of the different self-care practices and healing strategies that are integral for managing, coping with, and preventing professional fatigue syndromes such as empathy fatigue. Because each of us has our own unique personal and cultural identity, our approach to self-care requires a diversity of traditional and nontraditional strategies that are meaningful to us. This chapter has also highlighted the integration of healing strategies for the wounded soul that have been used for thousands of years by many indigenous cultures for healing the mind, body, and spirit of shamans and medicine men/women. Part III will offer specific guidelines and recommendations for integrating such indigenous or folk-medicine approaches. It is critical that creative approaches to self-care be explored by the individual. Cultivating solutions to complex problems of the mind, body, and spirit requires creative solutions and problem-solving strategies.

8

The Roots of Self-Care: An Overview of Western and Non-Western Approaches to Healing Empathy Fatigue

This chapter presents an overview of self-care practices that have been developed from a variety of traditional and nontraditional counseling approaches. The intention is to plant seeds that will grow and build resilient counselors. There are many personal stories of therapists at varying levels of development who have constructed a positive new future for themselves by taking care of their minds, bodies, and spirits. Additionally, this chapter is designed to stimulate thoughts, offer solutions, and offer guidelines for counselor educators, clinical supervisors, and professional counseling associations to help them develop models of self-care and support. Specific guidelines for the implementation of these non-conventional and nontraditional self-care approaches will be outlined in part III of *Empathy Fatigue*.

THE ROOTS OF SELF-CARE: AN EXAMPLE FROM THE NATIVE AMERICAN CULTURE

Native American medicine has been practiced in North America for over 10,000 years. Given that there are over 700 North American tribes (Native Languages of the Americas, 2007), various healing traditions have been described. There appears to be one common thread observed in most of these tribes and cultures. Primarily, healing is practiced as a very intense activity. The journey to become an Indian doctor, or medicine man/woman, involves an understanding that the healer at some point in time will become wounded and will require healing (Tafoya & Kouris, 2003). As in the Native American culture, many professional counselors in the West also encounter a wounded healer type of experience.

In some Native American teachings, it is said that each time you heal someone you give away part of your mind, body, and spirit. Eventually, the healer will need healing. Historically, in Native American medicine there is a significant personal and social transformation that must take place in order to restore harmony and balance in the person's mind, body, and spirit (Mehl-Madrona, 1997). Accordingly, physical, emotional, mental, and spiritual unease or diseases are not regarded as separate phenomena within Native American medicine. Healing does not take place in one-hour talk-therapy sessions or a visit to the physician's office to acquire a medical diagnosis and be treated with an inorganic pharmaceutical substance. Rather, Native American medicine uses ceremonial rituals for healing.

Historically, during the times when no modern medicine or mental health practitioners existed, the person who became "sick" visited the Indian shaman. This healer, together with the person who was sick, would journey to seek assistance from the power animals or spirit helpers. The healing ritual would last an hour or a week depending upon the type of treatment required. It was necessary that the receiver be an active participant in this ritual and take full responsibility for healing her/his mind, body, and spirit. The Indian shaman would work with the receiver until either that person was healed or there were no other healing approaches that could be facilitated. In most traditions, if the person was healed, this would be the only time the shaman could accept gifts from the sick person or his/her family. Imagine a healing system in today's modern culture where the therapist or physician would be paid only if the client/patient got better.

Native American healers have a rich tradition of healing the self and others using a community of healers. Rituals are practiced in the indigenous communities for the purpose of creating spiritual awareness and healing in order to accomplish a specific intention for the person who is sick (Mehl-Madrona, 1997). Particularly in Native American cultures, mental and physical wellness is achieved only when the mind, body, spirit, and community are in harmony. Achievement of the transformation of the soul takes commitment and persistence by both the giver and receiver of the healing rituals and by a caring community of providers. This is something that appears to be missing from the mental and physical health care system in Western culture.

Notably, compassion or empathy fatigue appears to have been observed thousands of years ago. Tafoya and Kouris (2003) describe the philosophy of healing based on the beliefs of tribes in the Pacific Northwest of the United States. The Indian doctor will ask family, friends, and other healers to sit in a circle around the person requiring healing. The "patient" is told to sit inside the circle. The Indian doctor then states, "One day you will sit in the chair yourself." This serves as a reminder to all those present that they are all part of the great circle, which has no top or head.

Health and healing rituals and ceremonies performed in the various indigenous tribes of North America have been foundational practices for thousands of years. In traditional Native American cultures, taking care of one's mind, body, and spirit is vital to living in harmony with oneself, the tribal community, and all things earthly. It is the way to live holistically and sustain balance with oneself and others, and the primary way to connect with the Great Spirit. In fact, health is not considered simply the absence of disease or physical problems. One may still have a chronic illness or health condition to deal with in life. Thus, sustaining balance is integral to the daily practice of living in harmony with one's mind, body, and spirit. Tragically, as various scholars have documented throughout history, Native American cultural practices of health and healing were nearly lost, driven to near extinction due to the White European settlers' expansion in various geographic regions of the country, their philosophy of ethnic intolerance, their conservative and narrowly defined religious and spiritual beliefs, their political ideology, their practice of European medicine, and many other factors involving cruel motives with destructive intentions. Indigenous groups in North America have for all practical purposes been fighting illegal immigration and terrorism since the late 1500s.

Despite these horrific periods in Native American history, many indigenous groups today have retained specific cultural practices for health and healing. Many tribes continue to use medicinal plants and herbs, maintain a variety of tribal customs and rituals such as the sweat lodge and pipe ceremonies, and maintain other holistic practices that integrate the mind, body, and spirit into daily practice. Whatever the degree of acculturation and assimilation in America of Native individuals and the tribes they belong to, many report that their cultural traditions do not discourage the use of conventional Western physical medicine or behavioral and psychological health practices.

One particular study deals with a group of American Indian women who were concerned with the prevalence of breast cancer and elected to receive periodic mammograms. This study found that most Native women integrate their indigenous cultural practices with the Western model of medicine for the purpose of regular breast cancer screenings (Canales, 2004). Similar studies have been carried out on diabetes among various American Indian tribes. In particular, the Yaqui tribe, which has slowly accepted modern biomedicine, found ways to integrate their indigenous health and healing practices with Western models of medical healthcare (De Vera, 2003). Although the etiology of diabetes among the indigenous people of Arizona is not precisely known, it is critical for the survival of the tribe to prevent this disease and seek treatment for it. It has been documented that Native Americans as a whole have two to five times the prevalence of diabetes as compared to other groups in the United States (American Diabetes Association [ADA], 2000). Some Native peoples believe that many chronic illnesses and diseases are part of a plague that was brought upon this continent by the "White man." The medicine man/woman, Indian doctor, or shaman is kept quite busy given the culturally bound philosophy of health and healing that prevails in some tribes. The American Psychological Association (APA) has recognized these philosophies of health and healing and has listed various mental health diagnostic categories, many of which are viewed as illnesses of the mind, body, and spirit (see *DSM–IV–TR*, Glossary of Culture-Bound Syndromes).

An analysis of ethnographic data from multiple sources reviewing self-care practices among Native Americans (see Canales, 2004; De Vera, 2003; Linehan & Osman, 2002; McCormick, 1997; Mehl-Madrona, 1997; Mijares, 2003; Moodley & West, 2005; Weil, 2005) reveals the following six themes:

1   Belief in both a Christian God and the Great Spirit is commonly expressed and practiced by indigenous peoples through prayers for health and healing.
2   The way to maintain one's physical and mental health is to integrate Western medicine with various indigenous cultural practices, rituals, and ceremonies.

3   Support is essential for survival, and a profound sense of inter-dependence and connection is recognized by being part of a family, extended family, tribe, and community.

4   Understanding the meaning and purpose of one's mental, physical, and spiritual health and wellness is a journey and one should accept this challenge.

5   There are multiple levels of consciousness and layers of meaning, and expressing oneself through mind, body, and spirit has the potential to transform one's harmony, balance, and overall well-being.

6   A considerable amount of time during one's day needs to be spent in activities that balance work and the management of one's integral health by taking part in leisure and recreational activities and taking brief rest periods.

Many well-intentioned non-Native people have approached indigenous healers, asking to learn how to perform ceremonies or rituals. It has been suggested by some tribal elders that non-Native Western healers clearly do not understand that performing the elements of the ceremonies and rituals is only a very small piece of the actual healing process. As an example of the fact that a certain activity may be only a very small piece of the whole, we can cite the Navajos, who are well known for their weaving arts, describe training younger individuals who are chosen as rug weavers. Only about one-third of the training and instruction involves actual hands-on demonstration of the tools and techniques required to produce a beautiful woven rug. The other two-thirds of instruction are spent showing the younger weavers how to care for sheep, honor the sky, embrace water and flowers, and glorify the earth (Tafoya & Kouris, 2003). In the Navajo culture, it is essential to have great respect for the earth and all living things.

Many Westerners do not totally comprehend that time spent honoring the earth and all its living things is just as important in the culture as weaving a beautiful rug. All parts and elements of the task are essential for understanding how things fit holistically. In other words, the tools and techniques for weaving the rug are not the essential elements or the career goal. Rather, understanding the process of living through harmony and balance is the focus of one's occupation in many Native American cultures. The philosophy of an approach that balances work, play, spiritual life, relationships, and personal time has not generalized well to the Western world.

THE ROOTS OF SELF-CARE: AN EXAMPLE FROM WESTERN COUNSELING AND PSYCHOLOGY

Research on facilitating wellness strategies for therapists has focused primarily on the negative costs of counseling interventions, rather than on the personal growth that is experienced when dealing with traumatized clients (Linley & Joseph, 2007). Cultivating self-care practices by nourishing one's mind, body, and spiritual well-being can be extraordinarily transforming. Embracing such a practice of self-care requires the professional helper to take up the path of transformation and continue to grow personally and professionally throughout the professional career. Optimizing professional growth and development is a long, slow, and erratic process (Skovholt & Ronnestad, 1995). Just as in the Navajo worldview, acquiring the tools, techniques, and credentials to work in a particular vocation results in merely an occupational title. In Western cultures, completing a degree and acquiring a professional counseling or psychology license may be a great personal and occupational pursuit. However, the achievement of a professional credential itself should not be the final outcome in one's career.

In actuality, the attunement phase or initiation of the shaman or spiritual healer only marks the beginning of one's journey on the chosen career path. To appreciate the journey it is necessary to maintain a focus on the path itself. Thus, healing partnerships with our clients/consumers *are* the journey. However, sustaining the journey can be a wearisome task for some because of the intense nature of working therapeutically with others. Thus, losing the meaning and purpose of our chosen life's work places us at risk for any number of professional impairment or fatigue syndromes.

There is a growing body of research in Western counseling and psychology that advocates self-care practices for mental health professionals (see Baker, 2003; Dlugos & Friedlander, 2001; Lawson & Venart, 2005; Miller, 1998; Newsome, Chambers Christopher, Dahlen, & Christopher, 2006; O'Halloran & Linton, 2000; Shapiro, Warren Brown, & Biegel, 2007; Skovholt et al., 2001). An analysis of the quantitative and qualitative literature suggests that the primary self-care treatment options for professional fatigue syndromes frequently involve the following six approaches and themes:

1   preventing, managing, reducing, and coping with the counselor's stress and anxiety levels;
2   enhancing the counselor's mind-body behavioral health to increase her/his self-management skills;

3   increasing the counselor's capacity for self awareness and mind-
    fulness, for the purpose of exploring stress and anxiety triggers,
    countertransference, and overidentification with clients/con-
    sumers;

4   utilizing wellness and lifestyle approaches for the purpose of
    monitoring and balancing the one's mind, body, and spiritual
    health;

5   cultivating connections through peer support groups, mento-
    ring relationships, clinical supervision, and professional associa-
    tions; and

6   learning how to balance one's professional role with one's per-
    sonal life outside of work.

Overall, the literature on Western counseling and psychology self-
care practices suggests that (a) we must first build personal insight and
awareness of the issues related to professional fatigue; (b) to function
optimally in our chosen career, we must learn how to create a balanced
approach to our social, emotional, cognitive, physical, spiritual, and vocational well-being; and (c) cultivating quality connections and natural
supports with other like-minded individuals will help sustain and monitor us in our professional competence.

INTEGRATING TRADITIONAL WESTERN AND
NON-WESTERN SELF-CARE APPROACHES

Today, an increasing number of professional counselors and psychotherapists are trained, certified, and licensed in a variety of models of
complementary and alternative or integrative medicine. Training and
certification programs have become more available for people wanting
to specialize in herbal medicine, acupuncture, yoga meditation, pet
therapy, sound therapy, and body energy work such as Reiki and massage. Moodley and West (2005) provide a comprehensive model for the
integration of psychotherapy and such healing approaches. West (1997)
proposes an integrated model of the "therapist-healer" that includes "the
use of one or more of the following: intuition, presence, inspiration, psychic, shamanic, altered states, spiritual healing methods, subtle energy
work, mediumship, channeling, use of spirit guides, and transpersonal
work" (p. 291). It would appear, from the outside looking in, that the
therapist-healer approach is utilized by only a small minority of counselors and psychotherapist. However, certain healing phenomena reportedly

occur with more frequency in client-counselor sessions but are only discussed within the confines of clinical supervision (West, 2003).

Prayer as Local and Nonlocal Healing Medicine

Prayer, including forms of denominational faith-based prayer and spiritual healing, constitute one of the more common integrative forms used within the therapist-healer model. Such approaches are used more frequently than reported within the client-counselor session. However, only 24% of secular therapists discuss using such approaches in a session (overtly or covertly) with their supervisor (Gubi, 2002). There is speculation that prayer, as a complementary spiritual approach, is perceived as unacceptable in traditional psychotherapy and that the counselor's competence, professionalism, and credibility would be called into question if it were used on a regular basis.

Depending upon the spiritual or religious belief system of healing, prayer is expressed and communicated in a variety of ways. Many indigenous and ethnic groups use words, songs, dancing, chants, or mantras to convey a certain quality of vibrational energy that resonates with the frequency of the planet and the heavens. For instance, in the Eastern tradition, the chant or the mystical word *om* is said to bring harmony within the universe. Prayer is composed of thoughts, emotions, and spirit-energy that takes on a certain vibration, frequency, and energy that can transcend the space-time continuum and travel a distance for healing. The field of quantum physics suggests that this energy is a type of divine consciousness. Dossey (1993) suggests that this divine consciousness is similar to the nonlocal mind, which is spread throughout the universe. For example, if prayer at a distance is intentional, it takes on the characteristics of omnipresence, omniscience, and omnipotence. The nonlocal mind theory as originated by Dossey demonstrates how the extraordinary power of prayer can connect with spirits and individuals instantaneously at any distance anywhere in the universe.

There are many other examples of how prayer is integrated within consciousness studies and traditional approaches to health and healing networks. The foundational work in this area is too extensive to discuss in detail here (see Byrd, 1988; Groff, 1981; Shealy & Myss, 1990; Worrall & Worrall, 1970). However, the Institute of Noetic Sciences (IONS, 2007) is one particular organization that has been at the forefront of facilitating, organizing, and leading training and research efforts in consciousness studies. It has assembled internationally known healers, medical intuitives, mystics, shamans, and other like-minded cross-cultural individuals and groups.

The use of certain spiritual practices is generally not discussed openly, because it may not be endorsed by some people or groups unless the counselor practices in a faith-based setting. If prayer or other culturally specific spiritual approaches are stigmatized within the counseling profession, then this will likely be a significant hurdle for professional counselors to overcome. Additionally, if such spiritual practices are not endorsed by counselor training programs, clinical supervisors, or counseling settings, then practitioners may not integrate such approaches within their own self-care practices.

The role of professional counselor can involve considerable responsibility. The resilient therapist needs to have good psychological, physical, and spiritual wellness. Thus, self-care practices should be viewed as an ethical obligation of the counselor because of the intense nature of working with clients/consumers, which can lead to an empathy fatigue experience. One of the most important ways to reduce empathy fatigue and cultivate self-care practices within the new paradigm of therapist-healer is to make contact with a shaman, healer, priest, minister, rabbi, spiritualist, or any other professional helper who can serve as a personal guide to bring wellness, balance, and harmony back to the soul of the impaired counselor. Pursuing a deep transformation of the self requires commitment to one's personal spiritual well-being and bringing meaning and purpose to one's occupational choice. Ultimately, when professional counselors nurture their minds, bodies, and spirits, they will be in a better person-centered space from which to help those they serve.

THE PROFESSIONAL COUNSELING ASSOCIATIONS' ROLE IN COUNSELOR IMPAIRMENT

Healing the minds, bodies, and spirits of professional counselors should be a collective responsibility among professional counseling associations, as well as counselor educators, clinical supervisors, and people in the counselor's work setting. Most counseling associations at the state, regional, and national level offer opportunities for personal and professional growth. This is typically done through continuing education activities. Equally important to members of counseling associations is the necessary support that can be offered for (a) the identification and prevention of counselor impairment, (b) building capacity for occupational and career wellness, and (c) increasing counselor resiliency strategies. Providing compassionate outreach for professional counselors is paramount in addressing the individual's mental, physical, spiritual, occupational, and professional well-being. Thus, it is incumbent upon professional counseling associations and organizations to maintain counselor competence and consumer protection while, at the same time, organizing task forces that can address specific matters of assessment, prevention, education, and holistic resources for impaired counselors.

Issues related to counselor impairment and professional fatigue syndromes (e.g., burnout, compassion, empathy fatigue) have received the attention of the Governing Council of the American Counseling Association (ACA), which established the Taskforce on Impaired Counselors (American Counseling Association [ACA], 2003). This task force was developed to assist counselors who are impaired by professional fatigue syndromes such as compassion or empathy fatigue and burnout. The goals of this task force are (a) to educate counselors on strategies to prevent professional burnout, (b) to identify resources for professional counselors, (c) to provide specific intervention and treatment strategies for professional counselors, and (d) to advocate within professional counseling associations at the state and national level to address issues related to impaired counselors. Lawson and Venart (2005) provide a working definition for the ACA's Taskforce on counselor impairment:

> Therapeutic impairment occurs when there is a significant negative impact on a counselor's professional functioning which compromises client care or poses the potential for harm to the client. Impairment may be due to substance abuse or chemical dependency; mental illness; personal crisis (traumatic events or vicarious trauma, burnout, life crisis); and physical illness or debilitation. Impairment in and of itself does not imply unethical behavior. Such behavior may occur as a symptom of impairment, or may occur in counselors who are not impaired. Counselors who are impaired are distinguished from stressed or distressed counselors who are experiencing significant stressors, but whose work is not significantly affected. Similarly, it is assumed that an impaired counselor has at some point had a sufficient level of clinical competence, which has become diminished as described above. (p. 243)

This definition highlights the intense nature of the work that counselors do and the potential impact it has on the individual's mind, body, and spiritual wellness. The challenge to professional counseling associations such as the ACA is to provide a coordinated effort with regard to self-care practices for impaired counselors. This task can be daunting for professional associations for several reasons. First, there are operational definitional differences in terms of what constitutes impaired counselor functioning. For example, organizations such as the American Psychological Association (APA) and the American Medical Association (AMA) have had a limited view of impaired professionals in the past. Their definition primarily centered on professionals who acquired substance abuse, addiction, and stress-related problems. Second, few models exist that have demonstrated a positive correlation between a reduction in counselor impairment and specific self-care treatment approaches that were sponsored, coordinated, or facilitated by professional associations. The outcome data do not appear to be found in the counseling literature or on organizational Web sites. Third, obtaining the financial resources and administrative support to coordinate such referrals has presented organizational problems in getting programs of self-care off the ground. Finally, given the compendium of counselor fatigue characteristics and the levels in severity of impairment, it is questionable at what point a referral needs to be made—if in fact the professional is acting in a competent, professional, and ethical manner. In other words, counselor impairment for some may be more observable outside of the professional's work setting (e.g., substance abuse issues seen by family, friends, and general public) as opposed to during work. Indeed, developing and structuring organizational policies and approaches to deal with counselor impairment can lead to professional organizational fatigue among the leadership.

Although good outcome studies can serve as a rationale and an empirical basis for developing wellness prevention/intervention strategies, there appears to be an overdependence on conventional stress reduction programs aimed primarily at decreasing job burnout. However, such approaches may not go deep enough to accommodate the professional helper's intense work environment. Much of the responsibility for increasing personal wellness should ultimately lie with the professional counselor. However, counselor educators and supervisors and professional counseling associations can share the burden of professional growth and development activities by providing guidelines for self-care practices.

Pursuing a graduate program in counseling does not always prepare the newer counselor for a menu of options for achieving an optimal level of well-being throughout the life-span of one's professional career.

Choosing the best-fit strategies and wellness practices for counselors in transition from graduate school to work plays a critical role in achieving optimal individual wellness. Many well-meaning and caring professionals have little or no preparation for what lies ahead in their career. Accordingly, counselor educators and clinical supervisors who fail to recognize the need for wellness approaches may in fact be unintentionally predisposing the new professional to problems of empathy fatigue by placing too much emphasis on counselor training and ethical behaviors at the cost of ignoring the professional's mind, body, and spiritual wellness.

Overall, advocating, leading, organizing, facilitating, and supporting self-care approaches has the potential to become the new primary care approach that professional counseling associations can offer as part of a comprehensive benefit system to its membership. Professional associations must understand the need for assessment, prevention approaches, and coordinated efforts for counselor impairment interventions. Dealing with these tasks has primarily been relegated to the counselor's employment setting and professional licensing boards. Some of these entities have responded in a punitive manner. However, new frontiers in professionally supported self-care practices should significantly reduce counselor burnout and empathy fatigue. Such an undertaking begins with leadership that is highly involved within its chosen professional counseling association.

A WELLNESS APPROACH TO EMPATHY FATIGUE

The skilled professional spends a large amount of time facilitating compassion and empathic attachments with clients/consumers. Accordingly, a holistic program of wellness is essential in maintaining a balance between self-care and other-care activities. This can often be quite a struggle for professional counselors. Pearlman and MacIan (1995) outline 10 helpful activities that trauma therapists can use to promote personal wellness. These include the following: (a) discussing cases with colleagues, (b) attending workshops, (c) spending time with family or friends, (d) traveling, taking vacations, pursuing hobbies, and watching movies, (e) talking with colleagues between sessions, (f) socializing, (g) embarking on an exercise program, (h) limiting case loads, (i) developing a spiritual life, and (j) receiving supervision. Such approaches would appear to work well within other counseling specialties as well.

Today, it is commonplace in the therapist's and healthcare provider's office to display resources regarding programs related to how to quit smoking, stop drinking alcohol, begin an exercise routine, and pursue weight loss, good nutritional habits, and stress reduction. There appears to be a new social-emotional consciousness among people wanting to make significant changes in their life, changes that will have positive outcomes. Despite the fact that there are multiple self-care treatment approaches available to the professional, some may not fit well into the individual's belief about wellness. Accordingly, wellness prevention approaches may not be a natural means to bring one's life back to harmony and balance.

For some clients and counselors alike, the precontemplation, contemplation, or action stage of change may be the typical developmental process used to cultivate a social, emotional, physical, spiritual, and occupational transformation into a personal plan of wellness. Although there are many studies of the physical, psychological, and psychosocial wellness of persons employed within private business and industry, little research has been conducted incorporating holistic models of wellness among professional helpers who have experienced professional fatigue syndromes.

In recent years, job satisfaction and meaningful work has become an important area of study in the field of organizational psychology, due to corporate downsizing, job reengineering, advances in technology, and job outsourcing, especially to overseas markets. Additionally, there appears to be an overabundance of online surveys and psychometric instruments to measure employees' personality types (e.g., persons prone to high levels of stress and cardiovascular disease, various psychopathologies), measure the multiple levels of intelligence required to perform work effectively and efficiently, and identify those employees showing promising leadership skills (Connolly, 2005). These preemployment and employee evaluations may result in better job matches but may not result in improved wellness.

Today, a much broader view of wellness is emerging that advocates implementing models of wellness among counselor educators and clinical supervisors (Myers & Sweeney, 2005; Witmer & Granello, 2005). Thus, applying the wellness philosophy for counselors in training can act as a prevention approach to professional fatigue syndromes, such as empathy fatigue, which may be experienced early on by preprofessional counselors. Integrating wellness approaches throughout the counselor education curriculum as well as the supervisee's practicum and internship experiences should increase psychological and psychosocial wellness. Broadly defined, psychological and psychosocial wellness encompasses factors related to the individual's self-concept, self-worth, self-esteem, academic achievement, spirituality, sense of belonging, social support from friends and family, and psychosocial adjustment to critical life stressors (Myers & Sweeney, 2005).

A theoretical and conceptual model of wellness, called the "wheel of wellness" (Myers & Sweeney, 2005; Witmer, Sweeney, & Myers, 1998), views five distinct factors as a measure of one's general well-being and total wellness. These factors include (a) the creative self—the combination of attributes that each of us forms to make a unique place for ourselves among others in our social interactions and to positively interpret our world; (b) the coping self—the combination of elements that regulates our responses to life events and provides a means for transcending their negative effects; (c) the social self—social support through connections with others in our friendships and intimate relationships including family ties; (d) the essential self—our essential meaning-making processes in relation to life, self, and others; and (e) the physical self—the biological and physiological processes that comprise the physical aspects of our development and functioning. The wheel of wellness builds upon work in psychology, behavioral medicine, and psychoneuroimmunology, and combines different theoretical perspectives from personality, social, clinical, health, and developmental psychological theories. The wheel of wellness model has been used extensively to construct different outcome measures of the individual's overall health and well-being and is the basis for the Five Factor Wellness Inventory (see www.mindgarden.com) measuring optimal lifestyle functioning. More recently, Myers and Sweeney (2005) reported on the results of an evidence-based model of wellness, the "indivisible self," which has grown out of their earlier work and provides a newer understanding of wellness within the constructs of the mind, body, and spirit.

At the center of many theoretical and conceptual models of wellness is the awareness of a supreme being or spiritual force that transcends the material aspects of life to provide a deep sense of wholeness or connectedness. This is referred to as spirituality. Spirituality is a critical factor in models of individual wellness, because many studies in the last decade suggest that there is a significant positive relationship between spirituality, mental health, physical health, life satisfaction, and holistic well-being or wellness (Chandler, Miner-Holden, & Kolander, 1992; Goleman, 2003; Goodwin, 2002; G. Miller, 2003; Vash, 1994; Weil, 1995).

The Building Blocks of Wellness: Cultivating Resiliency Early On

The building blocks for good mental and physical health begin early on in adolescent development. In *What Is Adolescent Mental Health?* (Stebnicki, 2007c), I delineate the adolescent risk factors that predispose youth to behaviors that are harmful to self and others. Truly, many youth today could benefit from a soul-retrieval or a revival of the mind, body, and spirit. Adolescents are exposed to incidents of violence at home, at school, and in their communities. Such violence is replayed on the nightly news, in movies, in video games, and on the Internet. Building resiliency in the face of multiple life stressors begins in early childhood and adolescence. Many developmental psychologists suggest that one's personality, perceptions, self-concept, and overall response to life are formed in early childhood.

Various state and federal government agencies are aware of the building blocks of wellness. In fact, public health initiatives have been delineated by the Institute of Medicine and the National Academy of Sciences as well as many other partners in developing youth resiliency. The leading health indicators in a federal government report (Institute of Medicine and the National Academy of Sciences [IMNAS], 2004) provide a map for community health initiatives that are designed to assist in focusing county, state, and federally funded programs that serve children and adolescents. Extensive efforts have been undertaken to develop leading health indicators that present significant challenges for community, state, and government agencies.

The following health indicators have been identified by Healthy People 2010 (IMNAS, 2004) as reflecting a major shift in public health concerns for both children and adolescents: (a) physical activity, (b) overweight and obesity, (c) tobacco use, (d) substance abuse, (e) responsible or irresponsible sexual behavior, (f) mental health, (g) injury and violence, (h) environmental quality, (i) immunization, and (j) access to health care. Additionally, the research shows that the most at-risk populations are minority youth. Thus, careful attention to culturally relevant programs is critical to maximizing the potential of such wellness approaches.

It is unfortunate that there are few blueprints to follow once the older adolescent transitions from high school to college, other than campus prevention and wellness programs. Additionally, it is regrettable that a personal plan of wellness is not always offered to graduate students during their course work or internship experience. Despite the fact that the wellness literature and various government agencies overwhelmingly support early intervention strategies, few counselor training programs, clinical supervisors, or professional counseling associations have taken a lead in providing counselor impairment prevention and intervention programs.

Identifying, preventing, and treating counselor fatigue syndromes will require a collective effort. Professionals just beginning their career should seek employer-friendly organizations that provide professional wellness opportunities and employee assistance programs that focus on building counselor resiliency strategies.

TOWARD A HOLISTIC MODEL OF COUNSELOR-CENTERED WELLNESS

The implications for integrating wellness approaches within counselor education programs and institutions are complex and far-reaching. Various outside factors (e.g., university policies, accreditation standards) can hinder the utilization of best practices within a holistic wellness agenda. There are multiple reasons why integrating holistic-wellness approaches becomes difficult. These include, but are not limited to, the following: (a) many counselor education programs have accreditation standards and curriculum guidelines to follow and have little if any room in their day-to-day structure for providing wellness-related strategies; (b) many counselors, rehabilitation agencies, and mental health organizations follow client treatment protocols that may not fit the professional counselor's training experiences, or may not allow for alternative and complementary approaches within the wellness model; (c) the system of mental health does not always support the impaired professional because such a person may be viewed as incompetent in treating clients/consumers; thus, some entities may deal with counselor impairment in a punitive manner; (d) there are not enough qualified professionals to competently offer the diversity of approaches that can comprehensively and holistically address wellness approaches to reduce empathy fatigue; and (e) there are various ideological, philosophical, and theoretical orientations to overcome in developing prevention and intervention strategies.

Despite these difficulties, there appears to be some support for wellness-based approaches from the various counseling associations that can guide policies related to the training and treatment of impaired professionals. The ACA has formed a task force to address such issues related to impaired professionals. This appears to increase the visibility of and support for health and wellness approaches. This support and advocacy has also been visible in some state counseling associations, which provide a network of peer providers (i.e., care networks) that will provide free counseling to their colleagues who have experienced counselor impairment or fatigue syndromes. These care networks offer a current model of best practices for professional counselors and counseling organizations that are interested in a holistic-wellness approach that bridges the gap between employee assistance providers and other traditional community counseling organizations. Supporting counseling professionals creates an organization-friendly environment for improving counselor wellness. Other professional counseling associations and policy makers must come to the table in a solution-focused manner to offer a comprehensive and integrated model of professional growth opportunities in order to manage such counselor impairments as empathy fatigue.

CONCLUDING REMARKS

This chapter has presented a review of self-care practices from a Western and non-Western perspective. Regardless of one's personal and cultural identity, it is essential to cultivate practices that build resiliency and coping ability. Each of us may have our own personal story of "a really bad day at the office" or our "most difficult client/consumer." However, it is critical that we construct new, positive stories to help us build a new future. Specific guidelines for the implementation of nonconventional and nontraditional self-care approaches will be offered in part III of *Empathy Fatigue.* Paying attention to the care of our mind, body, and spirit has the primary purpose of stimulating new thoughts and creative solutions. Implications will be offered for professionals, counselor educators and supervisors, and others interested in self-care practices.

PART III

INTRODUCTION

Shamans, priests, and other healers have known for hundreds and even thousands of years that there is a social, emotional, cognitive, physical, spiritual, and occupational cost to healing others. Drawing from different sociocultural and indigenous belief systems and folk traditions may be valuable for counselors wishing to pursue an emerging practice of self-care so as to prevent a wounded soul experience. There are a number of different indigenous belief systems that have been useful in developing the construct of empathy fatigue. It is important to discuss the rediscovery and integration of the various indigenous healing practices within psychology and counseling (Mijares, 2003; Moodley & West, 2005), because of the rich insights that these cultures offer for healing empathy fatigue in a mind, body, and spiritual sense.

To further explore the experience of empathy fatigue as it relates to the counselor's soul loss or wounded spirit, the following section will offer specific guidelines for self-care practices that (a) can be used by clinical supervisors to guide preprofessional and professional counselors in developing prevention strategies integral to the supervisee's mind, body, and spirit; (b) provide a self-assessment or functional assessment approach to recognizing empathy fatigue; (c) are integrative, complementary, or wellness approaches that are widely recognized in the prevention and treatment of counselor impairment syndromes; and (d) are nonconventional or non-Western folk-healing practices that have indigenous roots. Cultivating healing approaches to empathy fatigue requires creativity and presents the challenge of expanding one's menu of self-care options. The collective wisdom of ancient practices, combined with integral approaches for skilled helpers of the 21st century, should provide a path to healing the mind, body, and spirit of the professional counselor.

9 The Resiliency Advantage in Healing Empathy Fatigue

Inherent in the role of helping others in a person-centered environment is the professional counselor's challenge of coping not only with the client's wounded mind, body, and spirit but with the counselor's own as well. It is incumbent upon the professional counselor as well as the counseling profession as a whole to respond to the counselor's experience of empathy fatigue with resources that build resiliency and hardiness. There are excellent models of building resiliency that can be integrated into a program of self-care for the purpose of reducing the experience of empathy fatigue. For example, the research in posttraumatic growth (PTG; Updegraff & Taylor, 2000), resiliency (Seibert, 2005) and positive psychology (Csikszentmihalyi & Nakamura, 2002) suggests that many people have the ability to emerge from extraordinarily stressful and traumatic experiences and experience a new depth of understanding, wisdom, and compassion. Thus, mending the mind, body, and spirit has a lot to do with developing one's resiliency and finding meaning and purpose in one's chosen career.

FRANKL'S SEARCH FOR MEANING

Victor Frankl (1963), a psychiatrist who spent World War II in a Nazi concentration camp, was one of the first psychotherapists to discuss the extraordinary experiences of the people who survived the death camps of Nazi Germany despite hunger, humiliation, fear, deep injustice, and torture. Frankl, an existential theorist who introduced the most significant Western psychological movement of its time through his book, *Man's Search for Meaning,* provided a dramatic narrative of humankind's capacity for coping and resiliency despite the most horrific treatment imaginable. Logotherapy, an original psychotherapeutic approach that Frankl developed, provides a foundation for treating survivors of extraordinarily stressful and traumatic events. It may also bring meaning to the professional helper's experience of empathy fatigue.

The key proposition in logotherapy is to find meaning in one's existential pain and suffering. For Frankl, it was all about one's perception of one's circumstances in life and then changing this attitude toward an unalterable fate (e.g., life-threatening disease, chronic illness, loss of a loved one). As Frankl states, "suffering ceases to be suffering in some way at the moment it finds a meaning, such as the meaning of sacrifice" (1963, p. 179). He further suggests that one of the basic tenets of logotherapy is not to gain pleasure or avoid pain but rather to seek meaning in life. It is through the death camp experiences that he comes to understand that it is critical to find meaning in one's physical, emotional, and spiritual pain and suffering. In Frankl's final analysis,

> It becomes clear that the sort of person the prisoner became was the result of an inner decision, and not the result of camp influences alone. Fundamentally, therefore, any man can, even under such circumstances, decide what shall become of him—mentally and spiritually. (p. 105)

Frankl concludes that it is this spiritual freedom and freedom to make choices that cannot be taken away, even under the most brutal of circumstances. Thus, this is what brings meaning to life—finding meaning and purpose, knowing that we can make a choice in the present moment, and changing our attitude toward a critical life event.

BIOPSYCHOSOCIAL ASPECTS OF RESILIENCY

Today, a new science is emerging using a biopsychosocial approach to discover the resiliency and coping characteristics of those who have survived extraordinarily stressful and traumatic events. It is suggested in the research that persons who are more stress hardy and stress resistant have a higher capacity for emotions such as empathy. These individuals possess what Seibert (2005) calls the "resiliency advantage." Resiliency psychology has identified why some individuals are more stress hardy than others. You may want to begin an exploration of your own fighting spirit by challenging yourself and taking a resiliency self-assessment quiz online at www.resiliencycenter.com. Using the self-rating scale developed by Seibert and his colleagues, you will be able to ascertain your capacity for resiliency and subjectively measure whether you are in the low, moderate, or high range. Despite the subjective nature of this scale, you may check the validity of your score by asking two or more people who know you well to rate you using the same resiliency quiz items.

Many people in the positive psychology and resiliency movement suggest that there are certain personality traits that may have been inherited by some persons who have survived traumatic events in their lives. Other researchers suggest that one does not have to be born with such resiliency traits; rather, these attributes can be self-taught and learned. One aspect of building resiliency and positive coping skills is that the individual has the ability to make a conscious choice to do the very best he or she can to survive, cope with, and adjust to negative life circumstances no matter how difficult things can be.

There are many inspirational stories based on individuals who have overcome adversity. Individuals such as Lance Armstrong (prostate cancer), Christopher Reeve (spinal cord injury), Stephen Hawking (Amyotrophic Lateral Sclerosis [ALS] disease), and thousands of women who are breast cancer survivors have all found meaning and purpose in their lives. For a more personal and up-close look at the traits of resiliency, talk to people in your own community who have survived a chronic life-threatening illness or disability, lost their job and found another career, divorced a spouse that was having an affair, or lost their home in a fire or flood. Did you ever wonder how these individuals survived and were able to cope with adversity better than others? Herein lies the secret of the prison camp survivors in the stories told by Victor Frankl. It is paramount that we begin to believe in the resiliency advantage and teach such coping strategies to ourselves and new professionals. The ultimate purpose is to increase the professional counselor's mental, physical, and spiritual well-being and to avoid empathy fatigue. Cultivating positive coping skills and resiliency approaches can be learned early in one's career.

Most professional counselors I have spoken with feel that they could benefit from improved coping resources. One of the first places to begin developing resiliency skills is seeking support from a trusted colleague who already has a survivor mentality. Seeking help from a high-functioning empathetic individual who is quite resilient can help refocus your personal and professional life. Learning how to accept help from others and communicating your thoughts and feelings to another professional helper is basically what we ask our clients/consumers to do. An overabundance of research suggests that the better you become at recognizing, verbalizing, and managing your feelings, the less vulnerable you will be to professional fatigue syndromes such as burnout, compassion, or empathy fatigue. This is important, because there is a close association between our emotions and thoughts and our physical health and well-being. In other words, there is a physiological cost to uncontrolled emotions, whether these emotions are out of control, constricted, or turned inward. Clinical supervisors can model resiliency strategies for counselors in training and help them cultivate an optimal level of mental health functioning.

BASIC PRINCIPLES OF RESILIENCY

A consistent finding in resiliency psychology research is that the individual's attitudes and beliefs play a key role in the degree of resiliency that is exhibited or expressed. Resilient professionals almost always appear to possess an internal locus of control, are inwardly directed, are self-motivated, and thrive in adverse conditions. Anecdotal evidence from professional helpers who have bounced back from adversity in their lives due to divorce, loss of a loved one, or career transition, or those who have been survivors of traumatic experiences and have chosen to live in an optimal state of mental health functioning, shows that they have incorporated the following principles:

- *Making a Choice.* A choice must be made on a daily basis by counselors who must deal with their client/consumer's adversity. At the end of the day, counselors can choose not to take home all of their client's adversity and add this to their own wounded soul. The alternative is to choose more healthy thoughts and emotions. The act of choosing a healthier outlook is basically a choice to take responsibility for one's own thoughts and emotions. There will always be client/consumer adversity to deal with in the profession of counseling. So, not moving forward into one's own program of personal wellness would be self-defeating. The alternative would inevitably be bleak: constantly ruminating over the client's adversity at the end of the day. Thus, making a choice to change one's stream of thoughts and emotions about the client's adversity into a more positive mode can be very empowering for some therapists. Negative and destructive thought patterns must be replaced with a plan of personal self-care and wellness. To be successful, this must be reinforced and supported by colleagues and others in the counselor's environment. Accordingly, professional counselors need to create opportunities to help cultivate personal wellness and self-care approaches.

■ *Positive Thinking.* The power of positive thinking is about believing in yourself, having faith in your abilities, and having a high level of confidence that you can achieve a positive outcome with your clients/consumers. As counselors struggle with their own and others' adverse life circumstances, it is easier for them to see the barriers and obstacles to living from a positive frame of reference. Counselors may have many recurring negative thoughts about their client's life in general. However, this can turn into a self-fulfilling prophecy. Professional counselors need to practice positive thinking in a genuine and intrapersonal way, so that it can become a more routine and intentional way of living life in an occupation that often is quite stressful.

■ *Taking Self-Responsibility.* Shifting blame to others does not provide an opportunity for the therapist to develop resiliency behaviors (e.g., my clients drive me crazy sometimes by really pushing my buttons; if they think they have problems they should have seen my last session). Metaphorically, "When you point a finger at someone else, there are four fingers pointing back at you." Taking responsibility is a challenge for many counselors despite the fact that we recommend it to our clients. Many professionals were never taught how to take responsibility and for what. For example, some clients may be in denial about their son/daughter's substance abuse behaviors and may be enabling the adolescent. The consequences of the adolescent's bad choices may be hindered by a therapist who takes on the emotional responsibility. Taking self-responsibility can be learned and will generalize to other areas of the therapist's life. We all need to learn how to model self-responsibility and give up some control to the client. Allowing our clients to take safe risks and fail can be very therapeutic at times.

It can build resiliency and promote healthy choices. Meanwhile, we may learn how our clients can live without our assistance. Overall, we should be internally responsible for our own thoughts, emotions, and actions, and build resiliency traits.

■ *Self-Motivation.* Resilient individuals find their own unique style of internally motivating themselves at school, at work, at home, socially, emotionally, and in other ways. Persons who have had to spring forward and pull through from adversity demonstrate to others around them that they are in control of their life. They tend to have an increased level of emotional, physical, and spiritual energy. They are persistent with tasks that they take on and have an innate knowledge of how to achieve their life goals. Many resilient adolescents have had the opportunity to observe healthy role models in their environment. They were fortunate to have a coach, teacher, or religious or spiritual leader in their community, or others who cared about them and helped them overcome the more difficult challenges in their life.

Choosing Healthy Emotions

The intentional and conscious use of empathy during client-counselor sessions appears to be integral to the helper's ability to be with the client both verbally and nonverbally. To achieve an optimal level of therapeutic engagement, we should recognize that it is essential to approach our profession in an emotionally healthy, responsible, and effective way. The following six elements are offered as a way to build counselor resiliency:

1   Realize that your experiences, thoughts, and feelings are all interconnected and can affect you physically, emotionally, cognitively, and spiritually.

2   All thoughts, feelings, and emotions are naturally transpiring events that are important to embrace. This just let us know that we are human. What is more important is to be aware of how you express your thoughts and feelings to others and to pay attention to how these unfold in your own life.

3   It is okay to have negative, hurtful, or painful thoughts or feelings. We should not place a value or judgment on positive or negative emotions; they are all just emotions. Particular thoughts or feelings you have do not mean that there is something wrong with

you or that you are "abnormal." This is a natural cue from your mind-body that signals you need to communicate your thoughts, emotions, or experiences to someone else.

4   Verbalizing thoughts and feelings to a professional helper will improve your positive mood and will assist you in feeling better. Verbalizing thoughts and feelings will also help you feel centered or balanced. This may take some patience. Remember that expressing your thoughts, feelings, and experiences to others does not indicate that you are a weak professional. Everyone needs help from others throughout his/her life.

5   It is important that you ask others for help. We generally do not live in environments where we are totally isolated. It is okay to accept help and support from others for a while until you feel more in balance. Remember that even professional counselors and psychologists need someone to talk with to help in problem-solving critical life issues.

6   It may take multiple attempts to try and get in touch with your thoughts and feelings and express them appropriately. As time goes on, it will become easier.

The professional helper's search for meaning, purpose, and a means of dealing with adversity is an ongoing life task. The price of ignoring some of the basic resiliency principles is that we may miss the opportunity to resolve conflict, obtain good closure to specific life tasks, learn how to deal with the inter- and intrapersonal demands of stressors, and most of all, learn the art of how to be tough-minded optimists. Professional helpers cannot expect to read a chapter on the principles of resiliency without living it, by "walking the walk." We can help our clients/consumers acquire some degree of healthy success by implementing creative resiliency approaches. Most of all, we can model healthy choices, exercising the power of positive thinking, taking responsibility for things that we can control, and motivating ourselves for success. These are the essential strategies for building counselor resiliency.

CONCLUDING THOUGHTS

Inherent in the role of helping others in a person-centered environment is the challenge of dealing not only with the client's wounded mind, body, and spirit but with our own as well. It is incumbent upon the professional and others in the professional's environment to support self-care strategies that will assist in healing the helper's wounded mind, body, and spirit. Seeking resources that build resiliency and hardiness must be intentional and integrated into a program of self-care for the purpose of reducing the experience of empathy fatigue. Chapter 10 offers researchers, counselor educators, clinical supervisors, professional counselors, and others in the professional's environment guidance to identify key risk factors associated with counselor impairment or professional fatigue syndromes, particularly empathy fatigue.

10   An Assessment of Empathy Fatigue: Research Considerations

Many in the counseling profession do not recognize the characteristics associated with counselor impairment or any of the professional fatigue syndromes. It is essential that the counselor's employer, supervisors, peers, colleagues, family, and friends recognize the negative shift within the individual's mind, body, and spirit that may signal an empathy fatigue or burnout experience. There are multiple variables coexisting on the empathy fatigue continuum that can create a sense of ambiguous loss, grief, significant emotional distress, and interruptions in the professional's daily routines. Mostly, there is a sense of being in disharmony with one's mind, body, and spirit.

This chapter offers researchers, counselor educators, clinical supervisors, and professional counselors the resources for identifying key risk factors associated with counselor impairment or professional fatigue syndromes, particularly empathy fatigue. Self-assessments may serve as a screening and prevention tool to help the counselor achieve optimal wellness. Accordingly, the reader will be offered resources that include the following: (a) a self-care assessment, (b) a risk factor assessment, (c) research considerations for constructing an empathy fatigue assessment, (d) the Global Assessment of Empathy Fatigue (GAEF) functional assessment scale under development, and (d) resources for counselor impairment and fatigue syndromes.

SELF-CARE ASSESSMENTS

Numerous self-care assessments can be found in books, in articles, and on the Internet. Each has its own focus as it relates to one's personal, emotional, physical, and spiritual wellness. Most of the self-care assessments that relate to practitioners in the field of psychology and counseling appear to measure acute, cumulative, or secondary traumatic stress in the following domains: (a) cognitive, (b) emotional, (c) behavioral, (d) spiritual, (e) interpersonal, and (f) physical. Additionally, there are various specific self-care assessments that measure job stress and burnout, compassion fatigue, cognitive-emotional stress, coping skills, and individual resiliency. There are no current self-care assessments that measure the experience of empathy fatigue. However, one is under development at the time of writing this book.

Baker (2003), as well as many others, suggests that the core element in self-care assessment is to develop the following: (a) self-awareness—awareness of significant factors that hinder personal growth and development as a counselor; (b) self-regulation—a conscious and unconscious process of decreasing physical, emotional, cognitive, and behavioral impulses that creates a sense of maintaining balance in the mind, body, and spirit; and (c) balance—a holistic means of achieving mind, body, and spiritual harmony for the purpose of reconnecting to the self in relation to one's internal and external environment.

To begin the self-care assessment process, consider asking yourself the following questions as they relate to your experience of empathy fatigue:

- What things have I discovered about myself in regard to my experience of empathy fatigue?
- What life areas have I been challenged in as a result of my experience of empathy fatigue?
- What are some specific coping skills and other things that keep me in balance?
- What are some things I have learned about my coping abilities and resiliency for maintaining my chosen occupation?
- What specific resources have helped me get through adversity in my past?
- What sense, purpose, or meaning have I found as a result of my empathy fatigue experience?
- What advice could I give to my colleagues about dealing with empathy fatigue?

EMPATHY FATIGUE DOMAINS FOR CONSIDERATION

Stebnicki (2000) outlines a functional risk-factor assessment for empathy fatigue that may assist professional counselors and others in identifying and recognizing risk factors related to empathy fatigue. The items in this particular functional assessment were developed from a meta-analysis of counselor impairments and fatigue conditions noted in the literature. In the current development of an empathy fatigue measure, consideration will be given to content items that address the spiritual dimension. There are many areas it is necessary to address, in order to gather information on an individual. These include but are not limited to the following:

1   *Current and preexisting personality traits and states:* type A personality traits, unrealistic or high expectations, need for recognition, pattern of cynicism.

2   *History of emotional or psychiatric problems:* underlying mental health issues or behaviors that may interfere with the counselor's competency, direct or indirect exposure to critical incidents, lethality issues or harm to self and others.

3   *Maladaptive coping behaviors:* patterns of alcohol or substance abuse, increased use of tobacco, caffeine, food.

4   *Age- and experience-related factors:* younger professionals new to counseling versus older professionals' coping abilities, experience in working with different types of clients/consumers, experience in crisis response.

5   *Organizational and system dynamics at the counselor's place of work:* organization or system insensitive or unappreciative to the emotional needs of counselor, organization or system's openness to trying new approaches.

6   *Specific job duties of counselor in relation to the organization in which the counselor is employed:* direct service versus supervisory, caseload size, work overly demanding, time consuming.

7   *Unique sociocultural attributes:* values, beliefs, cultural identity that may be different from that of the organization/employer.

8   *Response to handling past critical and other stressful life events:* level of exposure to trauma or STS and the counselor's ability to cope, identification of any counselor isolation, detachment, or dissociative issues.

9   *Level of support and resources:* individual, group, or family support, ability to seek out assistance.

10 *Spirituality:* counselor questioning the meaning and purpose of life, occupation, spiritual and/or religious beliefs; anger toward God or religious affiliation, any spiritual emergencies.

A functional assessment approach is a valuable tool for counselors and researchers to assist in developing prevention and screening tools for counselor impairment conditions such as empathy fatigue.

Generally, in instrument development, well-developed domains and items should be able to predict low, moderate, or high degrees of the phenomenon that is of interest. For example, counselors who currently have issues related to mental health and substance addiction should theoretically be functioning in a high range of severity on the empathy fatigue scale that is under development. This would likely be due to the individual's poor coping abilities and resiliency skills. The counselor's work setting may be of an intense nature (e.g., psychiatric/substance abuse hospital, county mental health crisis response), predisposing the individual to acute levels of empathy fatigue. Likewise, counselors who have accumulated or ignored their stress associated with empathy fatigue may be reacting to the cumulative nature of the stress. There are also professionals who react to multiple hot buttons or personal triggers related to client countertransference and are prone to an empathy fatigue experience. Regardless of whether we are examining the acute, the cumulative, or the delayed onset reactions to empathy fatigue, the more expert counselor who has dealt with counselor impairment issues early in her/his career may be functioning with healthier coping and resiliency skills than the neophyte counselor who has perhaps not dealt with these issues. Accordingly, in the scenario we are considering, the level (i.e., low, moderate, high) of empathy fatigue that is present may be dependent upon the following: (a) the counselor's developmental level of competence, (b) whether the precipitating event has triggered an acute response, (c) the cumulative nature of a particular stressor as it relates to the person, (d) the counselor's previous coping abilities, or adaptive-maladaptive behaviors, and (e) the counselor's previous exposure to critical incidents.

Generally, there are multiple risk factors in empathy fatigue that complicate one's career goals and personal and professional relationships, and hinder one's capacity for personal coping and resiliency. Thus, consideration must be given to assessing empathy fatigue from a holistic perspective. Developing domains before scale items is essential in the scale development process. Factor analysis and other statistical procedures will assist in this process. The following domains by which to measure the construct of empathy fatigue are suggested:

- *Individual Traits.* Current and preexisting personality traits, any history of emotional or psychiatric problems, maladaptive coping behaviors.
- *Family.* Level of support and resources, family history of poor coping abilities, lack of clear expectations and rules for occupation or career.
- *Sociocultural.* Worldview, personal and cultural identity, choice of occupation, family and extended family members, coping resources, age, gender, race, ethnicity, disability.
- *Developmental Level.* Experience level of counselor: practicum, internship, postgraduate, or expert.
- *Occupational Setting.* Organizational and system dynamics, setting where professional is employed, specific job duties, responsibilities, and position within the organization.
- *Physical Attributes.* Medical—physical status, chronic illness, disability, health status, nutritional intake, lifestyle factors related to health.
- *Cognitive-Behavioral.* Dysfunctional thought patterns, ability to motivate oneself, flexibility in problem-solving tasks.
- *Religious-Spiritual.* Connection to higher power, God, spirit helpers, patterns of religious practices in terms of rituals, ceremonies.

CHALLENGES IN THE ASSESSMENT OF EMPATHY FATIGUE

An empathy fatigue functional assessment may be used as a self-care screening instrument. However, it is essential that any measure be based on the collective wisdom and observations of concerned individuals who are involved within the counseling and allied helping professions. The challenges in developing a functional assessment or scale with which to measure empathy fatigue are as follows:

1 There is no single "type" or "clinical profile" for an impaired professional. Rather, the fatigued professional should be viewed within the context of the individual and her/his environment.

2 A distinction should be made between countertransference, compassion fatigue, occupational stress, burnout, and other such constructs. The essential features of each of these have been compared and contrasted earlier in this book. However, various instruments (e.g., the Compassion Satisfaction and Fatigue Test, the Occupational Stress Inventory, the Maslach Burnout Inventory) have already been developed to measure such constructs. Some constructs and factors may be defined similarly or dissimilarly in different instruments.

3 The analysis of the critical pathways of empathy fatigue has been delineated in chapter 2 of this book. The individual who experiences an empathy fatigue reaction should be viewed on a continuum that ranges from low to moderate to high levels of self-reported fatigue.

4 Measuring an empathy fatigue reaction is a whole-body experience. Thus, one needs to measure its effects on the person's mind, body, and spirit.

5 The literature is replete with characteristics and symptoms that relate to one's mental health, physical health, and wellness. Thus, such factors, when identified in empathy fatigue, may relate to similar kinds of factors and domains. The similarities and differences in factors and domains are not known at this time because the present empathy fatigue scale is still under development.

6 There may not always be a causal risk factor associated with empathy fatigue. Professional helpers work with a variety of clients/consumers in diverse counseling environments. The presence of any one particular work setting (e.g., crisis response or career counseling) or client type (e.g., substance abuse versus grief counseling) may not predispose the counselor to an empathy fatigue reaction. Thus, empathy fatigue must be viewed in terms of its intensity, severity, chronicity, or persistence. It is not solely an acute reaction.

Overall, the theory underlying any measure (e.g., depression, stress, wellness inventories) must be studied carefully. Measures of counselor impairment and fatigue syndromes take time to develop. However, over time, developing a stable measure that has a sound underlying theory and predicts relationships between the variables of interest and the professional's experience of such variables appears to be a worthwhile course to pursue. This is because sustaining one's self-care and wellness is essential within the helping professions.

LIMITATIONS OF FUNCTIONAL ASSESSMENT AND SELF-CARE MEASURES

The limitations of functional assessment and self-care measures are numerous. In dealing with the theoretical construct of empathy fatigue, self-report scales should not become protocol driven or a "gold standard" for determining a diagnosis under the general category of professional fatigue syndromes. In other words, it is critical that functional assessments and other self-care measures take a balanced and responsible approach. This can be achieved by using a multidisciplinary group of diverse individuals across settings who collectively structure a checklist, screening items, or an inquiry into the low, moderate, and high risk factors that are observable in persons that may exhibit some degree of counselor fatigue. The ethical implications of impaired counselors may be involved here. Thus, interpretation of the results of any self-report or screening measure should be approached cautiously.

Many functional assessment instruments are "homegrown" in nature and should never supplant the collective wisdom of professional experts in the field or valid and reliable psychometric instruments (e.g., the Beck Depression Inventory II [BDI-II]; Minnesota Multiphasic Personality Inventory [MMPI]; the Alcohol Screening Instrument [ASI]) that are administered by trained and competent professionals working together in a multidisciplinary team. The functional assessment approach is a process that should result in the consistent assignment of individual characteristics that quantify certain behaviors by assigning some type of value to each individual trait or characteristic. The measurement process can be quite complex. It requires that the researcher attend to empirical guidelines for instrument or scale development for the purpose of quantifying the variables and the constructs of interest. Often, ongoing studies are required to strengthen the validity and reliability of a particular scale. This is necessary to yield any relationship to the variables of interest and devise a measure that is meaningful.

It is important to note that functional assessments and self-care measures are not psychometric or diagnostic instruments. They simply provide different perspectives on concepts that may be difficult to define (e.g., sense of ambivalence with regard to career, low energy and motivation to be compassionate with others). Operational definitions or agreement by skilled observers about particular phenomena of interest can help define, replicate, or compare different behaviors or characteristics that vary in degree, such as counselor impairment or fatigue syndromes.

Functional assessments and self-care report measures are largely based on personal observations, perceptions, values, beliefs, predictions, and the overall "worldview" of the evaluators'/observers' experience. They are based on patterns of behaviors that the researcher believes are consistent with helping professionals who may exhibit low, moderate, or high degrees of counselor impairment. The development and use of a functional assessment and self-care reporting scale is not an exact science. However, there are large numbers of clinical studies that have measured such constructs as compassion fatigue, burnout, depression, and occupational stress. Some of these measures describe such constructs with a good deal of accuracy and can predict specific patterns of behavior. At times, the warning signs of counselor impairment and risk factors for it are vague and elusive. Constructing items, conducting ongoing research in empathy fatigue, and delineating specific behaviors and traits appear to constitute one practical strategy for identifying early on the triggers that may lead to the phenomenon I refer to as empathy fatigue.

Most importantly, by the end of the day, after the professional helper is emotionally, socially, physically, psychologically, occupationally, and spiritually depleted, a score derived from taking a self-care measure matters very little in that person's life. Exhaustion becomes a trigger for survival and the professional helper must rise to the challenge of coping with adversity.

GLOBAL ASSESSMENT OF FUNCTIONING IN THE THEORETICAL MEASUREMENT OF EMPATHY FATIGUE

The Global Assessment of Empathy Fatigue (GAEF) is a theoretical measure, under development, of the overall experience of empathy fatigue. The GAEF is categorized according to five different levels of functioning. Level V indicates the highest and Level I the lowest level of empathy fatigue that would theoretically be experienced by the professional helper. The theoretical constructs involved in measuring this type of counselor impairment are currently being researched. As the GAEF is in its theoretical stage of development, the construct of empathy fatigue is being differentiated theoretically from other counselor impairment and fatigue syndromes. There is no empirical evidence as yet to report.

The intent and purpose of the GAEF at this early stage of development is to provide a means of viewing the overall level of functioning of professional helpers who experience empathy fatigue. The content developed for the five levels of functioning is based on a comprehensive review of the literature as documented in the list of references at the end of the present work. The characteristics of professional fatigue syndromes, such as burnout, compassion fatigue, and other measures of professional psychological distress, tend to be categorized according to seven distinct content areas: (a) cognitive, (b) process skills, (c) emotional, (d) behavioral, (e) physical, (f) spiritual, and (g) occupational.

Counselor impairments appear to involve a constellation of states, traits, behaviors, and other factors that encompass the person's impaired or fatigued reaction in the mind, body, and spirit. The reader should note that each individual experiences critical incidents and acute, cumulative, and daily stressors differently. Thus, some counselor characteristics may have more relevance than others. The theoretical continuum ranging from Level V (most impaired) to Level I (least impaired) hopefully can provide an anchor or benchmark for the optimal level of functioning for the professional helper within each of the content domains.

The GAEF should be used to rate the professional helper's current level of functioning. Because individual behaviors, states, and traits are often dependent upon the environment in which they are observed, observations by the individuals listed below should be documented. A time sampling method should be used because the individual may differ in experience of empathy fatigue with regard to events that take place at different times in the day (e.g., mornings, afternoons, evenings, weekends, before client sessions, after client sessions, every other day). Persons considering rating themselves and/or others using the GAEF should be open to the other self-assessment instruments that are available to measure such things as mood, affect, personality, stress, attitude, and job burnout, as well as other areas of mind, body, and spiritual well-being.

- *Self-Ratings by the Professional.* The individual him/herself may use the GAEF as a self-report measure.
- *Ratings by the Professional's Colleagues.* The professional may request his/her clinical supervisor, peer mentor, or other professionals to give independent ratings on the GAEF measure.
- *Ratings by Clients/Consumers.* Ratings may be carried out according to a well-designed scheme within the work environment that uses inter-rater agreement by the therapist's client/consumer

and/or a triad of raters (i.e., client, therapist, and independent observer).

- *Ratings by Independent Observers Outside the Work Environment.* The therapist may request ratings by close professional colleagues.
- *Ratings by Another Objective Individual.* The professional may request ratings by others (i.e., personal therapists) who are closely committed to the professional's personal goals of self-care and personal growth.

GAEF Rating Scale

Please rate the level of empathy fatigue that you have experienced primarily within the last two weeks:

Level V

- *Cognitively.* Counselor may exhibit diminished concentration, seems preoccupied, has disorganized thoughts, and attends to client in a quiet or detached manner.
- *Process Skills.* During therapeutic interactions, rapport and working alliance with client appear to be extremely strained or almost nonexistent. Counselor attending and listening may be almost nonexistent. Session primarily involves gathering basic information about people, data, things, and/or events with no attempts at processing client story. Counselor misses many opportunities to integrate client content, experience, and affect. Empathic responses not genuine. Counselor may be resistant, apprehensive, or show hypersensitivity to becoming involved therapeutically during session. Counselor may show resistance to facilitating client goals and avoid challenging client because of high degree of countertransference. Counselor may not use open-ended questioning, solution-focused probes, or brainstorming techniques for problem exploration.
- *Emotionally.* Counselor may exhibit diminished affective state, moodiness, very clear high and low emotions, sadness, tearfulness, appear emotionally depleted and/or exhausted. May feel extremely negative and pessimistic.
- *Behaviorally.* Counselor may exhibit physical signs of impatience, irritability, aggression, and/or hypervigilance. Poor eye contact. Vocal tone and pace of speech may be strained, erratic, slow or fast paced. May be cynical during interpersonal interactions with client.

- *Physically.* Counselor may exhibit shallow breathing, sweating, fatigue, discomfort while sitting, facial grimace indicating pain, feelings of dizziness, nausea, muscle tremors or twitches, severe headache, and/or disturbance in visual acuity.
- *Spiritually.* Counselor may lack meaning and purpose with regard to faith or spiritual beliefs and either communicate this in session or through internal dialogue during therapeutic interactions. May be totally detached from spiritual support.
- *Occupationally.* Counselor may be missing at least one day of work per week, canceling or not showing up for client sessions. Counselor avoids most meetings and colleagues at work, leaves work early every day, exhibits sick or cynical sense of humor, has difficulties separating professional work environment from home or personal relationships. May exhibit poor coping skills and show very little resiliency.

Level IV

- *Cognitively.* Counselor may exhibit diminished concentration, seems somewhat preoccupied, exhibits some slightly disorganized thoughts and attends to client in a quiet manner. Shows some degree of detachment in an on-and-off manner. May be irrational in his/her thinking.
- *Process Skills.* During therapeutic interactions, rapport somewhat difficult to establish and working alliance is not attained. Counselor attending and listening may be somewhat poor or much decreased from Level III attending and listening. Session may involve gathering basic information about people, data, things, and/or events with little attempt at and many missed opportunities for processing client story. Very little integration of client content, experience, and affect. Empathic responses may be superficial. Counselor may be somewhat resistant, apprehensive, or show little interest nonverbally in becoming involved therapeutically during session. Counselor may show increased resistance to facilitating client goals and avoid challenging client because of some degree of countertransference. Counselor may show little use of open-ended questioning, solution-focused probes, or brainstorming techniques for problem exploration.
- *Emotionally.* Counselor may exhibit somewhat diminished affective state, moodiness, slight mood swings, moderate level of sadness, may appear emotionally fatigued and/or exhausted. May feel negative and/or pessimistic.

- *Behaviorally.* Counselor may exhibit physical signs of being somewhat impatient, irritable, competitive, and/or very cautious. Eye contact is fair. Vocal tone and pace of speech may be somewhat strained, erratic, slow or fast paced. May be somewhat cynical in interpersonal interactions with client.
- *Physically.* Counselor may exhibit some shallow breathing, slight sweating, fatigue, some facial grimacing indicating discomfort while sitting, slight feelings of wooziness, lack of appetite due to upset stomach, occasional muscle tremors or twitches, moderate degree of headache, and/or disturbance in visual acuity.
- *Spiritually.* Counselor may lack some meaning and purpose with regard to faith or spiritual beliefs and may communicate this in session or through internal dialogue during therapeutic interactions. May sense some detachment of spiritual support.
- *Occupationally.* Counselor may be missing 2–3 days of work per month, calling to reschedule client appointments; avoids meetings and colleagues at work, leaves work early more days than not, consistently cuts session short, exhibits cynical sense of humor, has difficulties separating professional work environment from home or personal relationships. May be struggling and exhibiting decreased coping abilities and resiliency.

Level III

- *Cognitively.* Counselor may exhibit some diminished concentration, appears somewhat preoccupied, thought organization is somewhat loose. Focus on therapeutic process is fair but counselor may be attending quietly to many internal thoughts and feelings. Appears to be having an "off day."
- *Process Skills.* During therapeutic interactions, rapport with clients takes longer than usual to establish. Working alliance may be achieved more slowly. Counselor attending and listening is fair to good. Empathic responses more genuine than at Level IV. Session may involve gathering basic information about people, data, things, and/or events. Some missed opportunities in therapeutic interactions, and processing of client story does not capture all of content, experience, and affect. Counselor responses may contain elements of only basic empathy. Counselor may be somewhat resistant, apprehensive, or show little interest nonverbally in becoming involved therapeutically during session. Counselor may show increased resistance to facilitating client goals and avoid challenging

client because of some degree of countertransference. Counselor may show little use of open-ended questioning, solution-focused probes, or brainstorming techniques for problem exploration.

■ *Emotionally.* Counselor's affective state may be fair; slight moodiness, dysthymic, appears emotionally tired. May feel somewhat negative and/or pessimistic.

■ *Behaviorally.* Counselor may exhibit physical signs of being restless or impatient. Eye contact good but slightly inattentive. Vocal tone and pace of speech may be slightly strained.

■ *Physically.* Counselor may exhibit some tiredness, sighs of frustration with breath, some facial grimacing indicating discomfort while sitting, lack of appetite but yet somewhat hungry, occasional muscle twitches, slight sense of headache coming on, and/or eyes feeling dry.

■ *Spiritually.* Counselor may have some confusion regarding meaning and purpose with regard to faith or spiritual beliefs and may communicate this in session or through internal dialogue during therapeutic interactions. Some separation from spiritual support.

■ *Occupationally.* Counselor may be missing 1–2 days of work per month, exhibits some avoidance of starting session on time, hopes for client "no-shows," cuts session shorter than usual, makes excuses to try and leave meetings and work early, has only superficial contact with colleagues at work, exhibits inappropriate sense of humor, has some difficulties separating professional work environment from home or personal relationships. May be exhibiting some difficulties with coping abilities and resiliency.

Level II

■ *Cognitively.* Counselor may exhibit only slight problems in concentration, occasionally seems preoccupied, thought organization good but finds the need to continually refocus. Focus on therapeutic process is good. May be some response to internal thoughts and feelings. Thoughts of hopefulness and idea that tomorrow will be a better day than today.

■ *Process Skills.* During therapeutic interactions, rapport takes slightly longer than usual to establish but eventually connection in therapeutic process is good. Working alliance may take somewhat longer to achieve, but ongoing therapeutic work with client remains intact and stable. Counselor attending and listening is good. Empathic responses more genuine than at Level III.

Session goes beyond data gathering, content, or client story. Integration of client content, experience, and affect is good. Only a few missed therapeutic opportunities with client and empathic responses are at a somewhat deeper level but much more frequent than at Level III. Counselor may be somewhat hesitant to explore new areas for client support and resources. Counselor may show nonverbal incongruencies but appears to be fully involved therapeutically during session. Counselor may show increased interest in understanding countertransference but avoids dealing with the experience. Counselor may use open-ended questioning, solution-focused probes, or brainstorming techniques for problem exploration but could do better.

- *Emotionally.* Counselor's affective state may be good, has sense of dysthymic mood, and appears slightly emotionally tired. May notice self feeling slightly negative and/or pessimistic.

- *Behaviorally.* Counselor may exhibit physical signs of being somewhat restless or impatient but is aware enough and chooses to control behavior while at the same time being slightly uncomfortable. Eye contact good, vocal quality and pace of speech good but occasionally strained.

- *Physically.* Counselor may exhibit slight tiredness but actively takes steps to avoid such fatigue. May exhibit occasional sighs of frustration, but breathing is conscious; must use internal dialogue to relax; despite some discomfort while sitting, action is taken to correct this. Appetite and eating habits somewhat irregular but awareness is good and steps are taken to maintain appropriate nutritional intake. Muscles feeling slightly tense and counselor requires constant reminders to rebalance physical wellness.

- *Spiritually.* Counselor may have some sense of awareness of refocusing on meaning and purpose with regard to faith or spiritual beliefs. Attempts are made throughout the day to remain connected spiritually through internal purposeful dialogue. May feel some sense of separation from spiritual support but makes some attempts to become reconnected.

- *Occupationally.* Counselor may feel the need to take off 1–2 days of work per month, has thoughts of client "no-shows" but always conducts sessions on time and for usual duration, occasionally will make excuses for leaving meetings early, has minimal contact with colleagues at work, exhibits usual sense of humor but has difficulties transitioning to social self, has some difficulties separating professional work environment from home or personal relationships but is able to leave most personal issues at home. Better coping abilities and resiliency than at higher levels.

Level I

- *Cognitively.* Counselor may exhibit slight problems in concentration and thought organization. However, using various internal and external prompts is able to refocus on therapeutic interactions. May occasionally be more preoccupied than usual. Focus on therapeutic process is good but may be responding to internal thoughts and feelings more than usual. Fleeting thoughts that tomorrow will be better than today.
- *Process Skills.* During therapeutic interactions, rapport takes slightly longer than usual to establish but eventually connection in therapeutic process is better than at Level II. Working alliance may take somewhat longer to achieve than usual but ongoing therapeutic work with client remains intact and stable. Counselor attending and listening is appropriate. Empathic responses more genuine than at Level II. Session goes beyond data gathering, content, or client story, and integration of client content, experience, and affect is better than at Level II. A few missed therapeutic opportunities with client, and empathic responses are at a somewhat deeper level. Counselor may be somewhat hesitant to explore new areas of client support and resources but does better than at Level II. Counselor may show some nonverbal incongruencies; however, may become more fully involved therapeutically during session than at Level II. Counselor may show increased interest in understanding countertransference but feels uncomfortable thinking about the experience. Counselor may use open-ended questioning, solution-focused probes, or brainstorming techniques for problem exploration but could do better.
- *Emotionally.* Counselor's affective state is good but could be better, has sense of a slightly "down" mood, and appears somewhat emotionally tired. May catch self feeling slightly negative and/or pessimistic but initiates self-correction.
- *Behaviorally.* Counselor may exhibit physical signs of being somewhat restless or impatient but is aware enough to control this behavior. Eye contact good, vocal quality and pace of speech good but occasionally strained.

- *Physically.* Counselor may exhibit slight tiredness but actively takes steps to avoid such fatigue. May exhibit occasional sighs of frustration, but breathing is conscious. Must use internal dialogue to relax, experiences some discomfort so steps are taken to correct this sensation. Appetite and eating habits somewhat irregular but awareness is good and steps are taken to maintain appropriate nutritional intake. Muscles feeling slightly tense and constant reminders made to rebalance physical wellness.
- *Spiritually.* Counselor may have some sense of awareness of refocusing on meaning and purpose with faith or spiritual beliefs. After self-reassurance, a sense of connectedness is restored. May feel sense of separation from spiritual support so attempts are initiated to become reconnected.
- *Occupationally.* Counselor may feel the need to take off 1–2 days of work per month, has thoughts of client "no-shows" but always conducts sessions on time and for usual duration, occasionally will make excuses for leaving meetings early, contact with colleagues at work is less than usual, exhibits usual sense of humor but has difficulties transitioning to social self, has some difficulties separating professional work life from home life or personal relationships but is able to leave most personal issues at home. Better coping abilities and resiliency than at previous levels.

RESOURCES FOR COUNSELOR IMPAIRMENT AND FATIGUE SYNDROMES

American Counseling Association (ACA) Taskforce on Counselor Wellness and Impairment: www.counseling.org/wellness_taskforce/tf_resources. htm. The ACA is the largest professional counseling association in North America. This is a very comprehensive source for counselor self-care. There are multiple assessment and screening tools for professional counselors, including assessments of wellness, professional quality of life, and traumatic stress, and a variety of other assessments.

Gift From Within: www.giftfromwithin.org. Gift From Within is an international not-for-profit organization for survivors of traumatic stress. This particular organization is dedicated to PTSD survivors and advocates multiple supports from family, friends, and peers. Educational materials and a list of retreats, workshops, and online support are offered.

Green Cross Foundation and Green Cross Academy of Traumatology: www.greencross.org. Green Cross is a professional organization of traumatologists founded by Dr. Charles Figley and colleagues, who developed the foundational research and educational materials related to compassion fatigue.

Mark Lerner Associates, Inc.: www.crisisdoc.com. Dr. Lerner is a clinical psychologist and traumatic stress consultant with an international reputation in working with organizations and individuals that have experienced extraordinarily stressful and traumatic events in their lives. Dr. Lerner offers consultations, workshops, and educational and training materials designed for individuals and organizations after traumatic events.

The special resources in the Appendix of *Empathy Fatigue* have many more resources to offer the interested reader.

CONCLUDING REMARKS

The assessment of counselor impairments such as empathy fatigue is an ongoing process. Preventing counselor impairment may never be possible in some environments because of the intensity or nature of the work. Providing a safe environment so the client can disclose feelings of loss, grief, stress, pain, or suffering can have a psychological cost. Responding empathically and sensing our clients' level of emotions is not something that we can turn on and off. However, identifying the emotional hot buttons is essential for competent and ethical practice within the helping professions.

In chapter 11, the reader will be offered an understanding of how emotional hot buttons can begin to be triggered early in the graduate counseling program as well as in the postgraduate career in the helping profession. Thus, developing self-care practices must begin early on to identify and prevent counselor impairment or empathy fatigue. The individual in his/her early development as a helping professional will need guidance from a competent clinical supervisor who possesses a high regard for professionalism, competence, and integrity in the counseling profession. Thus, chapter 11 describes the roles and functions of clinical supervisors, counselor educators, and professional counseling associations in identification, prevention, and intervention for those experiencing counselor impairments.

11

The Role of Clinical Supervisors in Identifying, Preventing, and Treating Empathy Fatigue

Most counselor educators and clinical supervisors in graduate-level programs spend a good deal of time working on process and intentional interviewing skills, modeling counseling strategies and techniques, watching and listening to countless hours of video and audiotape recordings of client-counselor sessions. These skills are all essential for preparing counselors in training to establish a rapport and achieve a good working alliance with their clients/consumers. However, clinical supervisors need to take on more complex tasks. For example, supervisors may take on the roles of counselor educator, therapist, and consultant to facilitate the varied learning styles of supervisees. Clinical supervision is essential in assisting supervisees with issues related to personal growth and development. Thus, facilitating creative supervisory activities is of paramount importance in promoting good mental, physical, and spiritual health among preprofessional counselors. Many graduate-level clinical supervisors that do not practice in the field may have forgotten the day-to-day routines and the job stress as it relates to dealing with client/consumers who have intense interpersonal issues. The stressors that lie ahead for some counselors in training can result in career-ending injuries to their mental, physical, and spiritual well-being. Thus, it is incumbent upon clinical supervisors to pay attention to their supervisees' personal growth and self-care needs.

The development of self-care practices early in graduate counselor training programs has been increasingly recognized as essential content within the clinical aspects of the curriculum (Baker, 2003; Newsome et al., 2006; Weiss, 2004). Yet, few counselor training programs prepare preprofessional counselors to plan, organize, and self-initiate self-care strategies during their first clinical experiences and beyond. Newsome and associates suggest that the demands of the graduate curriculum, now 60 semester hours in some states, and the clinical requirements leave little room for facilitating self-care approaches. Many times, developing self-care practices is viewed as the responsibility of the supervisee rather than as the duty of the counselor educator and supervisor.

ETHICAL CONSIDERATIONS IN DEALING WITH SUPERVISEES' EMPATHY FATIGUE

Counseling and psychology as disciplines have struggled to address the issues of professional distress, empathy fatigue, and counselor impairment. The largest professional counseling and psychology associations in the United States, the ACA and the APA, have recognized this critical need to support professionals' personal growth and development. There has been a conscious and intentional effort by these groups, as well as by many other professional associations, to deal with matters of professional impairment, counselor burnout, distress, compassion strain, and empathy fatigue. This has been accomplished by publishing various risk factor assessments and providing a range of resources and strategies to deal with the counselor's/psychologist's impairments. However, there are many helping professionals that are not affiliated with any professional counseling and psychological associations. Thus, counselor educators and supervisors as well as professional associations may need to increase their efforts to reach impaired professionals. Many resources are available. However, counselor educators and clinical supervisors are the first line of prevention in recognizing professional impairment conditions. Thus, it is essential to integrate some of these self-care strategies into clinical supervision sessions.

Ethically, clinical supervisors are obligated to "render assistance to any supervisee who is unable to provide competent counseling services to clients" (National Board for Certified Counselors [NBCC], 2007, Section C. [h]). Thus, counselor educators and supervisors are encouraged to identify the characteristics of counselor impairment. Professional counselors themselves have a responsibility to seek out assistance if they are emotionally or physically impaired. The ACA *Code of Ethics* (2005), Section C.2.g, states that counselors shall "seek assistance for problems that reach the level of professional impairment, and if necessary, they [shall] limit, suspend, or terminate their professional responsibilities until such time it is determined they may be safe to resume their work" (p. 9). Section D.1.i of the Certified Rehabilitation Counselors (Commission on Rehabilitation Counselor Certification [CRCC], 2001) *Code of Professional Ethics for Rehabilitation Counselors* also states that "Rehabilitation counselors will refrain from offering or rendering professional services when their physical, emotional, or mental problems are likely to harm the clients or others" (p. 8).

Regardless of the professional code of conduct individuals are bound by, each appears to address counselor impairment to ensure that counselors (a) have the necessary and sufficient skills and competencies to provide services to consumers; (b) have reached an acceptable level of competency in the specialty area which they practice; (c) have the ability to control or cope with the personal emotional and psychological stress of their job or otherwise limit, suspend, or terminate their practice; and (d) possess enough self-awareness to assess the personal risk factors that may hinder their ability to competently and ethically interact professionally with their clients and consumers. Indeed, counselor impairment is a concern for the helping professions. Its prevalence is high enough to warrant inclusion in the ethical codes of conduct. Further, it is evident that counselor educators and supervisors must plan and anticipate for the likelihood that when counselors work with others at intense levels of service there will be a psychological, social, emotional, physical, spiritual, and occupational cost.

Ongoing personal growth and development to enhance supervisee wellness is an essential component of the supervision process (Stebnicki, 1998). Thus, the code of ethics as it relates to clinical supervision should not evoke thoughts of punitive actions. Rather, caring clinical supervisors should take on a supportive role that facilitates positive interpersonal working relationships with their supervisees, using a diversity of supervisory styles and approaches. The largest part of the time spent in the supervisory session deals with process and case conceptualization skills, as well as the discussion of boundary issues within the client-counselor relationship. However, it is essential that a good portion of the supervisory sessions should also focus on the personal stress experienced by the supervisee during client-counselor interactions. Analyzing the supervisee's countertransference, inappropriate reactions to the client, or other issues that border on unethical behavior needs to be handled by the clinical supervisor in a therapeutic manner. Not recognizing "the elephant in the room" can hinder client growth and progress. Thus, counselor educators and clinical supervisors should balance the role of the teacher-supervisor with that of the supervisor-therapist.

Developing Supervisee Wellness as an Ethical Obligation

Myers and Sweeney (2005) advocate for counselor educators and supervisors to assist graduate students and supervisees to develop wellness plans during their early stage of growth and development as professional counselors. Monitoring supervisees' personal growth and wellness is critical for preprofessional counselors as they gain experience. Applying a wellness-oriented philosophy to the preprofessional's mind, body, and spirit can act as a means of early identification and prevention of counselor impairment, burnout, and compassion or empathy fatigue among clinical supervisors. Thus, counselor training programs and clinical supervisors have the initial responsibility for monitoring the supervisee's healing involvement with clients/consumers at the same time as promoting self-care practices.

There are various foundational counseling textbooks within each of the counseling specialty areas. Regardless of the counselor's area of expertise, most supervisees are taught the foundational skills of how to (a) establish a client/consumer rapport through the skills of intentional interviewing, including attending, listening, empathic responding, questioning, probing, paraphrasing, and summarizing; (b) facilitate basic techniques and strategies to achieve a therapeutic working alliance with their client/consumer; (c) increase their ability to be objective, open, and flexible when serving clients from different racial, ethnic, cultural, gender, and disability backgrounds; and (d) empower clients/consumers with multiple resources and supports in a goal-oriented and solution-focused environment. Thus, in graduate-level counselor training programs, the largest part of the time is spent learning how to take care of others, with little time given to caring for oneself (Skovholt et al., 2001). One of the most essential elements in counselor training programs should relate to the stress of becoming a skilled helper and developing a program of self-care.

BECOMING A SKILLED HELPER

Making a commitment to a graduate-level counseling program can be quite a stressful life event for some students. There are many reasons why students choose counseling as their life's work. Many are attracted to the occupation because either they or a family member may have experienced significant life events such as loss, grief, sexual abuse, addictions, chronic mental, physical, or medical conditions, or permanent disability. Some individuals may simply have an intense personal career interest in working with others who have a variety of mental, emotional, social, interpersonal, physical, occupational, or spiritual health issues. Many have aptitudes for working in person-centered or human service environments providing direct services as opposed to working in administrative or supervisory roles. Whatever the reason for the individual's choice of this field, it is essential that clinical supervisors recognize the supervisee's (a) personal motives for choosing such a profession; (b) stress levels and countertransference issues, and the ways in which other emotional buttons may challenge the supervisee while working intensely with clients/consumers who have a variety of issues similar to those of the helper; (c) attitudes, values, and beliefs about the helping profession; and (d) long-term developmental goals in terms of personal and professional growth.

Clinical supervisors can assist supervisees to recognize their emotional hot buttons when working with certain types of clients. For example, working with high-risk adolescents (e.g., substance abusers and those with oppositional defiant disorder and low impulse control) is an example of a possible high-risk situation for the preprofessional counselor to encounter during a first experience, a situation that may result in a short-term experience of empathy fatigue. This is especially evident when there is an emotionally fatigued parent involved within a triad (i.e., adolescent client, parent, and counselor). Goodwin (2002) suggests that teenagers are a prime example of a source of "button pushers" that can easily wear down parents.

Preprofessional counselors are also at risk for emotional and physical depletion after intense therapeutic interactions within this triad. When dealing with high-risk youth, even the most understanding and empathic parent or preprofessional counselor will experience some degree of psychological distress (Stebnicki, 2007c). As a result, the preprofessional counselor may become overwhelmed by the experience due to a lack of opportunities to build counselor resiliency and coping skills. It will require some awareness, knowledge, and understanding of how the preprofessional can get her/his buttons pushed by the adolescent and the parent during therapeutic interactions. The parent's fatigue may transfer to the preprofessional counselor. This is a prime example of a scenario that will require a supervisor to help the supervisee make sense of the triad of interactions. Accordingly, the supervisee may need to act more consciously and intentionally during parent-adolescent interactions so that the supervisee can understand how his/her buttons are pushed. It is an opportunity for the preprofessional supervisee to begin the journey of building counselor resiliency strategies through self-care approaches.

WORLDVIEW, BELIEFS, AND VALUES
SELF-ASSESSMENT FOR SUPERVISEES

The following exercise may be used during the initial supervisory session for supervisees to examine their personal self-awareness and unique life experiences. More importantly, this exercise should provide an opportunity for supervisors to facilitate an awareness of supervisees' personal growth and developmental needs. Approaching these issues early on with supervisees emphasizes the need to develop self-care practices and cultivate strategies for counselor resiliency for the purpose of reducing empathy fatigue.

All of us have our own unique life experiences. Because we respond to others according to our own schemata (i.e., feelings, cognitions, values, beliefs), our personal gestalt has an impact on the therapeutic environment that we create for our clients/consumers. After the supervisory working alliance has been established, the supervisor should initiate an open discussion of the preprofessional helper's worldview. One structured way of doing this is to have the supervisee spend about 10 minutes briefly responding to the open-ended questions listed on page 141. Processing these responses with supervisees should assist them to become aware of their hot buttons early on. Supervisors should pay close attention to supervisees' responses and the ways in which their unique value systems, behaviors, feelings, emotions, personality, and goals for future clients/consumers may interact positively or negatively or contaminate the client-counselor therapeutic relationship. Supervisees' worldviews will ultimately impact their (a) theoretical approach, (b) expectations for their clients/consumers, and (c) overall therapeutic interactions within the client-counselor session. Clinical supervisors may begin their first supervisory session by having supervisees respond briefly to the following questions.

1   Some reasons why people go to individual and/or group coun-
    seling are...
2   Counselors can help others become more effective at managing
    their lives by...
3   Clients/consumers in counseling change when...
4   I believe that the responsibility (between counselor-client/
    consumer) begins with...
5   Highly effective counselors are ones who...
6   Ineffective counseling happens when...
7   Some reasons why clients/consumers do not benefit from coun-
    seling are...
8   If I had a client/consumer that was culturally different from me
    (e.g., in race, ethnicity, gender, sexuality, disability, religion, spir-
    ituality) I would especially be mindful of...
9   Counselors can take care of their own mental, physical, or spiri-
    tual wellness by...
10 If an ethical dilemma or conflict arose in a session I would...
11 Some of the personal issues that counselors may be challenged
    by are...
12 One of the most successful things that counselors can do for
    their own personal growth and development and to assist them
    in getting through a bad day is...

One of the primary tasks of the clinical supervisor is to facilitate supervisory approaches that will maximize the supervisee's ability to become
a skilled, competent, and ethical counseling professional. Thus, developmentally this appears to be the appropriate time to assist supervisees
in acquiring an understanding of self-care practices in order to continue
in their chosen profession and reduce the risk of counselor impairment
syndromes such as empathy fatigue. Although there are various out-
standing counseling texts available in counselor training programs, few
address the self-care essentials that build counselor resiliency. Accordingly, the supervisee's practicum, internship, and postgraduate experiences appear to be opportune times to develop counselor resiliency and
self-care strategies.

    One of the differences between the present work and other general
works on occupational stress and burnout is the discussion in the present
work of integral approaches that focus on the professional counselor's
mind, body, and spirit. Clinical supervisors cannot ignore the need to train
supervisees in the foundations, principles, philosophy, and skills of the

counseling process. However, interwoven with this process is the intense nature of the professional relationship between client and counselor. The individuals, couples, and groups that we serve have acquired conditions that affect their interpersonal, emotional, social, physical, relational, vocational, and spiritual wellness. Thus, it should be anticipated that there will be some therapeutic interactions in the supervisee and the client experience a parallel process. Anticipating such experiences provides an opportunity to implement empathy fatigue prevention approaches. Clinical supervisors can assist their supervisees in understanding what to do when such personal issues arise. Accordingly, a special emphasis should be given to empowering supervisees with resources for developing an ongoing practice of self-assessment and self-care. The purpose of such practices is to build counselor resiliency and lessen the possibility of future counselor impairment.

PLANNING THE SUPERVISORY SESSION

Much has been written lately on planning for the supervisory session. Supervisors may plan a portion of the supervisory session to assist their supervisee to acquire self-care skills through (a) self-exploring personal and professional growth potential in the field of counseling; (b) learning how to problem-solve a variety of client/consumer issues in a diversity of settings that include but are not limited to vocational and career, psychiatric, substance abuse, mental health, marriage and family, neuro-rehabilitation, and correctional settings, as well as a variety of other community rehabilitation, mental health, and institutional settings; (c) empowering client/consumers to take on maximum responsibility for developing their own individualized supports and resources; (d) examining and exploring the development of the counseling skills needed for practicing competently and ethically in a private practice therapeutic environment; and (e) developing supports that will help them avoid job burnout and empathy fatigue. Overall, supervisors can use practicum, internship, and postgraduate supervision as a time for supervisee self-exploration, self-assessment, and discussion of issues related to countertransference, counselor impairment, job burnout, and empathy fatigue. Developing empowerment strategies for preprofessional counselors is critical to counselor development and to the provision of opportunities to build counselor resiliency skills leading to better problem management.

Supervisee Analysis of Client-Counselor Session

There are various professional supervisory roles that can be utilized to facilitate supervision. Stoltenberg and Delworth (1988) describe a model that integrates the supervisory roles of teaching, counseling, and consulting. Essentially, this model suggests that supervisors need to attend to (a) the supervisee's process skills (i.e., what the supervisee is doing in the session that is observed by the supervisor); (b) the supervisee's case conceptualization skills (i.e., how the supervisee understands what is occurring in the session, identifying patterns, or choosing specific interventions); and (c) the supervisee's personalization skills (i.e., how the supervisee relates to the client, including congruence as therapists and the supervisee's ability to avoid contaminating the session with their own personal issues).

Despite the fact that most supervisees do not find it helpful when a particular supervision session focuses on their personal issues (Stebnicki, Allen, & Janikowski, 1997), this is an essential component of the supervision process and may be particularly relevant in a particular situation involving client-counselor interactions. Thus, the following questions may be posed to supervisees during an audiotape, videotape, or live review of a client-counselor session, but they are also essential questions to begin an exploration of characteristics and features that may predispose the supervisee to a compendium of counselor impairments such as empathy fatigue:

1   What was the most productive or dynamic part of your client session?

2   What was the most important or significant accomplishment of the client session?

3   In which parts of the session did you find yourself to be most challenged?

4   How did you respond or what did you feel when your client expressed specific recurring themes, feelings/emotions, and experiences?

5   Was there any part of your session where you felt the working alliance with your client was awkward or perhaps strained?

6   Did you notice anything about your client's verbal or nonverbal communication that may have been confusing to you?

After these sample questions are facilitated with supervisees, then perhaps, depending upon the needs of the supervisee and the client, the clinical supervisor may want to separate out the critical issues related to supervisee growth and development.

The case scenario of Jordan, a 24-year-old master's-level counselor supervisee, presented below, is an example of a supervisory session that requires the supervisor to deal with the supervisee's issues from a personal growth framework. Jordan is experiencing some degree of countertransference relating to his own history of substance abuse. In this scenario, the clinical supervisor's concern is not with Jordan's process skills. Rather, the supervisor is dealing with Jordan's countertransference issues from a positive growth perspective, as opposed to dealing with them in a punitive manner. Notice how the clinical supervisor is dealing with Jordan's risk patterns for future behavior, which may lead to counselor impairment.

CLINICAL SUPERVISION CASE SCENARIO: JORDAN

This scenario is offered as a guideline for conducting a clinical supervision session that is focused primarily on the supervisee's personal growth and development. As with all such scenarios, your responses may change depending upon the supervisee's developmental level and a host of other interacting variables. Additionally, you will likely be more comprehensive in your analysis and assessment of Jordan when conducting supervision within your particular setting. Thus, your reactions and goals for the supervision session will probably depend upon the setting, client population, and developmental level of the supervisee, as well as other factors.

Scenario Presentation. Jordan is a 24-year-old master's-level student who is doing his internship at an outpatient alcohol and drug program. Jordan's client Rick is an 18-year-old male with a diagnosis of polysubstance abuse disorder, oppositional defiant disorder (ODD), and attention deficit and hyperactivity disorder (ADHD). He had a minor relapse with regard to his former drugs of choice, cocaine and alcohol. Reviewing a videotape of Jordan's client-counselor session, you notice that Jordan exhibited an increased level of defensiveness in dealing with his client. Jordan's interpersonal interactions with his client appear to be those of a "critical parent" or "big brother," and this seems to have strained the therapeutic relationship.

Analysis of Videotape. You should provide a comprehensive analysis of the supervisee's videotape; verbal and nonverbal communication, and other relevant features. After reviewing the videotape, you hypothesize that Jordan's defensiveness may be caused by several factors: (a) Jordan has a personal history of substance abuse and he is experiencing increased levels of countertransference; (b) the counseling strategies and techniques that Jordan is using are not appropriate for this situation; (c) Jordan is a very inexperienced intern and lacks the appropriate set of process skills; (d) Jordan really does not like working with this particular mental health condition or in this setting; or (e) there is some combination of all the above.

Primary Supervision Issues and Planning for Supervision. You should state concisely the significant issues that need to be addressed during the supervisory session. In particular, the supervisor should assess Jordan's potential risk-level for future empathy fatigue or counselor impairment. Jordan appears to be a very immature 24-year-old, who has not dealt with his own issues of substance abuse. Although he is a good-hearted person and exhibits moderately good levels of interpersonal skills during client interactions, you will need to challenge Jordan's "critical parent" or "big brother" behaviors as well as the defensiveness he exhibits with this particular client. Additionally, he seems to react more gently or softly with other clients who have also relapsed into substance abuse but who are female. Jordan may unconsciously try and "protect" (or enable) his female clients. The primary supervision issues will likely be (a) how to challenge Jordan's thoughts, awareness, and behaviors during his interactions with this particular client, (b) how to select the most appropriate supervisory strategies to address the issues you noted during the videotape review, and (c) how to help Jordan generalize this learning experience to other clients.

Presupervision Session Plan. Describe how you will structure your supervision session with your supervisee. What supervision roles will you use? What supervision theories is this based on? What expectations will you have for your supervisee? What strategies/techniques will you use so that your supervisee can generalize this learning into other client-counselor sessions? How will you assess/measure whether you have been effective as a supervisor with regard to this particular issue? Are there any ethical or social-cultural concerns that you need to address?

Plan to use the integrated developmental model and other supervision techniques:

1   Be mindful of your own countertransference within the supervisory session.

   Rationale. You may react strongly to Jordan's critical parent voice.

Example Approach. Review the videotape together; be open and honest with Jordan...

2   First obtain Jordan's perception of his videotaped client-counselor session.

Rationale. Your view may be different from that of your supervisee. Also, if you first listen to Jordan's perception of his session, he may provide additional information concerning the supervisory issues. Also, you may need to provide feedback to Jordan or confront Jordan's countertransference behaviors.

Example Approach. Review the videotape together; use the Socratic method, role-play...

3   Try to gather more information on Jordan's personal history as a substance abuser.

Rationale. The information you acquire on Jordan's personal history should help you understand Jordan's background, and this may then be integrated into your chosen supervisory role.

Example Approach. Assess the severity of past and current substance abuse behaviors, hold a brief counseling session to increase insight, make possible referral to student mental health services...

Postsupervision Feedback and Observations. Be objective in describing how well your supervisory roles, approaches, or techniques worked. What are you using to measure how well you did? How well did your supervisee respond to the supervisory approaches you used? Is this an approach you would use again in dealing with this particular issue? Generalize this particular presentation to other supervisory issues—What other supervisee issues would this approach work well with?

During your supervisory interactions with Jordan, you became very conscious of the critical parent voice but may not have been aware of how fragile Jordan's ego is and how much self-confidence he lacks as a novice preprofessional counselor. Thus, you could have provided more support and encouragement during the videotape review. For example, in his session with the client, Jordan did use some good empathic responses, open-ended questions, and summary statements. But he became aware of his defensiveness during the session. You may have been able to provide supportive and specific feedback during the videotape review session. You believe that Jordan's awareness was increased when you tied in some of his personal/family history to the critical parent voice he was using with his client. Although you and Jordan did not dwell on these issues at length, you felt that this was a brief therapeutic moment. The most productive part of this session may have been when you transitioned from a therapist role into more of a teacher or trainer role. This seemed to take the pressure off. It also appeared to provide a better opportunity for Jordan to generalize the information to other client sessions. You believe that your Socratic method of addressing and challenging Jordan's belief about substance abusers in general was frustrating him. Thus, you soon became aware of his rigid thinking patterns, and had you persisted with this supervision method you would likely have strained your working relationship.

Overall, the clinical supervisor in this scenario is making intentional efforts to plan for supervision using a diversity of roles and strategies. A primary concern of the supervisory session is issues related to Jordan's personal growth and development. If this were not addressed immediately, Jordan might develop repeated patterns of the same behaviors in other client sessions. One can see that if the supervisor addressed Jordan as a "critical parent" this could hinder the supervisory relationship. Additionally, if Jordan's issues of countertransference were ignored or not noticed by the clinical supervisor, they might develop into a repetitive pattern. This would certainly hinder Jordan's personal growth and development; in addition, cumulative experiences of countertransference may lead to unprofessional counselor behaviors. A key aspect of this case scenario is that if Jordan were to obtain employment in a drug rehabilitation setting, his empathy fatigue buttons might be pushed by multiple clients. This would likely place Jordan at risk for any number of counselor impairment or fatigue experiences.

SUPERVISEE DEVELOPMENT

There is a plethora of developmental models in the counselor supervision literature. Each model has its own unique features for facilitating supervision within different settings, at different levels of supervisee experience, and using different theoretical approaches. As a result of this diversity of thought, authors differ in their conclusions regarding how supervisees and supervisors develop. Bernard and Goodyear (2004) suggest that the intense interest in supervision within a developmental framework may have been stimulated by Blocher (1983); Littrell,

Lee-Borden, & Lorenz (1979); Loganbill, Hardy, & Delworth (1982), as well as by several other authors in the late 1970s and early 1980s. This movement was followed by more comprehensive explanations of how supervisees transition through practicum, internship, and postgraduate professional experience (Bernard, 1997; Bernard & Goodyear, 2004; Stoltenberg, 1981; Worthington, 1987). Some developmental supervision models focus on the role of the supervisor, the dynamics of the supervisee, and the learning environment within the supervision session (Borders & Leddick, 1987). Others offer supervisors the traditional Eriksonian stages of linear development and a step-by-step process for problem solving, skill acquisition, and dealing with more advanced and complex issues in therapy (Russell, Crimmings, & Lent, 1984). It is beyond the scope and intent of this chapter to provide the reader with a comprehensive review of the literature regarding supervisee development. The interested reader will want to consult the references provided within this chapter for further information.

Healing Involvement Within the Context of Clinical Supervision

The primary focus of clinical supervision within a developmental framework is to prepare supervisors to anticipate and plan their supervision sessions as supervisees gain knowledge, awareness, and clinical experience. Consideration must first be given to the particular developmental level at which the supervisee therapist functions: novice, apprentice, graduate, established, seasoned, or senior. One particular developmental model of interest that appears to have implications for evaluating supervisee development and identifying potential counselor impairment fatigue syndromes early on is offered by Orlinsky and Ronnestad (2005). These authors provide a comprehensive model of the theoretical integration of psychotherapist development by describing two patterns of counseling practice: *healing involvement* and *stressful involvement.* As described by Orlinsky and Ronnestad, healing involvement "reflects a mode of participation in which therapists experience themselves as personally committed and affirming in relating to patients, engaging at a high level of basic empathic and communication skills, conscious of Flow-type feelings during sessions, having a sense of efficacy in general, and dealing constructively with difficulties encountered if problems in treatment arose" (p. 162). By contrast, stressful involvement "is a pattern of therapist experience characterized by frequent difficulties in practice, unconstructive efforts to deal with those difficulties by avoiding therapeutic engagement, and feelings of boredom and anxiety during sessions" (p. 162). These modes of therapist involvement are not mutually exclusive, because therapists may encounter one mode of involvement with some clients but not with others. This is a dynamic model by which to view therapists' overall practice. More importantly, it may provide a model for supervisors to view the early onset of at-risk counselor behaviors that may lead to counselor impairment.

For example, therapists who have very little experience at the graduate level and who function according to the stressful involvement mode of therapy are more likely to feel some therapeutic strain, facilitate protocol-driven therapy, feel insecure about their ability to deal with complex client issues, and experience less client success overall. In contrast, therapists who function according to the healing involvement mode are deeply absorbed with their client's interpersonal issues, are able to form a strong therapeutic bond, and are effective therapists overall. Thus, it can be predicted that beginning-level graduate therapists who function according to the stressful involvement mode of client contact will need much closer supervision than those who function according to the healing involvement mode. Many will lose their capacity to respond empathically to others and may become disillusioned with their chosen career.

Developmentally, the established therapist who experiences cumulative depletion or mental, emotional, physical, or spiritual exhaustion may be in a state of stagnation over time. This sense of depletion or exhaustion becomes accentuated if the established therapist has very little coping or resiliency skill. Such therapists may have to seek opportunities to experience "healing involvement" during therapeutic interactions. The cumulative effects over time begin to reduce the capacity for personal growth. Thus, planning for supervision and the selection of supervisory strategies must take into account the therapist's developmental level.

It is clearly recognized throughout the clinical supervision literature that both novice and more experienced practitioners require support, positive feedback, and direct involvement with the healing aspects of their client's therapy. Otherwise, supervisees may be at risk for any number of professional fatigue syndromes. Considering issues related to the supervision of graduate-level supervisees, Orlinsky and Ronnestad (2005) offer the following recommendations to counselor educators and supervisors:

1   Candidates selected for counselor training programs should have well-developed interpersonal communication skills and a warm empathic way of communicating with others.

2   Clinical work should begin early in the student's graduate training once the student has been provided with the initial orientation and basic course work in counseling theory and technique.

3   Theoretical and technical orientation to the counseling profession
should not be ideological or dogmatic in nature; counselor educators and supervisors need to be flexible and open and maximize
the supervisee's opportunity for facilitating therapy with a diversity of techniques and strategies.

4   Beginning-level therapists should be matched well with their clients for the purpose of maximizing client success in healing involvement and minimizing stressful involvement. Beginning-level
therapists should also be provided opportunities to work with a
diversity of groups and clients.

5   Supportive ongoing supervision should be coordinated throughout the supervisee's clinical experiences to ensure continued
growth and development. (p. 182)

Overall, candidates for graduate-level clinical training programs
should be selected on the basis of individuals' interpersonal skills, matu-
rity level, and capacity for empathic communication with a broad range
of individuals and groups. If counselor educators and supervisors truly
want to decrease the possibility of counselor impairment early in the
therapist's career, assisting the therapist to cultivate self-care approaches
early on is essential.

HIGH TOUCH PROFESSIONS AND
THE CARING CYCLE

Counselors, teachers, nurses, social workers, and psychotherapists are
members of a larger group of professionals that are at risk for an empathy or compassion fatigue experience. Naisbitt (1984) refers to this
group as "high touch" professionals, in fields where human contact is
essential to the health and well-being of the individuals they serve.
Counselors especially require regular support and attention. The career development needs of counselors are dynamic and require ongoing consideration for balancing self-care with other-care needs. This
process is described by Skovholt and colleagues (2001) as a "Caring
Cycle process [that] involves repeated empathic attachments, active
involvements, and felt separations" (p. 168). Skovholt and colleagues

(2001) suggest the following potential categories of hazards that can exacerbate problems involved in the difficult work that counselors do. An interpretation is provided for each of these categories:

Hazard 1: Clients have an unsolvable problem that must be solved. When clients become stuck and feel a sense of hopelessness, often counselors feel low self-efficacy and some parallel feelings of despair. It is difficult for professional helpers to make a solution-focused impact on a client's life and there is a tendency to try and "solve the problem" on behalf of the client.

Hazard 2: Not all clients are "honor students." Counselors have a natural tendency to desire clients who are motivated, have abilities and resources, and have few environmental problems. If this were reality, professional helpers would see rapid growth and feel very positive about the changes they facilitate with their clients. However, this is not reality, because many clients struggle with basic tasks and resources, and do not function well in their daily lives.

Hazard 3: There is often a readiness gap between them and us. Readiness for counseling is ultimately dependent on the individual's commitment and readiness to work toward change. Professional helpers expend a lot of emotional, physical, and spiritual energy trying to facilitate change. However, this is difficult to achieve, especially for the novice counselor.

Hazard 4: Our inability to say no. This is the tension we feel between our good intentions and the sense of turning our back on human need. There can be a struggle for the counselor's mind, body, and spirit. Turning our back is extremely difficult to justify from a moral, ethical, mental, emotional, and cognitive perspective. This is especially true for professionals in environments with extremely intense work and large caseloads.

Hazard 5: Constant empathy, interpersonal sensitivity, and one-way caring. Persons in high touch professions are successful because they are able to use their talents and expertise to work therapeutically with others. This can take tremendous effort and emotional energy. Many times the energy flow is not reciprocal between counselor and client and results in emotional exhaustion and mental, physical, and spiritual depletion for the counselor.

Hazard 6: Elusive measures of success. In helping relationships, the goals for therapy are often complex and outcome measures ambiguous. The problem for counselors is the assessment of what their client learned or achieved, or what they did to enact positive change. Success is a relative concept. It depends upon the observers who are involved with ratings or reports of "success."

Hazard 7: Normative failure. Many counselors' self-concept is wrapped up in the polar opposites of failure and success. The expectations we set for ourselves and our clients, our intense drive and determination to maintain high levels of empathy, commitment, and compassion, may not be enough to bring about client growth. This means that the practitioner must develop a realist view of success and normative failure and try to accept that this may be the nature of working in this particular occupation.

Skovholt and Ronnestad (1995) describe professional growth as a long, slow, and erratic process. It takes several years for some counselors to feel competent and achieve a high degree of self-efficacy. Clinical supervisors who understand this reality can plan supervisory sessions using a constellation of issues related to supervisee growth and development. Counselor supervisors must continue to be mindful that many professional counselors have highly satisfying and meaningful careers that may, nevertheless, follow a pattern of ebb and flow.

Incorporating some of the strategies in part III of *Empathy Fatigue* may assist clinical supervisors to keep the focus on the supervisee's mind, body, and spiritual development in order to maintain balance and harmony and reduce the risk of counselor impairment. However, good clinical supervision requires good supervision training. Most doctoral-level programs in counselor education require a course in clinical supervision. One particular approach, developed by Allen, Stebnicki, and Torkelson Lynch (1995), utilizes two components that are both didactic and experiential. The first component of the clinical supervision training consists of five elements: (a) developing a theoretical base for supervision, (b) cultivating self-awareness within the supervisor-supervisee session, (c) understanding legal, ethical, and administrative supervisory tasks, (d) providing experiential training of master's-level practicum or internship supervisees while they are being supervised by a senior clinical supervisor, and (e) planning strategies and techniques for the supervisory session.

The second component of training utilizes doctoral-level students as supervisors for master's-level practicum and internship supervisees. In this component, the doctoral-level supervisors are supervised by a senior faculty supervisor. The doctoral-level supervisors also receive peer supervision. This model utilizes a holistic approach that involves senior faculty supervising a doctoral-level supervisor, with the doctoral supervisor engaging in the supervision of master's-level counselors in training.

Overall, this model is similar to models of training in other doctoral training programs, but it presents a special emphasis on developing personal counselor growth within the supervisor-supervisee relationship. The supervisory time spent in personal growth activities can accelerate the supervisee's self-care practices. Optimal functioning as a professional helper requires constant attention to taking care of oneself and cultivating resiliency.

MODEL PROGRAMS OF SELF-CARE: MINDFULNESS AND WELLNESS PRACTICES

One particular model program facilitated by the counselor education and training program at the University of Massachusetts (see Newsome et al., 2006) utilizes the underlying philosophy of Jon Kabat-Zinn's Mindfulness-Based Stress Reduction (MBSR) Program (1990). The MBSR approach is based on the Buddhist concept of mindfulness. Supervisees are taught to shift their awareness to the here and now and cultivate states of consciousness that lead to an acknowledgment of the present moment and a transformation of their negative physical and mental state into a more desirable calm, peaceful, and relaxed state of being.

Applying a wellness philosophy to counselor education and training programs has also been successful in reducing the onset of the beginning stages of counselor impairment. Witmer and Granello (2005) suggest that such a philosophy promotes health and optimal well-being among both counselor educators and supervisees. This is achieved through wellness assessments and identifying healthier lifestyle habits. As part of this model, the program objectives are communicated to the supervisee's peers, as well as to the field placement in which practicum/internship supervisors are trained in the essential elements of nurturing a wellness-oriented environment.

There are many other approaches that could be utilized within counselor education and training programs to assist counselors in training to plan, organize, and begin a program of self-care. The self-care philosophy can be implemented as (a) a first semester course for counselor trainees, (b) a one-semester-hour seminar required for all new counselor trainees, (c) a model that is infused throughout the counselor trainees' curriculum, and/or (d) a personal development activity beginning with the pre-practicum and continuing through the practicum and internship.

CONCLUDING REMARKS

Empathy fatigue and other counselor impairments are natural consequences of working with others at intense levels of service. Clinical supervision is perhaps one of the most important aspects of graduate-level
counselor training programs. With such supervision, the individual's first
clinical experiences can be an opportunity to build resiliency and coping
skills for the future. Chapters 12 and 13 offer readers the foundations
of self-care practice. Breathing, relaxation, meditation, and visualization
strategies have been utilized in model programs of self-care. Maintaining a program of self-care is essential for life-long personal growth within
the profession.

12

Foundational Practices of Self-Care: Breathing, Listening, and Awareness Meditation

Modern self-care practices may have begun with the Human Potential Movement (HPM), which was nurtured in the social and intellectual environment of the 1960s. The HPM, a name that senior magazine editor George Leonard claims as his own (DiCarlo, 1996), has its conceptual roots in existential and humanistic psychology. The philosophy and ideology of the HPM suggests that human beings are capable of an exceptional quality of life filled with happiness, creativity, and fulfillment. If one can tap the extraordinary resources of the mind (the cognitive level of consciousness) then one has the potential to reach self-actualization, which is depicted by Abraham Maslow (1968) as the supreme expression of the individual's life.

Many psychologically well individuals who were tied to the HPM movement recognize Esalen, a resort setting in Big Sur, California, as the place of origin of the study and development of human potential (Vash & Crewe, 2004). Michael Murphy and Dick Price founded the Esalen Institute in 1962 with the collaborative influence of George Leonard. The purpose and intent of Esalen was for it to be a think-tank for intellectual ideas and discussion, theory development, and therapeutic training, and to be a strong influence on experiential activities. The HPM has come under criticism from various disciplines in psychology, medicine, and science that dismiss the movement as pseudoscience or psychobabble. The transpersonal psychology movement, which emphasizes the esoteric, psychic, and mystical forms of spiritual development, appeared to bring more credibility to the research related to extraordinary states of consciousness and human potential. Both the HPM and the transpersonal movement seem to have matured into today's New Age movement, which is heavily influenced by secular spirituality, complementary and alternative medicine, integral medicine, biopsychosocial models, and mind-body-spiritual approaches. Many of these approaches have been shaped by the ancient philosophy of China, India, Japan, and other Asian countries.

Decades of theoretical and experiential development have expanded these approaches and propelled a movement filling a unique niche in personal growth and self-care development. However, a major flaw in many of these self-care theories is the focus on the individual's own development. We have either ignored or neglected to give credit to our ancestors and the collective wisdom of indigenous cultures that developed the foundation of balancing and harmonizing our mind, body, and spirit. The basic structure of a gathering for ceremonies, rituals, conscious connections, and communal living is clearly absent from self-care practices. Consequently, we may have lost our focus in terms of the ultimate support system that extends beyond the family: our tribal communities.

There are more therapeutic support groups than ever before, in modern counseling, psychology, and health and wellness (e.g., Alcoholics-Narcotics-Emotions Anonymous, Diabetic-Cancer-ALS support groups, Al-Anon, and many other family support groups). Most groups, however, will meet for only 2–3 hours per week. For the remainder of the week, support group members and the professionals that facilitate these groups go about their daily lives and may be detached and isolated from their primary support system.

Taking care of the soul requires support in everyday life. It requires cultivating one's own sacred space. However, it is of paramount importance for professional helpers to receive a network of assistance from their earthly community of brothers and sisters. No human being is totally self-sustaining. Even Christian or Buddhist monks, who spend months and years practicing their devotions and living in silence, must channel their love and compassion to others at some point in their existence. Otherwise, the peak spiritual experiences, non-ordinary states of consciousness, and spiritual gifts of a deeper awareness would have little meaning and purpose.

The activities and guidelines offered in this chapter and others that follow bring us back to the roots of self-care; the philosophies related to meditation. Meditation is a stress reduction approach used by persons of many different Eastern and Western faiths. It has been used successfully in controlled research studies for persons with high blood pressure, cardiovascular diseases, migraine headaches, arthritis, and many other chronic conditions. Meditation has also proved to be helpful for persons that have addictive behaviors, anxiety, depression, and anger issues. There are literally hundreds of different types of meditations and each achieves its own purpose.

Many indigenous meditative practices can be facilitated by oneself or with a group of like-minded individuals. The foundational practices of cultivating awareness through breathing, meditation, awareness, journeying, and visualization have an immense spiritual energy that is greater than ourselves. They require us to honor the wisdom of and give reverence to the spiritual resources of indigenous groups that have cultivated such rich healing resources, from Africa to Appalachia and everywhere in between. The collective wisdom of those who came thousands of years before us can no longer be minimized or ignored. The special resource list in the appendix reflects the body of work presented in the material that follows.

BREATHING AWARENESS AND TAKING A CLEANSING BREATH

Breathing is an unconscious process that is essential for life. It connects the mind, body, and spirit and offers us opportunities to use our conscious mind and voluntary nervous system to modify our unconscious mind and involuntary nervous system. It balances sympathetic (involuntary nervous system) with parasympathetic (voluntary nervous system) activity. With each breath, we take in oxygen and release the waste product, carbon dioxide. Poor breathing habits can diminish the flow of these gases to and from the body, making it harder to cope with stressful situations in life. Most important of all, poor breathing habits can lead to physical and mental fatigue.

Breathing appears to be the guardian angel of all body systems. In many languages the same word is used for spirit and for breath: Sanskrit (*prana*), Greek (*pneuma*), Hebrew (*ruach*), and Latin (*spiritus*). Restricted or shallow breathing can reduce the efficiency of the brain and the nervous, cardiovascular, and respiratory systems. The emotional and psychological cost of restricted breathing is the creation of negative mood, affective, anxiety, and stress-related disorders. Some physiological benefits of taking a cleansing breath include lowering the blood pressure and heart rate, increasing circulation throughout the body, improving skin tone and physical appearance, and aiding in digestion.

Taking a cleansing breath is the most fundamental and important practice for physical, mental, and spiritual well-being. It is also one of the more critical aspects of (a) gaining control by harnessing the body's natural energy and metabolic system, (b) centering oneself for meditation and visualization activities, (c) sustaining focus and attention for cognitive and intellectual pursuits, and (d) integrating many other holistic approaches.

Dr. Andrew Weil (1995) is a major advocate of taking a cleansing breath to enhance the body's natural healing capabilities. He suggests within the principles of breathwork that individuals should make their breathing slower, deeper, quieter, and much more regular or natural. Remember that each breath you take should come naturally and automatically. For optimal breathing and cleansing breaths, the following directions should be followed:

- Lie down and get comfortable. Place a pillow behind your legs, directly behind your knees to take pressure off the lower lumbar region of your back. Now begin paying attention to your natural breath. Place one hand on your abdomen around your waistline and the other hand on your chest right in the center and notice how the air moves in and out of your body. Simply take notice of how you breathe in and out (inhale-exhale). Focus on your breathing pattern for about 1–2 minutes.
- Now that you are aware of your breath, exhale through your nose until all the air is out of your lungs. Now take in a cleansing breath of air through your nostrils for about 4 seconds, pushing air into your abdomen. Your abdomen should stretch outward as far as it will go. Do not breathe from your chest area. This is shallow breathing and is characteristic of persons in states of stress or anxiety. Draw in air through your nose and notice how your abdomen begins to rise, not your chest. You may hold this breath for a few seconds before releasing it in a slow, deep, quiet, and regular manner.
- Next, exhale through a small opening in your mouth. Your exhalation should last 7–8 seconds. This will take some practice because

the amount of air you exhale is related to the amount of air that you inhale. A good cleansing breath should last at least 7 seconds.

■ As you notice the air leaving your lungs through your mouth, you may want to make a "whooshing" noise. You may wish to create a one-word or one-syllable mantra to use quietly as you exhale. A mantra or a nonverbal "whooshing" noise will help you focus on the breath as you exhale. It is also a prompt for you to repeat this pattern. Examples of mantras that are used quietly during exhalation are "One," "God," "Love," or "Peace." Again, use something that is verbal or nonverbal, whichever fits best for you.

■ Continue taking deep breaths for about 5–10 minutes then return to your normal breathing pattern. Make sure that you find a quiet place, empty out your mind, take your time with this exercise, and concentrate only on your breathing. Try this for about 20 minutes per day in all, until it begins to feel natural.

LISTENING MEDITATION

In ancient spiritual-religious cultures, the sense of a peak spiritual experience and being one with a spirit entity was very natural. It required people to sit in silence and listen with all five bodily senses and then try and connect with their sixth or intuitive sense to achieve a deeper personal spiritual experience. Spiritually conscious communities today have a very different relationship to silence and listening with their third-eye chakra. For example, in the Christian church today, an activity that appears to be popular among younger Christians is the praise and workshop service. Some such services involve large video monitors and some are broadcast live via the Internet or public access television. This type of service may seem quite impersonal, especially for those who primarily connect with God in solitude. However, well-developed, spiritually focused Christians manage to experience both the praise and worship service and to find some time alone through the week for prayer and meditation.

The point of these observations is that we may have forgotten how to listen and experience our divine healer and spirit helpers through silence and solitude. We are not comfortable sitting in silence for long periods because of the lifestyles we have created for ourselves, watching movies and television, playing video games, surfing the Internet, and listening to music. These distractions do not help us create a sacred space.

The basis of spiritual grounding is learning how to be comfortable sitting in silence and creating a sacred space. First, we must make a commitment to finding a balance in our life with regard to our family, our job, and all the activities that fill our week. The hidden spiritual messages in our lives may be found in water (touch), wind (sound), cloud formations (vision), flowers (smell), food (taste), and deep meditation (using our intuitive sense). The first step in most meditative practices is to create a sacred space in the inner and outer environment to try and connect with spiritual states of consciousness. Be mindful of the following:

- After you have engaged in deep breathing for about 5–10 minutes, direct your attention to your natural outer environment. Listen in a nonjudgmental way to the quality, tone, pitch, or frequency of the sounds around you. It may help to close your eyes or tie a scarf around your eyes to help you focus while you participate in this listening meditation. After a while, practice screening out the external sounds.
- Some individuals may find it helpful to listen to a sound therapy, relaxation, or Reiki CD while facilitating a deeper state of conscious listening. However, do not focus your attention totally on the music or sound, as this will not allow the opportunity to develop listening skills using higher levels of consciousness.
- Check in from time to time by drawing your attention away from unwanted thoughts and sounds. Monitor your breath, making sure that it is deep, slow, and rhythmic. This will help you sustain your state of intentional solitude.
- Allow your creative imagination to experience both your inner and outer environment. Try and notice any non-ordinary physical sensations, mental images, emotions, or other vibrations that are present as you are in a state of deep listening.

Listening meditations should be cultivated based on personal needs. Individuals beginning a program of mediation may want to spend 15–20 minutes per day in this activity and then increase the time to whatever their schedule allows. This activity may take place within a meditation group, with or without a group facilitator. Participants should allow time to process their experiences at the end of each session. Peer support from like-minded individuals is an important component of sustaining any spiritual activity. Most importantly, keep a journal of your listening meditation experiences. It is essential that you review these experiences for personal meaning and insight.

AWARENESS MEDITATION

Awareness is being mindful of the present moment in a conscious and intentional way. It is a way of being conscious throughout our daily activities. Christians, Buddhists, Native Americans, and others emphasize that paying attention to our mind, body, and spiritual health is the quintessence of sustaining a path of wellness. It is *the* way to soften and open our hearts so we can communicate compassion and empathy toward others. An awareness of how our thoughts, perceptions, bodily sensations, and spiritual well-being affect us and others in our environment can provide us with invaluable opportunities to grow personally and professionally. As professionals, if we take time to notice how we respond to our colleagues, in therapeutic client relationships, and with our family and friends, then we are developing a discipline of self-observation.

It is essential that we should be open to cues from our natural environment that can provide us with immediate feedback. Approaching life in the present moment and observing the intentional choices we make will provide us with a qualitative measure of how we connect to our experiences. It allows us to be mindful of how our mind, body, and spirit live within us through a variety of stressful events. The question of *how we would like to be remembered after we pass on in life* requires some level of understanding of how we choose to react to people, to events, and under a variety of circumstances. We send a powerful vibration or form of energy to others that communicates who we are. As Kabat-Zinn (1994) suggests in his book, *Wherever You Go There You Are,* by feeling the present and living life fully in the moment, we can accept the truth of our interconnectedness with all things. Thus, being aware and mindful of our present life is simply the art of conscious living.

Unfortunately, many of us are unconscious in our response to life. Ignoring the way we communicate our energy to our internal and external environment denies us a process of self-observation and self-inquiry. For instance, if we are not mindful of the emotional-physical stress that we accumulate throughout the week, we become our stress. In some people, the stress response seems to show up long before they actually recognize that it is there. Thus, it presents a challenge to the individual's muscular-skeletal system as well as the emotions and psyche. Paying attention to our mind, body, and spirit in the here and now provides us with protection from experiencing stress that has occurred days, weeks, or months before we recognize its negative effects. We can become more resilient if we live in the present moment. Our mind, body, and spirit have a way of helping us let go or forget the intensity of our past stressors. Likewise, acceptance of the present moment assists us in coping with events that may be days, weeks, or months in our future.

The anticipation of future stress, worry, or anxiety may be a particular challenge for some. It may be a belief system, perception, or attitude that is inextricably linked to our mind, body, and spirit. As a result, we may experience muscular-skeletal conditions such as tension and pain that seem to originate from an unknown cause. When negative, toxic, or irrational thoughts, perceptions, attitudes, and beliefs become chronic and persistent, this becomes integrated into our physiological and emotional well-being. Soon we react to our physical and emotional fatigue, pain, and other sensations that promote the empathy fatigue response. Integrating the breathing and listening meditation into a purposeful activity of self-care is critical to letting go of the social, emotional, physiological, perceptual, spiritual, and occupational tension that becomes incorporated into our daily self-destructive routine. The following guiding principles may assist you in integrating progressive physical relaxation activities with meditations of the mind and spirit:

- Begin by integrating deep breathing and awareness meditations with this activity to release any tension or stress that you are holding in your body. After you have centered yourself and are either lying down or sitting comfortably, scan your body for tension. Notice which area(s) of your body has (have) the most tension and stress.
- As you take-in a deep breath, visualize yourself replacing your tension and stress with a purifying, cleansing, spirit-like energy.
- Hold this breath for a few seconds then exhale through your mouth and visualize removing any unwanted, negative, or toxic energy held in your body.
- Continue scanning your body for about 15–20 minutes for any tension or stress and use a good cleansing breath to purify your mind, body, and spirit.

CONCLUDING THOUGHTS

The majority of traditional progressive muscle relaxation activities are facilitated using a pure physical-emotional or cognitive-behavioral experience. Incorporating the spiritual dimension into such an activity may add a deeper meaning and purpose for some individuals. Also, in traditional models of progressive muscle relaxation, there is a tendency to adhere to a structure that begins with multiple body parts, joints, muscle groups, and so forth. This can become a lengthy procedure and frustrating for some individuals. Another adaptation of this traditional approach would be to use 3–4 major areas of the body that may be the most tense (e.g., head, neck, shoulders, stomach) and then cultivate a concentrated awareness within these particular areas for purification, detoxification, and letting go.

Chapter 13 should open doors to deeper dimensions integrating the mind, body, and spirit into wellness. The practices of guided and contemplative meditation and visualization integrate other bodily senses (i.e., sight, hearing, touch, smell, taste). These advanced approaches tend to create other opportunities for journeying into our interpersonal and spiritual wellness.

13

Foundational Practices of Self-Care: Guided, Contemplative, Walking, and Visualization Meditation

Meditation practices have the ability to provide the transformative path or journey to healing empathy fatigue. Meditation is a simple yet powerful means for developing an inner wisdom of our mind, body, and spirit. The practice of meditation is not an invention of one particular culture or religious/spiritual belief system. Meditation itself is not a doctrine or religion and it takes on as many different forms and approaches as there are people, problems, and cultures of the world. The research on meditation is quite extensive and it is beyond the scope of this chapter to comprehensively discuss the research and its application. However, there are several recent qualitative studies worth mentioning on the use of mindfulness-based meditations for training beginning-level mental health therapists (see Newsome et al., 2006; Shapiro et al., 2007).

These studies have strong implications for integrating self-care practices, particularly in clinical supervision settings. Most notable are several themes that emerged among counselor supervisees who experienced mindfulness meditation training during the first semester of their graduate program. Supervisees noted a significant short-term impact on their physical, emotional, attitudinal, spiritual, and interpersonal awareness. As a result of mindfulness training, the supervisees' clients also benefited. The supervisees reported they had (a) increased comfort with silence during client sessions; (b) more focus and attention to the therapeutic process; and (c) a change of attitude about the mind, body, and spiritual connection within the health and healing aspects of their self and clients. Other studies suggested that mindfulness-based training enhanced supervisees' capacity to (a) be more mindful and aware of the present moment; (b) reduce overidentification with client problems; (c) focus on reducing negative self-thoughts; and (d) decrease their stress level to enhance psychological well-being and mental and physical health. It has been shown in hundreds of other studies dealing with a variety of consumers, clients, and patients that persons who practice meditation possess greater physical, mental, and spiritual well-being. Most importantly, meditation increases our awareness, compassion, and empathy toward others.

Meditation has certainly become popular in the United States during the last few decades and has been used by sports psychologists to enhance athletes' focus, promote the relaxation response, and improve performance. It has also been used as a complementary, alternative, and integrative medicine approach to decreasing pain among persons with chronic illnesses and disabilities. Meditation has also been helpful for individuals with a variety of mental health and substance abuse-related disorders.

Many Westerners associate meditation with Buddhism. Although meditation is central to all Buddhist practice, however, it is also practiced by members of many of the world's other religious groups, including Christians, Hindus, and Muslims, and in many other cultures of the world.

Daily meditation is the cornerstone of a healthy mind, body, and spirit. There are as many types of meditation as there are people in the world, because meditation is an individual path to deepen your awareness, compassion, inner peace, and empathy with others. Meditation is very different from the cognitive-behavioral types of activities or mental tasks that we perform. It is a higher level of consciousness; the experience is like floating out of body. With daily practice you will develop the ability to observe your thoughts, your emotions, and your physical and spiritual well-being.

Remember that meditation can be done either individually or in groups of like-minded people. The following guidelines can help you get started on the path to achieving higher meditative states of consciousness:

- Find a comfortable space where you can either sit or lie down and bring your attention to your normal breathing. Try not to think about each breath and do not try to control or change your normal breathing pattern. Rather, just be with the experience of your body and observe your breathing.

■ Let your mind, body, and spirit feel free and natural. Allow any passing thoughts, sensations, or experiences to bubble up and float into the vastness of the universe.

■ Be open to the idea that you are living in the moment. Watch how the "now" or the present moment unfolds before you. During calm meditative states, there is no yesterday or tomorrow; there is only living for this moment. Be mindfully aware of the silence. Find your own quiet space and let go of any worry, fear, tension, or stress that you are experiencing in the present moment.

■ Give yourself permission to allow any unwanted feelings or sensations to dissolve into the vastness of the universe. Allow your mind and thoughts to come together in your heart. Without specific intention or request, just whisper to yourself, "May I be at peace," "May I dwell in my heart," "May I be healed." Create your own statement of compassion.

■ Communicate with an open heart and bring in messages of love, compassion, and kindness; feel the vibrations of warmth, happiness, joy, and wholeness. Draw in this wholeness and with each breath try and deepen this experience and nurture these feelings and experience. Seek out the loving kindness and compassionate spirit within yourself.

There are other popular types of meditation that achieve the same goals. These include guided, contemplative, and walking meditation. Each meditation can be tailored to meet your own unique needs. You may also decide on your personal intention for engaging in such integral approaches. The following well-accepted meditations provide other opportunities for your journey in healing empathy fatigue. A brief description is provided for each. Be open to the resources in this book to expand your knowledge, awareness, and skills of experiencing a more holistic way of living through meditative practice.

GUIDED MEDITATION

Guided meditations are typically done while listening to an audiotape of sounds and/or voices. Usually the individual follows a structured session of meditation from the voice on the audiotape. The use of sound as therapy is typically incorporated into this structured meditation. Sounds from the earth (e.g., ocean, wind, animals, other natural sounds) or music of the ancient masters of chants, drumming, or indigenous instruments will certainly enhance the guided meditation experience. During guided meditations, your rational mind may create unique images. Distracting sounds in the environment may pull your attention away. However, the plethora of pleasant images and sensations may be explored and re-created in greater detail with each session. Use your mind, body, and spirit to listen and to guide you. The challenge with this type of meditation is to sustain a focus of intention. The purpose is to cultivate the relaxation response, develop a sense of enlightenment, seek answers to difficult personal problems, and enhance the interconnectedness of your mind, body, and spirit. Despite multiple sessions with the same guided meditation, whether live or by CD, you must be receptive at all times to the possibilities of acquiring new, unplanned, unsought-after information and experiences. Those new to meditation may not understand how the shaman journeys using the same repetitive drumming each time, or the Sufi dances to the same rhythm and dance. Individuals can have completely different experiences in each session. However, be open, sit back and relax, pay attention, and be open to the new insight and energy that may appear to you in your guided experience.

CONTEMPLATIVE MEDITATION

Father Thomas Merton (1961), a Trappist monk and one of the most prolific writers and theologians of 20th-century spirituality, notes that contemplation meditation is one of the highest expressions of humankind's intellectual abilities and spiritual life. It is acquiring the gift of a spiritual vision at the highest levels of consciousness. One particular form of contemplative meditation requires the individual to fix her/his eyes on a chosen object that can be held in the hand. Natural objects such as stones, shells, pieces of wood, candles, leaves, or other natural items seem to work best with this meditation. In Native American spirituality, all things on the earth are connected to one another. Thus, plants, animals, and people all deserve equal respect. As you examine the object, notice its color, texture, size, and shape. Allow yourself to become immersed in exploring this object as though you have never seen such a thing before. Communicate a message of unconditional love and kindness, open your heart to expressing love, compassion, warmth, happiness, joy, and wholeness. Feel the vibrational energy between you and the item you have chosen. In Father Merton's most widely read work, *New Seeds of Contemplation,* he states that "the contemplative is not isolated in himself, but liberated from his external and egotistic self by humility and purity of heart" (p. 66). To truly communicate esoterically with the vibrational energy of the item or object you have chosen, you have to understand that life holds not only mystery for us, but also clear solutions. Planting and cultivating the seeds of contemplation reveal the light within the darkness hiding in our soul. Observing a dance while in contemplative meditation (as in Sufi dancing) provides us with another opportunity to sit in silence and listen for our inner voice of experience to emerge and bring us new awareness.

WALKING MEDITATION

Walking meditations are undertaken by seekers who are on a transcendent spiritual journey. Many of the major stories in the Jewish and Christian scriptures involve walking as a spiritual journey. For example, Moses and his people journeyed to the Promised Land; Joseph and Mary walked to Bethlehem. There are hundreds of Native American stories that make reference to journeying in the desert, over mountains, or through the forest in search of some meaning and purpose from the Great Spirit. Making the choice to take that first step on your journey to heal empathy fatigue provides a very powerful message. In a walking meditation you are never alone. There have been others that have walked before you on (and off) the path. Walking meditations are inward journeys. The actual physical path you may be walking on may prepare you for good cardiovascular health. However, the goal of this type of meditation experience is not to arrive at some destination. Rather, you will be preparing your mind, body, and spirit for an ongoing journey; one of continuous exploration and discovery.

There has been a resurgence in the use of the labyrinth for meditation, prayer, and celebration. A labyrinth is a circuitous path (which looks like a maze from above) that people have used for walking meditations for thousands of years. Although labyrinths take many shapes and forms, they are more than mazes, because the path always leads the person back to the center. It is a highly spiritual experience that has mystical connections with most of the world's religions and spiritual belief systems. Schaper and Camp's (2004) book, *Labyrinths from the Outside In: Walking to Spiritual Insight—A Beginner's Guide,* provides a rich resource for understanding the spiritual significance of the labyrinth. This work offers guided meditations in walking and provides instructions for constructing a labyrinth. There are well over 500 labyrinths in North America; these involve interfaith activities based on walking meditations. They are 21st-century symbols of modern spirituality that connect with the ancient past, even further back than Stonehenge or the ruins of Troy.

Walking meditations can be done indoors or outdoors. However, they seem to work best in natural environments, such as in the woods, on the beach, on a walking trail, or in other natural areas. Whether you are walking a labyrinth or engaging in some nonstructured walking meditation, here are some tips to follow:

- Assess the terrain and weather conditions before you go on your walk, making sure that you have the necessary footwear, water, clothing, and other appropriate supplies.
- Be aware that you are not training for a 10-kilometer run or walk. Walking meditations are contemplative activities that draw your attention to the path you are on. This type of meditative activity focuses on the quality of the experience, rather than how far or how fast you should go.
- Make sure that you pay attention to your breath, stride, pace, and overall experience of achieving meditative states of consciousness.

The walking meditation is an inward journey. Be intentional about the spiritual path you want to take. You have chosen to be active and have heard the call to move. Trust in the journey and be open to the idea of seeing, hearing, feeling, and experiencing life with a different perception or an attitude of gratitude.

VISUALIZATION

Visualization uses the creative power of your imagination for the purpose of health and healing. There are as many visualization experiences as there are people. This approach requires the sensory integration of sight, sound, touch, smell, and taste along with your creative imagination.

Be open to the possibility that you have the energy, awareness, and creativity to cultivate a better future for your mind, body, and spirit. Begin your visualization experience much like other activities, being mindful of your breathing, taking full natural cleansing breaths, and concentrating on being in a state of total relaxation.

Developing Your Senses

Your visualization experience may begin with the development and exploration of your different senses using the following:

Sight. Create a visual image, an imagined or a real experience from your past, present, or future that you feel positive about, and try to achieve a peak visual experience of beauty and awe.

Sound. Concentrate on a pleasing sound that you are familiar with in your environment. This could be the sound of a comforting voice, sounds in the natural environment such as waterfalls, birds, ocean waves, wind blowing through the trees or wind chimes, or the still silence on top of a mountain.

Touch. Give your attention to something that you cannot see or hear. Tune in to a very pleasant physical sensation, an object, person, or item in your natural environment. You may focus your attention on something that you have created in your imagination. Feel the texture of this sensation of touch. Contemplate the texture (smooth, rough, prickly) and the temperature (cool, hot, warm), and sense the energy that surrounds this object.

Smell. Focus on a pleasing smell or aroma with which you have come in contact. Notice how your body reacts to and experiences this particular smell and the way it was recorded in your olfactory memory. Be aware of any natural smells in your environment (ocean water, wild flowers, fresh mountain streams) or smells that you associate with special occasions (Christmas cookies, birthday cake) or with daily moments of surprise (the scent of freshly baked bread, fresh-cut flowers).

Taste. Center your attention on your mouth and tongue. Become aware of your taste buds and explore the peak sensations that you have experienced using the sense of taste. These sensations may be the taste of salty ocean water, wild mountain berries, or a favorite fruit.

Some individuals may find it is much easier to develop certain senses than others. That is fine; allow yourself time to develop this holistic experience.

Analysis of Your Visual Sensations

As you develop your sensory awareness of sight, sound, touch, smell, and taste, begin exploring these senses at a deeper level through meditative states. First, be aware that it is quite normal for you to experience (a) some images and sensations that are easier to visualize than others, (b) images that may be unwanted or that you want to avoid or suppress, (c) images that are hard to distinguish from others, and (d) images and sensations that are difficult to explore in any depth. Your attempts to cultivate and bring alive your five senses may take some practice. Some experiences may be much easier to develop in your memory than others. The following sections contain recommendations to increase your visual experiences.

Strengthening Your Visual Memory

Patrick Fanning (1994) in *Visualization for Change* discusses ways to increase your visual memory. He suggests opening a drawer in your kitchen, bedroom, or closet and studying the objects that you see inside. Do this for about 10 seconds. Now close your eyes and see if you can remember the objects that were in the drawer. See if you can remember how these objects were organized or what their shapes were. Notice some blank spots in your memory that are hard to fill in. Now open your eyes and re-examine the objects and see what was missing from your visual memory. Close your eyes again and try to see with your "third eye" or use your intuitive sense and see how many more objects you can remember.

Barbara Brennan (1988) in *Hands of Light: A Guide to Healing Through the Human Energy Field* discusses her visual techniques using high sense vision to raise the vibrations and energy level within individuals for the purpose of seeing body auras. Regardless of one's approach to meditation, the natural inquirer hungers for ways to develop the intuitive senses, to look introspectively. The challenge for those who practice various types of meditation is to integrate all body systems into the total experience of the mind, body, and spirit.

CREATIVE VISUALIZATION AND NEW DISCOVERIES

As you use visualization, imagine yourself as a free-floating video camera that has total control over camera angles, sounds, lighting, close-up or far away shots, or other special effects. As you become the lens, create your visual image, complete with all senses. Think about a special house you once lived in, a special flower you found on a walk or in your own garden, vacations in the mountains or on the beach, or other things in your environment. Discover new things about your visual image. Imagine that you have the technology to walk 360 degrees around these images. Look at the objects from all angles: the right side, behind, above, and so forth. Continue using your special technology to rotate the image, zoom in and out, make it smaller, larger, make it spin, make it disappear or reappear. Be playful, creative, and imaginative, and integrate creative meditations into your visualization experience.

Creating a Visual Image of Your Special Place

As you learn different visualizations for meditative purposes or to visualize different career goals, relationships, or problem situations at work, it is important to create very positive, wellness-connected types of places, activities, events, and peak spiritual experiences that can be integrated into your mind, body, and spirit. There are enough negative and unwanted images in movies, television, video games, and on the Internet. Be aware that some of these images may pop into your creative visualization from time to time. However, daily or weekly meditative practice will strengthen your focus and attention to those images that represent a strong sense of safety, security, personal physical, social, emotional, and spiritual comfort. The following is a self-guided visualization that may help you channel your mind, body, and spirit into a simple place where you are free to enter into a sacred environment that you create.

- Begin your visualization experience by creating a special place that is warm, comforting, safe, inspiring, or spiritual. Think of a place you can go to in your mind to release tension and stress. Your special place may be real or imagined.
- Create a special place that is unique to your personality; one that is tailor made for your life; a special place that makes a statement of who You are.
- Think about a special place; it may be a favorite room in your house (or dream house), a place at the beach, on top of the mountains, or in a desert or forest.
- Take a look around your special place. Walk around your place from different angles. You are the person in control of the special effects or structure of this environment.

■ Use all five senses to describe your special place and walk around so that you can become comfortable. Know intuitively that this is your place to go and release tension or stress in your mind, body, or spirit.

■ Make an area where you can store things in your special place. This may resemble a treasure chest, a hand-made bag, a hollow in a tree, or a steel-reinforced lock-box or safe.

■ Be aware that you can store anything in this special place, such as an emotion, a life experience, or an object such as a fishing rod, boat, or whatever. You can always go back to retrieve this thing that you have stored in your special place, to bring you comfort.

CONCLUDING REMARKS

There are untold numbers of meditative activities that one can engage in. One does not have to be involved in Buddhism, Christianity, Judaism, or Native American practices to reap the benefits of increasing the resiliency and hardiness necessary to work within the helping professions. The material presented in this chapter reflects a long history of research within the behavioral health movement for the purpose of effectively treating chronic illnesses and diseases that range from chronic pain through mental health and substance abuse conditions to life-threatening diseases such as cancer.

The overall purpose of breathing, relaxation, visualization, and meditation is to create new pathways for healing the mind, body, and spirit. Finding the healer within oneself is a highly empowering act of self-care. This is especially relevant for those who have experienced some degree of empathy fatigue in the profession they have chosen. Chapter 14, which follows, is an expression of finding the healer within oneself to creatively problem-solve issues related to empathy fatigue or professional impairments. Gaining access to one's inner voice experiences or sensing a divine presence in the soul can be extraordinarily meaningful for many who wish to explore a higher dimension of consciousness.

14 Counselors as Modern Day Shamans: Finding the Healer Within

Finding the healer within oneself is a journey unto itself. Carl Jung once remarked that it is easier to go to Mars or the moon than it is to penetrate one's own being. Searching for your inner guide requires that you break through a spiritual opening in your soul and connect with God, your higher power, the Great Spirit, or the Supreme Being. This being or power can be accessed primarily through higher states of consciousness, in which your mind, body, and spirit are in a deep, transcendental meditative state. Some can break through this spiritual opening through a shamanic journey or by learning how to listen to their inner voice or guide. Regardless of the technique chosen, the purpose of journeying to higher states of consciousness is to gain access to your inner guide, who is noetic, wise, and all-knowing.

Fanning (1994) suggests that your inner guide can be someone extraordinarily meaningful to you, someone who is deceased and has passed on, or someone that you have created out of myth or legend. Inner guides come in many different energy forms and from a diversity of cultural beliefs. They may appear in dreams, as a vision, a voice, a sixth-sense experience, or a symbolic gift. Your inner voice experience may involve synchronicity, as described by Jung's concept of "meaningful coincidences," when two or more events occur at the same time but could only happen by statistical chance (see Campbell, 1971).

The good news is that everyone has an inner guide to access because this is an innate characteristic of being human. Despite the fact that we are earthbound by gravity in our physical bodies, the powerful thoughts of creativity and imagination can transcend the fabric of space and time and bring us into other dimensions. Dreaming is just one example of the places to which our conscious mind, body, and spirit can take us. Many people choose not to go there. Einstein likely created the mathematical theory of relativity long before he wrote it down on paper. The Wright brothers invented their flying machine long before they left Ohio and moved to Kitty Hawk, North Carolina, to experiment with test flights. Similarly, our beliefs, wisdom, and creative imagination are actualized in our daily lives long before they manifest in some state of reality or in ordinary waking states of consciousness. Before we act upon the creative and imaginative inner voice, a higher wisdom, awareness, or state of consciousness must be accessed. This can be achieved by an intentional breakthrough into the spiritual realm.

BRIDGING THE GAP BETWEEN THE SPIRITUAL ORDINARY AND THE NON-ORDINARY

The Dalai Lama (1999) in *Ethics for the New Millennium* suggests that many great movements of the last hundred years (e.g., democracy, liberalism, socialism, technology) have failed to deliver the global benefits that were first hoped for. He is speaking of the way our thinking, feeling, and day-to-day existence are guided by what we believe to be the truth of science and technology and the laws of our social-political-legal system. Seeing our unsuccessful attempts to legislate morality and decency in human behavior, His Holiness calls for a spiritual revolution.

Thoughts of a spiritual revolution should benefit all of humankind. These heartfelt intentions should drive to the emotional, physical, and spiritual core of those engaged in the helping or caring professions. Essentially, self-care practices require more than cognitive-behavioral approaches to deal with our stress and improve our coping. They require a spiritual revolution within us. Spiritual approaches drive to the core of our very being and are an essential part of healing empathy fatigue. It is the recognition and awareness of how to bridge the gap between "spiritual ordinary" and "spiritual non-ordinary" experiences that will connect the mind, body, and spirit to achieve harmony and balance.

Those dedicated practitioners who follow a religious faith or a diversity of spiritual beliefs can journey back to the core reason why they came into the helping profession initially. There are many who believe that we are all spiritual beings with the capability to access non-ordinary states of our spiritual consciousness, journey to other spirit-worlds we have created, and return safely with some higher wisdom, awareness, and purpose. If we are open, mindful, and allow ourselves to be objective witnesses to our higher states of consciousness, then great things can happen in our lives and in the lives of people we serve. These spiritual occurrences do not take place through the use of our rational intelligence and cognitive beliefs. Rather, they are whole-body experiences. They are expressions of the mind, body, and spirit.

The other good news is that we do not actually have to be shamans, yogis, mystics, mediums, or spiritualists to gain the "right of entry" into higher states of consciousness or to access our inner spirit guide. These states and guides are available to mortal beings with guidance from spiritually highly developed mentors or guides. Our guides can be found both in our inner and outer environments. Our mentors can facilitate opening doors into other dimensions so we can have direct access to the Buddha within, or hear the voice and wisdom of God or the Great Spirit revealing a vision. For some, journeying is beyond the reach of the rational mind and transcends natural understanding. For some, reaching higher dimensions of spirituality is akin to being contacted by UFOs and aliens. However, dealing with matters of religious or spiritual significance is very earthly in nature; it is just as natural as breathing. Finding the shaman or spirit guide within is a deep and vital experience to which we should be open on the path of healing empathy fatigue.

Deepak Chopra (1995) talks about finding a spiritual guide in his book titled *The Way of the Wizard,* after Merlin the Magician's teachings. Chopra provides 20 spiritual lessons for learning how to tap into a spiritual source that exists within all of us. A few of the inspirational lessons he offers using the metaphor of the "wizard" are as follows: (a) everything the wizard sees has its roots in the unseen world; (b) the body and mind may sleep, but the wizard is always awake; (c) the wizard has centuries of knowledge that are compressed in revelatory moments; (d) when the doors of perception are cleansed, you will begin to see the unseen world of the wizard; (e) human order is made of rules but the wizard's order has no rules; it flows with the nature of life; and (f) seekers are never lost because the spirit is always beckoning to them. In the 20th lesson, Chopra suggests that the best a person can do for the world is to become a wizard. Metaphorically, Merlin the Magician may have much to teach professional helpers. In becoming a "wiz" at transcending empathy fatigue and interpreting the "20 Lessons" for the inward journey, Deepak (or Merlin) might suggest that "First, you will experience miracles in the state called cosmic consciousness.... Second, you will perform miracles in the state called divine consciousness.... Third, you will become the miracle, in the state known as unity consciousness" (p. 166). The health and wellness of the world depends upon using the creative powers of imagination to break through into the spiritual realm for purpose and connectedness.

FINDING THE SHAMAN WITHIN

Professional helpers are much like indigenous shaman healers. We are all counselors, coming from a variety of specialty areas, who work with individuals and groups of people that usually have problems of an intense nature. Many clients are bound psychologically, socially, emotionally, or behaviorally, or have personality features that create drama in their lives. They may sometimes recognize their problem issues only on the surface level, so they need a shaman of sorts to act as a guide. As the modern shaman probes deeper into the lives of the client/consumer/patient's consciousness or psyche, the competent practitioner may notice that the mind, body, and spirit are disconnected, giving us clues as to how to bring the client back to a state of wholeness. The fact is that many clients with mental health conditions (e.g., depression, anxiety, substance abuse) have associated physical conditions (e.g., headaches, low back or shoulder pain, arthritis, lethargy, endocrine disorders) and may have an existential or spiritual urgency to deal with in their life (e.g., having no clue as to the origin of the pain, blaming God for the condition). Thus, the client is trying to find meaning and purpose, and the professional helper, just like the shaman, must deal with the interconnectedness of the individual's mind, body, and spirit to try and bring the individual back to balance or harmony.

Father Morton Kelsey (1986), an Episcopal priest and prolific writer in psychology and theology, states that "our society doesn't emphasize ways of dealing with spiritual reality; shamans are desperately needed to guide people who are searching for a way to encounter the divine that will transform their lives" (p. 219). Father Kelsey further suggests that modern shamans must be trained in listening and compassion in order to be able to establish a trusting relationship with others. Nouwen (1972) explains in *The Wounded Healer* that the modern shaman needs to be articulate, compassionate, and contemplative. Such people must be willing to use their own pain or wounds to assist others who are in search of wholeness. Ultimately, we will have difficulty helping our clients if we cannot be empathic toward their pain and suffering. However, there is a cost to being compassionate and empathic at this level within a relationship; this is the experience of empathy fatigue. Accordingly, the modern shaman must seek guidance from an inner spiritual guide in order to be able to assist others along their journey.

LESSONS FROM OLD WORLD SHAMANISM

For tens of thousands of years, the practice known as shamanism has brought health and healing to persons from many different cultures around the world. Evidence for some of the first shamanic practices has been documented among the Tungus people of Siberia. Harner (1990), a Western anthropologist, has written extensively in this area and has gathered a plethora of extraordinary stories of shamanistic practices all over the world. He states that "shamanism represents the most widespread and ancient methodological system of mind-body healing known to humanity" (p. 40). Basically, shamans (both men and women) were individuals appointed by their tribes to go between ordinary and non-ordinary states of consciousness to acquire knowledge, power, and spiritual help to assist in healing the mind, body, and spirit of the "patient" or tribal member. Shamans are keepers of an extraordinary body of ancient knowledge and techniques that can be used to achieve and maintain the mental, physical, emotional, social, and spiritual well-being of the self and others. Interestingly, many shamanic methods are very similar all over the world. In Mircea Eliade's (1964) classic work, *Shamanism,* the author states that shamans from Asia, Australia, Africa, and North and South America all had similar roles and techniques despite being separated by oceans and continents for thousands of years.

In old world shamanism, long before there were medical doctors (to diagnose and treat physical ailments); counselors, psychologists, and psychiatrists (to diagnose and treat emotional, mental, and cognitive disorders); and organized religious practices, there was the shaman who treated all conditions. He or she was responsible for maintaining the mind, body, and spiritual well-being of the members of the tribe. Some shamans may have followed a family path and been born into the role. Others were chosen by the Great Spirit to be healers and then confirmed by members of the tribal council based on their reputation for healing work. Training or an apprenticeship to become a shaman sometimes required many years of learning how to acquire power and achieve non-ordinary states of consciousness. This was accomplished by journeying in the lower, middle, and upper worlds or other dimensions, to seek out spirit helpers or power animals for the purpose of health and healing. Most shamans had to go through intense initiation experiences that mirrored death and rebirth. Some training was brutal and required initiation by fire or water, wrestling with demons, or the use of psychedelics that drove the shaman apprentice into a state of madness. It was essential that the shaman understood the mental, physical, and spiritual pain and suffering of the persons with whom they were in a healing relationship. A wounded healer experience was essential for healing practice and understanding how to travel into "a dark night of the soul."

Carlos Castaneda, the Peruvian-born writer (1925–1998), described his training in Native American shamanism and claimed to have met a Yaqui shaman, Don Juan Matus, in 1960 while on a shamanic journey. While working on his master's and doctoral degrees in anthropology at the University of California, Los Angeles, Castaneda wrote three books describing this experience. Castaneda's works have sold more than 8 million copies and have been translated into 17 different languages. One of his most widely read books, *The Teaching of Don Juan: A Yaqui Way of Knowledge* (1968), describes some incredible journeys that were taken through the use of psychoactive substances. According to Castaneda, one of the most significant aspects of a person's life is the mastery of awareness and control of the various ordinary and non-ordinary states of consciousness. This is much like the Zen Buddhist philosophy in terms of the discipline and techniques used to achieve higher levels of mindfulness. Castaneda was perhaps most criticized for his inconsistencies in describing his communication with Don Juan in non-ordinary states, and the authenticity of the contents of his works was questioned. Castaneda was also criticized for his psychoactive drug use to achieve higher states of consciousness, although he used more natural mind techniques later in his life. There are numerous accounts of powerful shamans who journeyed in a natural state without the use of any hallucinogens (Robinson, 2005).

Perhaps proving the actual existence of Don Juan is irrelevant. What is important is that Castaneda provided a modern paradigm for the achievement of the heightened states of awareness and intuitiveness that lead to personal knowledge. These states were attained through Castaneda's intimate relationships with his spirit guides, which appeared to be very empowering. Thus, journeying into other worlds may provide individuals with ways in which to rebalance and harmonize their mind, body, and spirit for optimal wellness.

SOUL LOSS

According to shamanic practices, one of the major causes of mental, physical, and spiritual illness is soul loss. When soul loss occurs, it is believed that the vital essence of the person's life-energy must be retrieved to heal the affected portion of the mind, body, and/or spiritual self. To heal soul loss, the shaman performs the ancient spiritual rituals of soul retrieval so as to bring wholeness back to the person involved. Ingerman (1991), in *Soul Retrieval,* suggests that many times, our soul or spirit feels drained in the presence of another person who has sucked the energy out of us. She advises us to avoid giving away our spiritual energy to others. By calling upon your power animal or spirit helper and visualizing a healing light, you can create a boundary that protects you from another person's negative energy. The modern shaman can certainly relate to soul loss or develop a wounded soul experience.

In old world shamanic cultures, it is believed that many persons hold past extraordinary stressful and traumatic events in their physical bodies. These are centered in the various body systems (e.g., the nervous, endocrine, immune, cardiovascular, and respiratory systems). The intuitive modern medical and mental health professional can see how this blocked energy plays out physically in our clients or patients. We observe our client's flat affect, depressed mood, poor grooming, and slow, halting, or stuttering speech patterns, and get the sense that the client has carried this burden for quite some time. Our clients tell us how poorly they are coping and functioning in life. If we truly want to move toward integrating the spirit energy into our mind and body for healing empathy fatigue, then we must not only pay attention to our clients but be mindful of the countertransference we may be experiencing during therapeutic interactions. For some modern shamans, there is a soul loss experience that affects their spiritual energy. Keeping our spiritual boundary strong will protect us from any unwanted force that could permeate this field of energy, causing our soul to be weakened.

INTEGRAL WORK AS NEW WORLD SHAMANS

In indigenous cultures, all shamans worked together in healing ceremonies. They were not in competition with one another, as is seen in the modern competition for clients/consumers in private practice settings by counseling and psychology professionals and treatment programs using both medical model and integrative medicine approaches. It is said that one shaman's healing technique may not be effective in healing all types of mental and physical conditions, chronic illnesses, diseases, or disabilities. Many times it took a community of shamans to facilitate a healing path or cure for the individual. Perhaps there are lessons to be learned in how to integrate medicine with complementary and alternative practices. Working together to promote and facilitate healing practices for others may assist in avoiding a soul loss experience.

Many native healers today will use both Western medicine and indigenous healing or folk-medicine modalities when it comes to complex illness. However, the tribal healer is consulted first to communicate with the spiritual world to seek a cure for the individual. Legitimate healers rarely promise to "cure" the individual, although the element of hope is present when the shaman begins his/her rituals and prayers. As the healer enters a trance state, she/he is open to listening to the spirit world so as to receive instructions on the diagnosis and treatment of the person's illness.

Reeve (2000) has studied the Caboclo indigenous community of the Lower Amazon Basin. She interviewed the families living in a modern Caboclo community about their integration of both indigenous and Western methods for maintaining their health and treating illnesses. Reeve reports that the role of the local healer is critical within the belief system of this indigenous group, because physical illness is perceived as having supernatural causes. Thus, the trusted healer of the community is the most credible resource for the tribe, because the healer is able to access the spirit world for the diagnosis and treatment of chronic illnesses and diseases. Non-Caboclo healers in nearby communities may also be consulted, depending upon the patient's needs. Some healers will refer nonspiritual illness to a Western-trained medical physician. Overall, curing practices are strongly tied to social identity and association with a vibrant community of healers. This is very different from the system in which the individual goes for treatment into an urban clinic where there is a very impersonal relationship with the physician and other health care workers. In Caboclo society, both shamanic and Western health and healing practices can work together for the good of the person.

In indigenous healing modalities, the shaman has a very close personal and spatial relationship with the individual who needs to be healed. Because medical technology is not used in shamanic cultures (i.e., no stethoscope, blood pressure cuff, thermometers), the shaman has to diagnose and treat the individual "up close and personal" using the shaman's intuitive sense. It would not be unusual for the healer to lay an ear on the individual's chest to examine the cardiovascular and respiratory systems, examine the skin and muscular skeletal system at specific locations of the body, and use techniques that are intensively hands-on or directly above the body for the examination, manipulation, and treatment of the illness.

Despite the fact that the prevalence of some diseases is on the rise in indigenous groups, Western medicine should not be considered an acceptable substitute for indigenous practices. Disease is on the rise in such communities because of poor sanitation, inadequate diet and nutrition, and very little immunization and disease prevention programs. Western medicine on its own cannot solve such problems. Although physical health may be on the decline in some indigenous groups around the world, Westerners have much to learn about mental and spiritual health within these communities. For instance, there appears to be a strong ethnic/racial identity with an enriched community of caregivers and healers. This certainly serves as a protective factor for the tribe and for its individual members. The lifestyle itself in indigenous groups may have less stress associated with it because of less concern about custom-built housing, credit, competitive employment, and competitive sports. There is also a lack of exposure to radio, television, movies, the Internet, and video games, and to a host of other stress-producing events such as crime and violence. Perhaps it is time to reinvent such a world and take another look at our essential needs so that we can enhance our minds, bodies, and spirits.

Today's shamans are very different from old world shamans. Most are urban or suburban shamans who are alternative practitioners. Very few have the financial means to break away from conventional occupations and relocate to an area of the country with like-minded people. Most people do not find social isolation very rewarding. Harner (1990) has engaged in revitalizing the foundations of shamanic cultures by developing a specific training program in "core shamanism" through a nonprofit organization, the Institute for Shamanic Studies. The training approach is respectful of the many indigenous people that have practiced shamanism. Interestingly, the core philosophies and beliefs are presented primarily to Western-born workshop participants. This is done without the stereotypical use of features like indigenous dress, such as one might see in *National Geographic* magazine. Harner has drawn upon his anthropological background to communicate the central beliefs and practices of the collective wisdom of many indigenous shamans. The Foundation for Shamanic Studies (FSS, 2007) facilitates ongoing workshops for beginning-, intermediate-, and advanced-level shamanic training. Harner has developed a program that is meaningful within a Western healing context and facilitates training in the various healing ceremonies and rituals that are common to many shamanic cultures. There are many other resources provided in the appendix to the present work that the reader may review in the project of integrating indigenous healing techniques with typical Western counseling and psychotherapy.

MUSCLES OF THE SOUL

Professional helpers who experience empathy fatigue may have been exposed to extraordinarily stressful and traumatic events through the lives of their clients/consumers. Engaging in empathic relationships at such intense levels certainly places the individual at high risk for empathy or compassion fatigue. However, as we have learned in parts I and II of *Empathy Fatigue*, professionals who do not work in crisis response or disaster mental health may still acquire a counselor impairment of sorts. They accumulate their clients' levels of stress over time and later decide that they need a rapid career change. In actuality, all they may really need is an attitudinal change. Individuals who emerge from job burnout do so because they have developed an attitude of hardiness and resiliency. The inner resources these individuals have tapped into include humor, intuition, patience, creative imagination, and compassion, just to name a few. Seaward (2006) suggests that in times of highly stressful experiences, a person can either become a victim or emerge gracefully by letting go and moving on in life. To develop the inner resources needed to become hardy and resilient, Seaward introduced what he calls "muscles of the soul." The following is a brief description of the muscle groups required for developing muscles of the soul:

- Compassion: unconditional love toward self and other.
- Courage: being brave enough to move forward after adversity.
- Creativity: involves primarily imagination but requires inspiration and work (perspiration); it is a synthesis of imagination and ingenuity.

- Curiosity: seeking out information, options, and ideas for your life's journey.
- Faith: encompasses the mystery in divine nature but requires optimism and love.
- Forgiveness: having the capacity to pardon others when we feel violated or when we have made mistakes. It is not allowing someone to go free after being violated or victimized; rather, it is having an attitude of compassion for ourselves.
- Humbleness: a trait we can call upon to serve others before ourselves; but mostly we should treat others as we would want to be treated.
- Humor: one of humankind's greatest blessings, used to intentionally enhance our mood by invoking its healing power.
- Integrity: a code of conduct, a pledge to the highest ideals even in the face of adversity, striving to be truthful and not to take the easy way out.
- Intuition: use of sudden insights, inspiration, enlightenment.
- Optimism: being positive in times of adversity, not ignoring reality but seeing the best in a bad situation and learning from this.
- Patience: the ability to wait until intuitively you know the time is right, the power of stillness.
- Persistence: trying until all conceivable options have been attempted, but with good heart.
- Resiliency: bouncing back from adversity; this requires faith, optimism, self-reliance.
- Unconditional love: extending love and compassion from your heart without conditions or expectations; the hallmark of the "muscles of the soul" model. (p. 73)

If we have the opportunity to listen to the philosophy and principles of the world's greatest shamans, sages, mystics, or spiritual healers, we may hear words of wisdom that have been reflected in muscles of the soul. This wisdom has come from God, the Great Spirit, or some divine source that has communicated the foundations for living in wholeness to all cultures throughout the centuries. It is our journey to find the healer within.

ANGELS AS MESSENGERS OF THE HEALER WITHIN

St. Thomas Aquinas, the 13th-century theologian, suggests that the universe would not be complete without angels. They are important means to intercede between God and our mind, body, and spirit. Angels can be accessed as we sit in silent meditation and engage in contemplative living; they emerge from within. Cultivating an angel guide is an essential resource for tapping the healer within ourselves, because such guides empower us with inspiration, knowledge, awareness, answers, and solutions, and help us develop a resilient spirit so we can move forward in life. Angels are part of a new cosmology that awakens us, channeling a vital source of health and healing (Fox & Sheldrake, 1996; Hauck, 1994). Modern shamans can use all the spirit helpers they can discover.

There has been a rebirth of angels in Western culture. The resurrection of angels can be seen in television shows, movies, and literature, and in popular culture as evidenced by angel calendars, T-shirts, coffee mugs, jewelry, garden icons, and many other items marketed to those individuals who are mindful of angels' existence. Some authors comment that we are going through a period of "angel mania." Thomas Moore (1996), who has lived as a monk for 12 years in a Catholic religious order and is a prolific writer in psychology and theology, suggests that we should not speak of angels in a literal, materialistic, or metaphorical sense. Rather, it is important to respect them and understand that they may have more meaning to us if they remain anonymous and stay hidden in the invisible world.

The commercial success of angel mania may be a reflection of the fact that our culture desires a higher spiritual plane and access to higher levels of consciousness. For many people, angels represent messengers from God. They are very real spiritual entities that can be called upon to heal our minds, bodies, and spirits. Some people may perceive angels as symbols of a supernatural power that is heavenly and cannot be accessed here on earth. Others perceive angels as powerful natural spiritual advisors that exist throughout the universe. Indeed, angels embody a divine healing light that can stir our imagination in times of meditation and are a means of accessing our inner voice experiences.

Although the references to angels in this chapter are based primarily on Judeo-Christian writings, there are other ancient world religions, cultures, and racial and ethnic groups that have integrated angels into their spiritual belief systems. Extensive personal interviews completed by Wester-Anderson (1994) report that some people have had a multicultural experience with angel contact. Some angels appear as Asians, Africans, or indigenous people. There is no doubt that those who have encountered angels have had a peak spiritual experience that has enriched their life holistically.

It is difficult to provide proof in matters of divine faith, spiritual contact, and unseen supreme beings. Individuals either accept or reject certain religious or spiritual principles based on their belief system. However from a culture-centered perspective, being open to different spiritual perspectives links us to the same shared reality that enhances the mystery of our origin (e.g., where we came from before birth; where we will be going after death: see Pedersen, 2000). For many people, where we came from and where we are going is an existential question that begs for a rational explanation; although none can be given from within the scientific paradigm. By opening our hearts to the abundance of pure healing energy, we can access the ancient wisdom and collective consciousness of peoples who lived long before us. Discovering a divine messenger can provide us with a felt sense of purpose and spiritual empowerment.

Historically speaking, angels have been around since the beginning of time. They were part of the spiritual belief structure and mythology of ancient Rome, Greece, and the Middle East. Human beings have always had mystical experiences, including visions of some sort of angelic or divine being. This is depicted in numerous paintings by artistic masters of previous centuries (e.g., Hieronymus Bosch, *Paradise and Ascension Into the Empyrean*, 1504; Gustave Doré, *The Vision of the Empyrean*, late 1800s; Raphael, *The Three Theological Virtues*, 1507; Raphael, *The Transfiguration,* 1520). Some European art has depicted angels as mythical creatures that fly, play musical instruments, and communicate messages from heaven.

Today, angels stir our imagination and souls. They play a central role as heavenly messengers and they are sacred entities that are at our disposal for guidance and protection. Many of us have learned as children that angels bring a feeling of comfort, warmth, compassion, and security. They are an extension of God's love and represent all that is good in the world.

Raymond Moody (2005), an internationally known award-winning scholar, qualified in both psychiatry and psychology, is the leading researcher in near-death experiences (NDEs). He has interviewed over 1,000 people since the 1960s on the subject of NDEs and has sold more than 13 million copies of his books on the topic. In most documented cases, Moody states, persons who go through an NDE typically report the following: (a) a death occurs either through surgery or by natural means; (b) the individual goes through a tunnel immediately after death and encounters all those individuals (i.e., family, friends) who have passed on; (c) the individual meets a divine, angelic entity accompanied by a warm, radiant, divine type of light; (d) the individual receives some communication from this angelic source concerning a significant message about his/her life on earth, and finally; (e) the individual makes a choice to return to the earthly physical body or stay with this angelic source. Most individuals decide to return to their physical body on earth to take care of some unfinished business. Westerners experience grief, death, and dying very differently from indigenous peoples. Many indigenous groups view death as a part of life and honor those who have passed on by engaging in rituals and ceremonies. For many indigenous peoples, remembering those who have left their physical bodies is a way of bringing meaning and purpose to the cosmos and understanding the interconnectedness of all things.

Regardless of the cultural experience of death, the transformation that takes place within the individual after an NDE could be described as a soul recovery (McKenna, 2000), in which the person has radically redefined her/his sense of purpose and meaning in the world. Such a peak spiritual experience could have happened only in another dimension of space and time. It may be similar to the experience of conscious sedation administered by an anesthesiologist. Ken Wilber (2006) might view this level of consciousness as a "subtle state experience of intense interior luminosity accompanied by a sense of universal love" (p. 91), according to his model of integral spirituality. Wilber suggests that at this level of consciousness the individual may interpret a spiritual-religious experience as magical, mythical, rational, pluralistic, or integral depending upon the individual's stage of spiritual development. Nonetheless, transformative experiences can occur within any dimension of spiritual life. One could say that there is no angel of death, only an angel of life. It should come as no surprise, to those who believe such an entity exists, that angel messengers can offer us guidance in our health and healing.

THE HUMAN ENERGY FIELD AND REIKI AS A SELF-CARE PRACTICE

The Human Energy Field (HEF) has been described as an expression of God's divine light or as a source of universal energy that surrounds every living thing. It has been recognized for thousands of years and recorded in many esoteric teachings; for example, it is found in the ancient Hindu Vedic texts and has been passed down through the spiritual practices of indigenous peoples such as Native American medicine men/women, by Tibetan, Indian, and Japanese Zen Buddhists, and in the kabbalah, the Jewish system of mystical theosophy. A manifestation of the HEF can be seen in numerous religious paintings of Christ in which he and other spiritual figures are surrounded by a divine light. Barbara Brennan (1987), a physicist who once worked for NASA, has studied and practiced healing techniques using the HEF and her hands for healing illness. In Brennan's signature work, *Hands of Light,* she explores energy medicine and provides a practical guide to healing through human touch. She describes a seven-layer auric body system that exists among all humans and is consistent with the seven energy vortexes or body chakras of Japanese Reiki.

To understand energy medicine, we first need to discuss how the body creates and responds to electrical, magnetic, and electromagnetic fields such as are emitted by light, sound, heat, chemical reactions, and gravity. It is this energy produced within our bodies that can be used to create wellness and heal chronic mental and physical illnesses. A fundamental law of physics, Ampère's Law, states that when currents flow through conductors such as wires or living tissues, a magnetic field is produced in the surrounding space. Since living tissues are conductors of electricity, our heart, muscles, brain, and peripheral nervous system have the capability of generating a healing effect within the biomagnetic field (Oschman, 2002). Brennan has the ability to sense this human energy field, in terms of seeing different colored lights or body auras, feeling various changes in skin temperature, and in other intuitive ways. Individuals who are trained in energy medicine are able to sense the patient's energy blockage and flow. When the energy vortexes or body chakras are open and free flowing, the person's mind, body, and spirit are said to be in harmony. Thus, there are specific locations within the HEF that are responsible for our mental, emotional, physical, and spiritual well-being and can be manipulated through therapeutic touch techniques to help achieve individual optimal health and healing.

There is no doubt scientifically that our bodies emit chemical and electrical impulses. This process is activated through different body systems (e.g., nervous, respiratory, cardiovascular). The presence of the HEF is evident in various types of biomagnetic measurements such as CAT scans, PET scans, and MRIs. Modern medical technology has produced some life-saving and pain-reducing devices based on electrical impulses, such as transcutaneous nerve stimulators (i.e., TENS units), cardiac pacemakers and defibrillators, lasers, and pulsing magnetic field therapy, to name just a few.

The point is that all living things contain a pulsating energy source that vibrates at its own frequency. An exploration of how to channel such human energy can be used in one's self-care practices for cleansing the body aura, much like taking a deep cleansing breath. Oschman's (2002) research into hands-on therapies such as Reiki, acupressure, aura balancing, and other aspects of ancient Eastern medicine suggests that master practitioners are able to project a very strong biomagnetic field that stimulates the opening of the body chakras. Most ancient stories begin at the point where the energy source for a human being is intense enough and vibrates at the same frequency within the body's *ki* (Japanese) or *chi* (Chinese). Accordingly, the physics of energy medicine creates a biomagnetic field that can induce a flow of energy into human tissues and cells, thus creating a healing effect.

Masaru Emoto's (2004) best seller, *The Hidden Messages in Water,* suggests that projecting positive emotions onto another individual can have enormous potential in human health and healing. Emoto, a Japanese scientist, has demonstrated the effects that positive and negative forms of energy (emotions and thoughts) have on molecules of water. Using high speed photography, he showed how the energy of emotions could change the consistency and patterns of water crystals. In Emoto's work, when the words "love" and "gratitude" were communicated, the most beautiful crystals seemed to form within the water. The point that Emoto is trying to make is that expressing thoughts, words, and feelings of a high empathic nature (as counselors do) can change the heart of others in our environment from a negative attitude to one of gratitude. Emoto's theory, very briefly described here, suggests that since our physical body is 90% composed of water, emotions of a high empathic nature can change the physiological composition of our bodily fluids. Expressing empathy can positively affect our emotional, physical, and spiritual states. Based on the principles of the HEF and the biomagnetic energy field, Emoto suggests that for every negative emotion there is an exactly opposite positive emotion that can be communicated. This can be done in our own self-care as well as in the care of others. In other words, we can replace the emotion of hate with gratitude, anger with kindness, fear with courage, anxiety with peace of mind, and stress with presence of mind. Much like the water of Lourdes in France, which is said to have miraculous healing powers, the power of love, compassion, empathy, and gratitude can perform miracles on the individual's mind, body, and spirit. As Emoto states, "The focus of the human race has been drawn away from that which cannot be seen, and towards the obvious physical world" (p. 80). Despite all the technological advances we have created in our culture, perhaps we have been myopic when it comes to the divine energy field that is all around us.

REIKI AS A SELF-CARE APPROACH

One particular approach to healing within the HEF is the practice of Reiki. Reiki is emerging as a vital energy medicine approach and is based upon one of the most ancient healing methods known to human-kind (Honervogt, 1998; Mitchell, 1994; Rand, 2005). It has been developed primarily as a hands-on healing approach and has its foundations in both Eastern and Judeo-Christian philosophical beliefs. Today, in Western complementary, alternative, and integrative approaches, Reiki practitioners work alongside other body manipulation specialists such as chiropractors, osteopaths, massage therapists, and holistically centered physical therapists. Multiple studies have been done in major teaching hospitals around North America that use Reiki to treat persons with chronic illnesses and other diseases. A collection of these studies can be reviewed online through the International Center for Reiki Training (ICRT, 2007). The interested reader is encouraged to review this material as well as other credible sources.

The healing technique of Reiki was discovered by Dr. Mikao Usui (1865–1926), a Japanese monk and Christian theologian who studied the hands-on healing miracles of Christ. He also studied the ancient Indian language of Sanskrit as well as the original writings of Buddha (Honervogt, 1998). Dr. Usui, the original Reiki grand master, discovered Reiki through a peak spiritual experience and handed down the Usui form of Reiki to just two other grand masters; a Japanese physician, Dr. Chujiro Hayashi (1870–1941), and Mrs. Hawayo Takata (1900–1980). Mrs. Takata brought Reiki to the United States in 1938 and trained just 22 other masters. Although Reiki is a rich source of spiritual energy, it is not a religious practice and has no doctrine to follow.

In Japanese, *rei* means soul, spirit, or universal god. The word *ki* means energy, breath of life, or life force. For 5,000 years, the Chinese people have referred to this energy as *chi*, a form of spiritual energy that manifests itself in plants, animals, humans, food, water, air, earth, sunlight, and all living things. Loosely translated, in Japanese Reiki means "universal life force" or "self-healing." The primary intention of

Reiki treatment is to promote natural physical and emotional health and healing through a hands-on approach that serves to tune, balance, and revitalize the body's own energy. It is a safe and natural treatment that can reduce stress and enhance immune functioning.

How Does Reiki Work?

Reiki is a therapeutic touch technique that involves Reiki practitioners in gently placing their hands on the body in a particular pattern to channel the Reiki or universal life energy to the different chakras or parts of the body that function as focal points for spiritual energy. The Reiki practitioner acts as a conduit to channel the natural healing or universal life energy in a powerful and concentrated form through the use of therapeutic touch. A typical Reiki session lasts 30–45 minutes and, when combined with other therapeutic approaches such as breathing, visualization, and meditation, can last up to one hour. The overall purpose of Reiki is (a) to balance and harmonize the body's energies, (b) to support the body's natural ability to heal itself, (c) to release emotional blocks, and (d) to facilitate and increase the body's ability to achieve calm and meditative states of consciousness.

Reiki treatments are administered primarily to help the mind, emotions, and body to relax and feel less stressed and to achieve increased mental, physical, and spiritual wellness. The Reiki practitioner does not diagnose any medical or physical conditions or perform any medical procedures or treatments; nor can he/she prescribe any pharmaceuticals. A competent, ethical, and certified Reiki practitioner must recommend that you seek a licensed physician or allied health care professional for any medical or physical condition(s) that you may have concerns about.

How can Reiki help persons with empathy fatigue achieve an optimal level of wellness? First, it is important to be open to the idea that the body has the natural ability to achieve higher states of mind, body, and spiritual wellness. Reiki, used in conjunction with other complementary or integrative medicine approaches, can help reduce stress, enhance immune functioning, and restore balance in one's mind, body, and spirit. Reiki can be administered by a Reiki practitioner or by using self-Reiki approaches. Once nonpractitioners are taught the specific locations of the body chakras and the hand positions to be used, they may begin experimenting with their energy field to heal their own mind, body, and spirit. There are multiple online Web sites that teach the hand positions and body chakras to persons interesting in working within the HEF. The interested reader may consult the references within this section or use an Internet search engine to search "Reiki hand positions" for images and illustrations with which to begin the practice of self-Reiki.

Regardless of the many testimonials of those who have received Reiki treatments from practitioners (Honervogt, 1998; ICRT, 2007; Mitchell, 1994; Rand, 2005), it is most important that professional counselors be empowered with self-care practices that promote their own mental, physical, and spiritual well-being. Taking advantage of the ancient wisdom of energy medicine and integrating ancient healing practices into the daily routine can help restore balance to the mind, body, and spirit.

JOURNEYING TO FIND YOUR INNER GUIDE

Your inner guides can take many different forms and may present themselves as angels, wizards, priestesses, Zen monks, wise older individuals, friends or family members who have passed on to a heavenly dimension, Greek goddesses, animals, or some divine radiant energy that has no form or shape. It is up to the individual to decide. Your inner guide is there to assist you in problem solving or advice giving, or guide you to other resources. It is available to you to serve your greatest need.

Your inner guide serves as a channel or vessel for communicating messages to you through a much higher divine source in the universe. It has no ego or agenda but is there to serve you. Consulting with your inner guide may bring up hidden feelings, content, or experiences that cannot be accessed in ordinary conscious states of being. Thus, it will be useful to facilitate the breathing, meditation, and visualization activities as described previously. Be open to the idea that it will be difficult to access your inner guide through the rational mind. It will take some creativity and openness. Also, it is essential that you search for inner guides with noble intentions, not to have the winning state lottery numbers revealed to you.

Your inner guide most of all knows all your thoughts, your feelings, and everything that you have experienced and will experience in life. This is an awesome power at your disposal, which may reveal bits and pieces of information with each journey, or perhaps all at once. Your guide may reveal information or communicate with you in the most unsuspected or unanticipated moment. So be still and listen and use the following suggestions to call upon your inner guide:

- Before seeking your inner guide, create a sacred space that will enhance the experience. Make sure that you are free from all material and physical distractions. Create good Fung Shui in your environment. You may want to listen to some indigenous music or have aromas present to enhance your experience.
- Get in a comfortable position by sitting or lying down, closing your eyes, and relaxing. Begin with good intentions, asking a deep question for your guide. Keep the question simple but rich in content.
- Begin the breathing and relaxation activities presented previously. As you gain deeper states of consciousness, begin using the techniques of guided visualizations that can assist you in identifying a particular shape or form. Use all of your senses to come in contact with your inner guide. If this is a guide that you have intentionally journeyed for at some other point in time, or that was revealed to you in a dream, then seek this guide if it was helpful to you in your past.
- Be open to the idea that you may have to search a variety of paths to come into the presence of your guide. Shamans will journey to special places called the lower world, middle world, and upper world to find their spirit helpers, guides, and power animals.
- Once you have experienced what you believe to be the presence of your inner guide through your meditative journey, try to communicate with this entity. First ask, "Are you my guide?" You may have to ask several times, and if this is not your guide, then ask for help in finding your guide.
- Once you have a felt sense that you have found your guide, remember that there are many ways to communicate with your helper, both verbally and nonverbally. Make sure that you sit in stillness and are open to the messages that you receive.
- Allow your self to return from your journey and then write down the answer or response that you received from your inner guide. It is best to keep a journal while going on your journeys.

CONCLUDING THOUGHTS

The Dalai Lama (1999) recognizes from personal experience that constant exposure to others' suffering and being taken for granted by the individuals we serve can stimulate feelings of helplessness and despair. He suggests that if such feelings are "left unchecked, this can lead to insensitivity towards others' suffering. If this starts to happen, it is best to disengage for a short while and make a deliberate effort to reawaken that sensitivity" (p. 129). Professionals who work in a variety of counseling settings are at risk for acquiring a counselor fatigue experience. It may be in one's own best interest and in the interest of one's client/consumer to disengage for a short while. One does not have to work in crisis response or disaster mental health to be emotionally, physically, or spiritually affected. Empathy fatigue is the result of a stress and grief reaction that accumulates over time. Thus, it also takes time and practice to develop self-care strategies. The professionals who have emerged from job burnout or an empathy or compassion fatigue experience have done so because they have developed a positive attitude of gratitude toward their clients and toward the good work they themselves do. Developing this type of hardiness and resiliency requires a deeper level of consciousness, to cultivate one's inner resources. Part III of *Empathy Fatigue* has offered specific strategies for self-care. The implementation of self-care practices requires constant attention to the path of one's mental, bodily, and spiritual wellness. Chapter 15 will offer specific guidance on how to begin the journey and stay on the path of wellness. It will provide the reader with a prevention program of sorts, which offers guidelines for handling the ebb and flow of traveling on and off the path.

15

Show Up, Pay Attention, and Be Open to the Outcomes: A Three-Step Personal Growth Program to Restore Harmony and Balance

During my master's and doctoral programs, I had the opportunity to be mentored by one of the most skillful, compassionate, empathic, and insightful persons I have ever encountered in the counseling field: Dr. Harry Allen, now professor emeritus, Southern Illinois University–Carbondale. Dr. Allen, who preferred to be called "Harry," was not only a highly creative and enlightened rehabilitation counselor educator and productive researcher, but he also had a reputation among his peers as an extraordinary practitioner, a shaman of sorts. Harry developed a graduate-level foundational counseling pre-practicum course that he called the "Empathy Lab." As a matter of practicality, the Empathy Lab prepared students how to respond to real client issues during their practicum and internship experience. Harry would begin the first class of the semester by telling students "there are only three things that you need to do in this course: Show up; pay attention; and be open to the outcomes." There was little explanation beyond this mantra, from what I remember. However, as the semester went along I began to explore and process exactly what he meant by these three simple things.

Truly understanding Harry's mission, vision, and purpose for the Empathy Lab required participation in various experiential activities throughout the semester. The Empathy Lab, as I experienced it, facilitated my own interpersonal awareness of self and others; it cultivated

197

an increased understanding of my own emotional IQ and the way I experienced my clients' thoughts and feelings, moment to moment. The lab also provided me with the opportunity to acquire the foundations of the helping profession, which included responding to others with a high level of empathy and compassion; establishing a genuine and trusting relationship with others; and learning strategies that helped build a working alliance with my clients. This was accomplished through videotaped client-counselor role-plays and other relationship-building person-centered techniques. Most importantly, I had the opportunity to learn from a highly intuitive person who could empower others to nourish their spirit for the purpose of serving others in the world compassionately and empathically. It was also an opportunity to learn how to grow personally and professionally in the helping profession. The Empathy Lab was something that one would need to experience at first hand to gain the full range of lessons that it taught.

Through these experiences were born the principles of the three-step program I call the Personal Growth Program (PGP). This is truly where self-care approaches need to begin for the prevention of empathy fatigue: in one's graduate-level clinical experiences.

THE PERSONAL GROWTH PROGRAM: A THREE-STEP APPROACH TO HEALING EMPATHY FATIGUE

The Personal Growth Program (PGP) is a dynamic, interactive, and solution-focused approach to exploring your own interpersonal growth and development as a professional counselor. It provides an opportunity for early identification and assessment of, and recommended interventions in, issues of counselor impairment such as empathy fatigue. This approach, which has undergone several revisions, is based on my personal observations and case studies from my experience as a rehabilitation counselor educator and clinical supervisor, researcher, and private practitioner since 1995. Most importantly, the PGP provides a model for beginning and maintaining a program of self-care.

Because the essential job function and scope of practice for profession counselors requires that professionals work in a very person-centered environment, it is critical to deal with potential issues related to counselor impairments such as empathy fatigue. Current and future clients/consumers seek professional services and require the highest level of attention, compassion, and empathy. Accordingly, the PGP challenges professional helpers to show up, pay attention, and be open to the outcomes. More specifically, the PGP invites professional helpers to participate in various interpersonal growth and self-awareness experiences, integrating the self-care strategies offered throughout this book and particularly in part III. The PGP requires one to make a commitment to self and others in an intentional way, to ask for help from trusted colleagues, and to develop effective self-care practices while working with clients/consumers that have intense and critical needs.

For some professionals, several hours or days may pass between intensive interactions with professional colleagues or treatment team members. Given this isolation from peers and colleagues, professionals may be vulnerable to the experience of mental, physical, spiritual, and occupational fatigue. Cultivating a program of self-care may help present opportunities for personal awareness, growth, and hope for changing the thoughts, feelings, and behaviors that have been transferred to professionals from their clients/consumers.

One of the unique features of the PGP is that it employs both a group and an individual approach. Thus, it is recognized that personal change can be accomplished either individually or in a peer support group setting. A stage-change approach is used with the PGP to deal with problems and opportunities that relate to counselor impairment or empathy fatigue. Basically, the PGP invites you as a professional to change something in your life (e.g., way of thinking, feeling, perceiving others, work behaviors). This is very similar to the therapeutic stages of change that you may have observed with your clients/consumers. To begin your journey, please review the questions included in this three-step approach. You may find it useful to have a journal or diary to record and process your feelings, thoughts, and experiences.

Step One: Show Up and Be Present

Showing up is the first step in any structured self-care program. If you began by reading the introduction to *Empathy Fatigue* and have made it this far, then you have shown up: so you are welcome. The primary emphasis in this step is for you to be physically, mentally, and spiritually present in the here and now. Invite yourself to be open, honest, and flexible, and begin to conceptualize how you can deal more effectively or creatively with some specific issues related to the work you do. The issues may concern your sense of depletion or exhaustion. You may be an individual just beginning your career and anticipating some future occupational stress. Showing up challenges you to be mindful of the issues that may hinder your progress.

To begin this process, pay attention and be mindful of the things you want to change in your life. Find a quiet place in your home, or outdoors, or go on a retreat and invite yourself to explore the following questions:

1   What do I currently feel, emotionally, physically, spiritually, career-wise, educationally, academically, and in my relationships with others?
2   In which areas of my life do I want to grow?—What do I want to transform?
3   What can I do to change or grow in specific life areas?
4   What are some of the things that I need in order to achieve my goals?
5   How will I know when I've arrived and have reached the goal I set out to accomplish?

In this first step, please be open to the idea that you can choose a more conscious and intentional way of living and being mindful in the moment with yourself and others. The information provided throughout *Empathy Fatigue*, particularly the guided activities in part III, can contribute to your program of self-care. You may have already developed a program of self-care; however, being creative and incorporating other activities may inspire your mind, body, and spirit in other ways.

Step Two: Pay Attention and Be Mindful

Paying attention and being mindful is actually more than working on a cognitive level of awareness and understanding. It requires a shift in level of consciousness in which you become aware of your feelings, emotions, and mental and physical wellness. Paying attention to your deeper levels of consciousness through such activities as meditation will help you cultivate a felt sense of meaning and purpose for your life. It may open the door to other dimensions and help you access your intuitive sense of a divine presence that can assist you in cultivating the practice of self-care. You do not have to consider yourself a spiritual person in order to benefit from quieting your mind, body, and soul. There are so many distractions throughout our day that quieting the mind, body, and soul becomes as difficult as exercising, dieting, meditating, and engaging in other wellness activities. If you are already engaged in a program of wellness or personal growth, then you are nurturing your body. To nurture your mind requires that you begin paying attention to the different levels of consciousness at a much deeper level than ever before. You also may want to identify your unused opportunities and resources by starting with a variety of structured or nonstructured self-guided activities.

The primary emphasis at this stage is for you to communicate your plan of action to yourself and others in your environment. To begin this process, it will be helpful to keep a daily journal or diary. Documenting your thoughts, feelings, emotions, cognitions, and experiences will allow you to analyze the different levels of your consciousness. If you exercise your mind the way you exercise your body, then you will be developing a fit and healthy mind. After you have written down any thoughts, emotions, or experiences, then you should interpret, translate, and find meaning in your journal entries. You may want to seek out another person or a group of peers with whom to share and discuss your personal journal.

Some individuals may pose a question in their journals. Others may state a plan of self-care that has a specific measurable goal and/or objective supporting personal growth. If you are not the type of person that approaches life with specific behavioral objectives but you live one day at a time, this is okay too. Each person will find her/his own way of paying attention and being mindful by proposing a plan of self-care. At a minimum, you should begin learning how to pay attention, live life more consciously, and be more aware of your thoughts, feelings, and behaviors.

For some, writing down their life's obligations to self and others or developing a vision statement will help bring some meaning and purpose into the good work they do with others. So clear a space in your life and begin to visualize how you want to feel emotionally, physically, spiritually, and in other ways. Be creative in finding new ways to approach old problems. Since this is your personal journey, you make the decision on how to disclose your vision, goals, and plans for change.

Step Three: Be Open to the Outcomes and Experiences

In this step you will want to review your PGP journal and search for any significant themes or information that you may have overlooked. Review your journal notes and try to read between the lines. Search beyond the literal meaning of what you have written. Review your notes for any daily progress, creative ideas, or successes you have documented. Explore your journal entries for any challenges or obstacles that you may have encountered on your wellness journey. Remember that in most situations outside of the uncontrollable (e.g., weather conditions, chronic health conditions, disability, or socioeconomic status) we create most of our own obstacles.

There is an old Hindu story of a monkey and a coconut. A group of hunters wanted to capture a monkey, so they tied a coconut to a tree, drilled two small holes on each side of the coconut, and then planted/ baited the coconut with a banana. They waited for hours and then finally a monkey approached. He slipped his hands through the two small openings on each side of the coconut and grabbed the banana with both hands. However, the monkey could not pull the banana out of the coconut because his hand was in a fist. If the monkey let go of the banana, he could easily free his hands. However, his desire to try and pull the banana from the coconut was much stronger than his will to let go. Basically, the monkey was so consumed with holding on so tight, trying to pull the banana from the coconut, that he forgot how to free himself. Thus, the hunters caught their monkey (Pirsig, 1976).

It is essential that we are aware of things that can trap us, know how to get unstuck once we are in the midst of things that can harm us, and learn how to let go. Our critical thinking and problem-solving skills are much more sophisticated than those of a monkey. However, sometimes we get stuck, like the monkey in the Hindu parable. So we must make ourselves open to the outcomes by conducting an open and honest assessment of our self-care and PGP progress. It is essential that we explore ways to let go and grasp the things in life that can nurture and support our minds, bodies, and souls. Expanding our list of options, resources, and natural environmental supports will help us become unstuck.

GETTING STARTED: STAGES OF CHANGE IN PERSONAL GROWTH

So there you have it: the three-step program. In reality it is difficult to begin a program of any type. It requires commitment and motivation to begin a program of self-care. Holistically, it requires care of our body (e.g., an exercise program), care of our mind (e.g., reading a self-care book), and care of our soul (e.g., attending a church service, yoga, or meditation group). We should not be satisfied with a plan of exercise and nutrition alone as our self-care approach. It is a great start. However, we must be mindful of the fact that optimal functioning requires us to feel whole in our minds, bodies, and spirits.

It sometimes takes a few weeks or months to get started. Many counselor educators, researchers, and clinicians emphasize that individual change and personal growth do not occur spontaneously. There are large numbers of personal testimonials in books, articles, and online that discuss significant life changes others have made to ensure the survival of their mental, physical, and spiritual well-being. There are qualitative studies in peer-reviewed journals that report spontaneous remission from a chronic medical, physical, or mental health condition. In many of these studies, the person involved provides details of a profound spiritual transformation. Others provide testimonials about the wellness and lifestyle changes they have achieved.

The PGP does not propose that you attempt a rapid journey into mental, physical, or spiritual health. This would be unnatural for most people. You are smarter than the monkey in the Hindu parable. Some of you may want to consider the PGP, as an opportunity to begin the experience of extraordinary personal growth and/or transformation. Such a rehabilitation of the mind, body, and spirit typically occurs over time. It is essential that we are mindful of the baby steps to wellness that we can take. At a minimum, it is essential that you empower yourself by taking responsibility for seeking out multiple resources and support systems that will assist you in accomplishing your goals or vision for personal change and growth.

If you are a future professional counselor, you may have to facilitate personal growth by discarding older emotional baggage. If you are an experienced professional, you may want to look at the ways in which your ego, self-esteem, sense of self, body image, or other issues stand in the way of rebalancing your mind, body, and spirit. Whatever stage of professional developmental you function at, it will be helpful for you to go back and review the principles of resiliency. As the resiliency literature suggests, every negative action, feeling, and thought involves a physiological cost to your mind-body resiliency. Likewise, the literature in spirituality suggests that every negative action, feeling, and thought involves a cost to your spiritual resiliency. Thus, a resilient mind, body, and spirit are essential to your well-being, especially if you work intensely with others in person-centered environments.

QUESTIONS THAT CULTIVATE A DEEPER MEANING AND PURPOSE

Healing compassion or empathy fatigue requires much more than reading a self-help book or attending a workshop on counselor burnout. Some of the most prolific spiritual leaders of our time strongly believe that transformation of the mind, body, and spirit occurs when we create a place in our consciousness that takes us to a much deeper level than ever before. Access to the human spirit comes from a meditative or nonordinary state of consciousness, not from ordinary, everyday states of consciousness.

The following existential and spiritual questions may be helpful to you as you begin cultivating your program of self-care. Some of these questions have been developed through personal interviews (see Elliott, 1996) with some of the world's greatest spiritual healers (i.e., Mother Teresa, Norman Vincent Peale, the Dalai Lama, Ram Das, Rabbi Zalman Schachter-Shalomi). Listening and paying attention to your inner voice experiences by asking the following questions may bring you a higher level of wisdom and insight with which to begin your journey into wholeness.

Questions Using the Deeper Reaches of All Five Senses

Ask yourself the following questions:

1   On what main beliefs, truths, or values do I base my life?
2   Do I believe in a divine source of power, great spirit, or supreme being who ultimately has compassion for my life and its purpose? How do I experience this spirit entity?
3   How would I characterize or describe the ultimate purpose of my life?
4   What is the highest ideal that a person can reach in life?
5   How have I achieved or attained a goal that I really desired? What was the process I went through to achieve this goal for myself?
6   What has been or what is the greatest obstacle to obtaining what I want in my life?
7   Do I see myself achieving the ultimate happiness or harmony in life? If not, what are some things that may be obstacles to this?
8   What is the meaning or purpose of my life at this moment?

9   If I could change anything about my life, what would I want to change?

10   What advice has a family member, close friend, mentor, consultant, or spiritual leader given me with regard to my particular life issues? Has any of this been valid?

11   If I could meet anyone throughout history, whom would I want to meet? What would I want to know about or ask this person?

12   What was the most significant thing or event (positive or negative) that ever happened in my life? How did this affect me and what lessons did it teach me?

13   Some people believe that certain things interfere with reaching personal growth. What things have I noticed in my life that have hindered my ability to achieve?

14   If I had only a few days left on earth before I passed on to some other dimension, what advice would I have for my friends, family, children, or others?

15   If I had only a few days left on earth before I passed on to some other dimension, what would I want others to know or say about me when I'm gone?

Now that you have had an opportunity to review these 15 questions, you might notice how difficult they are to answer in a direct or concrete way. Some are deeper questions that require extraordinary thoughts, feelings, cognitions, insights, and reflections that may challenge you. There are no right or wrong responses to these questions. In fact, many clients/consumers you have served have probably asked you such questions indirectly. Perhaps they asked themselves such questions at a subconscious level, particularly when their lives were in crisis or when they experienced pain, suffering, loss, or extraordinarily stressful events. Despite the uncertainty that exists as we contemplate the nature of these questions, it is critical that we probe the deeper reaches of our mind, body, and spirit. A journey of inner healing requires that we come out of the darkness and into the light to face the fear of changing our lives.

SOLUTION-FOCUSED QUESTIONS: GETTING TO THE CORE OF THE PROBLEM

Highly skilled professionals know the importance of implementing the right strategies to facilitate client change. After professional helpers listen to their clients' stories and assess their motivation for change, they may choose specific counseling theories and techniques that help the clients put their chosen plans into action. Before this process begins, however, it is essential to have a direction that will lead clients to successful coping or problem-solving strategies. If you are acting as your own therapist, you may want to use similar strategies for yourself. The following solution-focused questions are offered to the self-therapist (yourself) for direction so that you may have a clearer idea of what you would like to change:

- What is it that you would like to change?
- Given your present situation, what changes in your life would make sense?
- If you made these changes, what would you be doing differently in your life right now?
- What would these changes look like?
- What particular behaviors, thoughts, emotions, and experiences would you be doing or feeling differently?
- What would you be doing that you are not doing currently?
- What resources would help support your goals/vision?
- If you no longer had these issues, what would others perceive as different about you?

STAGES OF CHANGE IN SELF-CARE

The following model is based on stages of change theory. Prochaska and DiClemente (1982), Prochaska, DiClemente, and Norcross (1992), and their colleagues did the foundational research in this area, explaining how individuals progress through five different stages of change to transform their patterns of simple and complex behaviors. The model offered here is designed to assess, predict, and monitor activities that relate to one's self-care as a professional helper. It follows the five stages proposed in the foundational research: precontemplation, contemplation, preparation, action, and maintenance.

The intent of this proposed model is to predict patterns of negative or unwanted thoughts, behaviors, emotions, cognitions, and personality states or traits that may be observable by self and others. The purpose of integrating the PGP with a stage change model is to enable you to assess and predict some of the challenges posed by the self-defeating and unwanted behaviors, thoughts, or experiences that may hinder your ability to achieve optimal wellness of your mind, body, and spirit. This particular stage change model makes the assumption that the professional has acquired some level of counselor impairment, burnout, compassion, or empathy fatigue. If you are not experiencing any of these issues, then you may want to start a group to help other professionals who may be experiencing empathy fatigue.

Precontemplation

Issues at This Stage. At this stage, you are typically not interested in changing certain behaviors, thoughts, feelings, and emotions. You are likely denying that you have any significant problems in life. Basically, you are not motivated to act at this time. Cognitively, you may feel somewhat disorganized and detached from your colleagues, friends, and family, because you are too preoccupied with the disharmonious internal dialogue or interplay between your mind, body, or spirit. There may be a sense of emotional exhaustion where you feel vulnerable or not securely attached to your family, friends, relationships, or job. You may also feel a sense of mental, emotional, social, physical, spiritual, and/or occupational depletion. Your career and day-to-day routine may feel meaningless. You may have a sense that "this is the career I've chosen so I just have to manage it."

Typical Feelings Experienced at This Stage. At this stage, you may feel that there are no possibilities for natural supports or a system that can provide a foundation to nourish your mind, body, and spirit. You may exhibit a pattern of negative thinking that creates problems for yourself and others around you. You would like to see others change, rather than be forced to change yourself. You may be coerced or forced into change because of poor coping abilities and choices you have made (e.g., driving under the influence [DUI], divorce, chronic mental and/or physical illness). This may lead to further resistance and defensiveness.

Check-In Self-Assessment. Ask yourself, do I become defensive or resistant when discussing certain aspects of my mind, body, or spirit with others? Do I tend to avoid relevant and important information about the health and wellness of my mind, body, and spirit? Do I avoid taking responsibility for trying to harmonize or rebalance my mind, body, and spirit? Do I intend to do something about these issues in the next few days, weeks, or months? When do I anticipate that I will make a commitment to change?

Interventions. Share and communicate your sense of how out of balance your mind, body, and spirit are. Discuss these problems with someone close to you. Try to understand your reason for wanting to avoid change or resist personal growth. Ask yourself solution-focused questions such as "How would things be different if I . . . ." Make some attempt to achieve a small commitment toward personal change or growth.

Contemplation

Issues at This Stage. At this stage, you may struggle to understand why your life is so out of balance. Stress and anxiety may be at their peak because you are experiencing the need for change. You begin to understand that change and growth require some kind of commitment from your mind, body, and spirit and that these must work in concert with one another. You may have to give up a self-destructive lifestyle habit, negative thoughts, self-defeating emotions, or some other negative behavioral pattern, personality state, or personality trait.

Typical Feelings Experienced at This Stage. At this stage you may be premature in your actions regarding change or you may have a fear of failing. Be cautious, because many individuals search for the perfect solution to their problem and attempt to make changes that are not natural to them. Many will change a self-destructive lifestyle habit (e.g., quit smoking, stop drinking, reduce poor nutritional habits). However, these changes may be superficial, because it is necessary that your mind, body, and spirit work in concert to achieve an optimal level of well-being.

Check-In Self-Assessment. Ask yourself, am I willing to discuss this with someone else without blaming others? Am I interested in being educated or increasing my insight and awareness about my particular issues? Do I intend to take action on this? Does this problem behavior, thought pattern, or dysfunctional coping ability serve some higher purpose in my life?

Interventions. Become aware and conscious of issues by balancing your mind, body, and spirit. Attempt change through a program of self-care involving breathing awareness, relaxation, meditation, or visualization. Notice how this impacts your life (i.e., job, relationship with others, lifestyle habits). What things must realistically be approached first? Identify some triggers, responses, or obstacles that could hinder your ability to change and rebalance your mind, body, and spirit.

Preparation: Building a Foundation for Success

Issues at This Stage. If you are truly at this stage, you will make a commitment to taking action in the very near future. You will recognize this by developing a plan of action or a clearer vision of the purpose and meaning of the good work you do with others. You begin to take the path and make the necessary initial first steps in taking action.

Typical Feelings Experienced at This Stage. You may make a premature leap into change. This may be due to a vague plan of action or perhaps you feel that your mind and body are ready, so why shouldn't your spirit follow along? You may feel that you are being pushed into personal change or growth because your professional impairment is so great that it is affecting your job, marriage, or mental, physical, or spiritual health. You may not be ready to make difficult life decisions and transitions. Another problem at this stage that should not be ignored is a very unsupportive environment. You may also lack the resources to support your change or growth.

Check-In Self-Assessment. Ask yourself, am I making excuses for not changing myself or achieving personal growth? Are there some real issues that I cannot control (e.g., brain chemistry, hormones) when it comes to rebalancing my mind, body, and spirit? If I do change something in my life, have I considered the consequences of this change? What would I be giving up? What challenges would possibly lie ahead for me? Do the positives of change clearly outweigh the negatives? Am I focusing on the future benefits of change? Have I developed some specific ideas about how to change my behaviors, thoughts, or feelings?

Interventions. Increase your commitment to acting by making a public commitment or asking others for help and support. Document a plan that has specific goals/objectives, meaning, and purpose for your mind, body, and spirit. State a clearer vision with specific start and completion times. Prepare your environment so it can support personal change and growth. Take responsibility and hold yourself accountable.

Action: Attempting Change

Issues at this Stage. At this stage, you will clearly recognize that you are making an honest attempt to change your behaviors, thoughts, emotional reactions, or maladaptive (codependent) behaviors, as well as your environment. The ultimate purpose is to achieve optimal wellness and much better control over your mind, body, and spirit. Other persons and supports in your environment should also notice these changes. Most persons require assistance from a support network of family, friends, or colleagues. If you are at the action stage of change, you will not be shy about asking for help from others.

Typical Feelings Experienced at This Stage. You may feel hopeful. The chances of resisting or terminating a plan of personal mind, body, and spiritual growth are less because you have prepared yourself much better at this stage. Thoughts of failure may be sporadic, but your confidence abounds because you have transitioned through the previous intense feelings and have made some sense and meaning of your thoughts, emotions, and experiences. At this time, anxiety about making personal change and growth may not be a dominant feature of your mind, body, and spirit, because you have already taken action. You may become less impatient or frustrated with the small changes or progress you have witnessed. You may feel less overwhelmed by making changes. A small step backward is viewed as a slip rather than a full-blown relapse. You have more good days than bad while at work, during therapeutic interactions with others, or in interpersonal relationships. Any slip you experience is not interpreted as a complete failure or disaster. Giving up is not a consideration, because of the level of success you have achieved. A very supportive environment is also responsible for your success at this stage.

Check-In Self-Assessment. Ask yourself, am I continuing to actively pursue personal change and growth in my behaviors, thoughts, emotions, environment, mind, body, and spirit? Am I using my plan, supports, and other resources to my advantage? Am I empowered to neutralize or counteract any doubts or issues with regard to my well-designed plan? What incentives am I using to sustain or reinforce my personal change or growth? Does my plan actually feel as if it is working? Do I feel better emotionally? Physically? Spiritually? Cognitively? Does my life have more meaning and purpose? Do I feel somewhat more in balance with my mind, body, and spirit?

Interventions. Use a variety of settings or environments to structure your interventions. Try to avoid or minimize your exposure to negative elements, people, or places in your life, knowing full well that you are the person empowered to control and maintain the balance of your mind, body, and spirit. Design your plan so that you can identify and interrupt negative thoughts or chains of events, which may be environmental, cognitive, behavioral, social, emotional, physiological, spiritual, or occupational. Have a deeper awareness of things you can control in your life and things you cannot.

Daily Maintenance and Preserving What Works

Issues at This Stage. At this stage, you make an honest and genuine attempt to sustain long-term personal change, growth, and commitment to your plan of mind, body, and spiritual well-being.

Typical Feelings Experienced at This Stage. Typically, there may be protective factors or strategies that worked well for you at one point in time. Recognize that these may not be working currently. Progress or advancement within the plan of action may be viewed as a success by yourself and others. Be mindful that sometimes you may rationalize, celebrate, or reward yourself prematurely. This could cause back sliding. Thus, be aware that achieving mind, body, and spiritual wellness is not an end goal. Maintaining a balance in your life is an ongoing process.

Check-In Self-Assessment. Ask yourself, do I know how to cope with high-risk situations in my plan? Are my mind, body, and spirit aware enough to know what to do if I have a slip or relapse? What elements of my plan do I need to modify or adjust to fit with my changing life needs? Am I continually being open and flexible to other possibilities and outcomes? Am I being creative enough to have a good level of self-fulfillment?

Interventions. Be open to the idea that there is no one correct way to do things. Try to view any slips or relapses as lessons to be learned. Understand that your goals and objectives may include a long journey on which staying focused and in balance is a major accomplishment. It may be helpful to return to baby steps again. Most important of all, your plan of action must change as you grow and develop.

BRAINSTORM STRATEGIES FOR ACCOMPLISHING YOUR PGP

Brainstorming is a technique that psychologist Gerald Egan (1998) uses to help people move beyond problem solving and thoughts that are overly constricted or narrow. It is a tool to help people develop both opportunities and possibilities for a better future. A good brainstorming session should empower you with the resources to take control of your life, anticipate any obstacles, and plan for a more functional and healthy future.

Egan has several prerequisites before facilitating a brainstorming session. These include (a) suspending your own bias and judgment about how the world functions; (b) encouraging a quantity of ideas no matter how wild they may seem to be; (c) coming up with as many possibilities as imaginable, then dealing with the quality or realistic aspects of the solution later on; and (d) stimulating others by combining one solution with another, which ultimately will create new ideas. Be mindful that brainstorming is an ongoing process, because as you develop as a person, you will try out new behaviors, see what works, and hopefully make adjustments in your plans. Dr. Egan suggests that during brainstorming sessions, you should form probes that are based on the following solution-focused questions:

How: How can you get to where you would like to go and how many different ways are there to accomplish what you want to accomplish?

Who: Who can help you achieve your goal and who can serve as a resource for you to accomplish this goal?

What: What resources, both internal and external, can help you accomplish your goal?

Where: Where are the places that can help you achieve your goal?

When: When should you act in order to achieve your goals?

One way of cultivating a program of self-care is to invent a better future. You may want to test the insight and awareness that you have already gained by asking yourself the following solution-focused questions. Notice that these questions are all future oriented. This will assist you in the action and planning stages.

- What would this problem situation look like if I were to manage it better?
- What changes in my present situation/life would make sense?
- What would I be doing differently with regard to my problem situation if I made the changes that I would like to make?
- What things would make life better for me right now?
- What things/feelings in my life would I like to eliminate right now?
- If I eliminated certain things in my life, what would that feel like?
- When do I plan on making these changes?

Discover Multiple Resources

A good brainstorming session should bring about some positive changes in your life. One essential component of the PGP is making sure that you have access to multiple resources with which to begin or maintain your self-care program. Here are a few resource suggestions:

- *Individuals.* Seek help from a qualified physician for problems involving chronic health conditions: for other problems, consult other professional counselors, spiritual leaders, folk healers, acupuncturists, message therapists, Reiki practitioners, close friends, family members, or others you can identify that can cultivate one-on-one healing.
- *Role Models.* Seek out persons who have been successful in healing others. Search for others who have the wisdom, knowledge, advice, and counsel you seek. Think about those persons in your environment who have been through what you have been through, emotionally, physically, medically, spiritually, and occupationally, and talk with them.
- *Communities/Groups.* Seek out communities and groups that are therapeutic and supportive. Create your own support group. There are also numerous legitimate online support groups and chat rooms.
- *Eco-environment.* Seek out geographic locations (e.g., mountains, rivers, lakes, oceans) that can help you connect with the earth or the natural environment.
- *Technology.* Seek out assistive devices or other technology that will empower your independence, knowledge, and wisdom.
- *Professional Associations and Organizations.* Seek out professional associations and organizations that adhere to your philosophy and ideology with regard to your profession, health, and wellness. Many of these organizations have networking, video-education, and training opportunities at distance. There are also face-to-face or online discussion groups and other activities that can help you achieve your goals.
- *Model Programs.* Seek out specific model programs that can assist you in achieving your goals. Some universities and teaching hospitals provide opportunities for people to become involved in study groups with regard to nutrition, weight loss, exercise, smoking and alcohol cessation, and many other wellness and lifestyle enhancement programs.

OPTIMIZING YOUR MIND, BODY, AND SPIRITUAL HEALTH

Optimizing your PGP may require that you make a commitment in writing to begin your journey along the path of wellness. Be open to the idea that your PGP may be a long-term building project and there may be live issues that challenge your ability to achieve personal growth and development. Andrew Weil (1995) in *Spontaneous Healing* proposes that there are specific areas in a person's life that create obstacles to health, healing, and wellness. Many of the areas listed below are things that we have direct control over. Weil has met with healers throughout the world to try and discover what can optimize our natural healing system. He suggests that illness is not caused purely by a deterioration of our physical wellness. Rather, our mind, body, and spirit interact to affect our overall healing and well-being. This belief represents a non-Western medical and mental health system of health care. We do have some degree of control over our lives. It takes responsibility, motivation, persistence, and support from others to achieve an optimal level of wellness. Dr. Weil is an advocate of taking responsibility for our overall health and healing. Weil proposes that the following areas can help us achieve an optimal level of functioning.

Weil's Proposal to Optimize the Mind, Body, and Spirit

Lack of energy. Energy supplied by our metabolism (the conversion of food to chemical energy) is essential for health and healing. An adequate nutritional intake, good digestion, and proper breathing to increase energy are all within our control. Overwork, overexertion, inadequate rest and sleep, and addictions (too much alcohol, too much caffeine, and too many cigarettes) can all pull energy away from our physical being. Ultimately, a healthy mind is sacrificed because of poor concentration, focus, and other attention deficits that cause a drop in performance.

Poor circulation. Our natural healing system depends on the circulation of blood through our body to bring nutrients to our systems and organs. Circulation can be enhanced by following a healthy diet, getting enough exercise, and not smoking.

Restricted breathing. Restricted breathing can reduce the circulation and metabolism, and interfere with the natural healing system in many other ways. The brain and nervous system especially require the use of good cleansing breaths.

Impaired defenses. Natural healing is unlikely to occur if the body's defenses are weak. Decreased immunity occurs when we have acquired

(a) persistent or overwhelming infections, (b) toxic forms of matter and energy in our immune system, and (c) multiple stressors due to various mental health conditions. We can protect our immune system through good mental and physical health practices.

Toxins. Toxic overload is much more common than you think. We take in toxins through the food we eat, the water we drink, the air we breathe, and the use of pharmaceutical products, as well as unhealthy thoughts, feelings, and emotions. Toxic overload may be a significant cause of allergies, cancers, autoimmune diseases, and a variety of other conditions. Educating ourselves about the various toxins we are exposed to on a daily basis is essential for good health.

Age. It is not necessarily true that everyone who grows old will have lower immunity and become sick and diseased. There are many cultures of the world that exhibit extremely healthy older individuals. The number one risk factor associated with age may be the American lifestyle.

Obstruction of the mind. Our thoughts and feelings have a major impact on our physical health. Persons who have acquired mental health conditions (e.g., depression, anxiety, substance abuse, stress-related disorders) become physically ill at much higher rates than individuals that are mentally and spiritually healthy. Thus, it is critical to maintain good mental health.

Spiritual problems. Many other world cultures believe that harmony must exist between the mind, body, and spirit. Thus, improving one's spiritual life is a protective factor. It is essential to maintain a balance of the mind, body, and spirit (Weil, 1995, pp. 129–135).

DEVELOPING GOALS AND OPPORTUNITIES FOR PERSONAL GROWTH

There are three kinds of people in this world: (a) list people—those who like to write out lists of things to do and may need concrete and structured plans to live by so they feel in balance with life; (b) non-list people—those who do little preparation ahead of time, but when the time is right, they can get down to business and achieve at an optimal level of functioning; and (c) combo people—those who combine both structured and non-structured ways of living, depending upon the situation and setting.

Developing concrete goals and objectives may not be a priority for you. It may work for others but not for you. Just the thought of structuring your day with a "to do list" may really turn off your mind, body, and spirit.

Regardless of your style of making commitments, you may benefit from reviewing the following examples of goal-opportunities that some others have committed themselves to and used to optimize their minds, bodies, and spirits.

I make an important distinction between *problem issues* and *goal-opportunities*. If you are always dealing with a problem situation or issue, then you tend to be focused on things that you are trying to avoid, reduce, or decrease in your life. However, if you can reframe your "problems" into goals and opportunities, then your focus will be on things you can increase, draw closer to, and feel motivated by in your life. So, take this opportunity to review some sample goal-opportunities listed below.

Examples

A. Identify the goal-opportunity from your list (or non-list) of things you want to change.

   Example. I do not feel focused during therapeutic interactions with my clients. I feel overly anxious at times and can never seem to break away from my emotional stress.

B. Turn the problem issue into a specific goal-opportunity by stating the issue as something that needs to be done differently.

   Example. I need to begin a program of stress management using different meditation approaches. I would also like to begin journaling and then analyzing what I've written.

C. For each goal-opportunity, create a short-term objective that is measurable.

   Example. You may want to state your short-term objectives in terms of the following:

   - Frequency (e.g., I will meditate using a guided meditation/relaxation tape for 15 minutes a session, twice per day—once in the morning and once in the afternoon)
   - Intensity (e.g., I will rate myself after each meditation session and during client sessions using my own peace-compassion scale, ranging from 1 to 10)
   - Duration (e.g., I will use a guided meditation approach every day for two weeks with the anticipation that my stress levels will decrease during my client sessions)

■ Amount (e.g., I will monitor the scores on my self-rating peace-compassion scale and try to decrease my stress level by 10% each day)

D. List multiple support systems and resources to help achieve your goal-opportunities.

Example. I will alternate the use of three different guided meditation tapes. I will spend a portion of my lunch break in meditation. I will ask my spouse for some quiet time so that I can focus on my self-care. I will review my journal entries daily so I can bring some meaning to this experience.

E. List observable indicators of improvement. Make sure to include items that are measurable, along with feelings, thoughts, behaviors, and experiences.

Example. My peace-compassion scale rating has decreased from an 8 at work to a 5 this week. I feel less distracted and more focused during client sessions. I also have an increased sense of compassion and empathy for the people I serve. Reading my journal entries helped me clarify why I chose this profession.

F. List a plan of action for maintaining your goal-opportunities by specifying multiple resources and opportunities.

Example. Buy new meditation tapes with a variety of visualization and contemplative meditation experiences. Start a meditation group with my close friends or colleagues. Search for a yoga or tai chi instructor.

WORKING WITH PERSONAL GROWTH: A PROCESS GROUP APPROACH

Purpose of Group Work

The purpose of facilitating or being a member of a process group is to cultivate a caring community of like-minded individuals that are having difficulties dealing with professional issues such as empathy fatigue. Individuals function most of their lives within group settings, especially those in the helping professions. However, there may be few opportunities for therapists who work in private practice settings to be involved in a process group. So a process group can be very beneficial for these particular professionals. The primary purpose of an empathy fatigue process group is (a) to provide a safe, secure, and confidential environment so professionals can release their emotions in front of others who have the same or similar feelings, reactions, and experiences of empathy fatigue in their professional lives; (b) to provide support to peers and colleagues and identify individuals within the group that may require more intensive help or special attention; (c) to provide a resource for recommitment to education and personal growth opportunities; (d) to share information, resources, and other supports with group members to assist them in building coping and resiliency; and (e) to cultivate seeds of hope by building a caring community of other professionals that may be dealing with empathy fatigue.

Choosing a Group Facilitator

It is strongly suggested that during the first process group meeting, group participants select a facilitator or leader. In some cases, groups may choose a cofacilitator. Sometimes it is healthy for a group to rotate group facilitators. This can be arranged so that each week a different person can be prepared to lead the group or group activity. Regardless of what your group chooses, the primary task of the group facilitator is (a) to lead, present, or facilitate guided activities for the week; (b) to take responsibility for keeping the group structure and rules intact; (c) to ensure that the group as a whole is moving in a solution-focused direction; and (d) to model a cohesive environment that enhances positive interactions for the purpose of reducing empathy fatigue and increasing positive support and resources outside the group.

Basic Protocol

Consider forming peer groups of approximately 6–8 participants that all have similar interests or associate with each other on a regular basis. Group participants should choose a facilitator or be in agreement that the facilitator will be chosen on a week-by-week basis. The facilitator should (a) make sure that all participants introduce themselves or check in with the group; (b) discuss group rules, attendance, goals, issues of confidentiality, and the overall group process; (c) obtain consensus from the group on what issues will be dealt with and what is to be accomplished within each session; and (d) focus on positive coping strategies, attitudinal healing, and wellness among the group participants, with the goal of reducing empathy fatigue.

Group Rules and Guidelines

1   *Maintain Confidentiality.* This is absolutely critical in developing trust among group participants. Building a working alliance is essential for disclosure and trust. Talking outside the group regarding others' personal issues is unethical and violates personal privacy. Persons who violate such rules should not be asked back unless there is a consensus among participants that they should.

2   *Be an Active Listener.* Every group participant has something important to say. It is essential to listen carefully to the other group participants. Listening with compassion and empathy demonstrates respect for others in the group and will help you understand their points of view on a particular issue. Other members also want to express their thoughts and opinions. We forget this group etiquette sometimes. Be open to the idea that we may learn something from our colleagues, although we do not always have to accept their views.

3   *Express Your Own Ideas.* You also have something important to say. Sharing your thoughts, feelings, and experiences with the group on a particular topic will make a contribution and may stimulate other creative ideas.

4   *Communicate Honestly, Concretely, and Openly.* Giving positive feedback to other group participants is important. You can accomplish this by being genuine and communicating openly and honestly with others. As a group participant, you can expect to receive from the group what you are willing to contribute. How you respond to others also affects how they respond to you.

5   *Problem Solve as a Team.* Problems are best solved when working together cooperatively with others. When conflicts or problems arise, think of creative alternatives and options to keep the group moving in a positive direction.

Suggested Group Protocol: A Three-Phase Approach

Since the individuals in your empathy fatigue process group may have many years of experience as group facilitators, be mindful that too many leaders can be toxic to the group process. If each participant takes responsibility as a group facilitator, then each is empowered with the same responsibility for a healthy process group environment. I offer below a three-phase group structure to help initiate specific activities. This protocol also serves as a way to monitor the progress of your process group. Be mindful that the three-phase protocol is flexible and should be designed for your particular agency, organization, and interests. Each phase will vary depending upon the participants in your group. Some groups may take several sessions to complete one particular phase, while others may take longer in other phases.

Phase One: Opening and Emotional Check-In

1   Assuming that the group rules and structure have been fully determined and discussed, the group facilitator should provide an opportunity for each participant to give a check-in. Individuals should be allowed 4–5 minutes each to disclose a particular issue, emotion, or experience that they are struggling with as it relates to their empathy fatigue. The purpose of the check-in is to allow all group members to become aware of how each participant is currently functioning and what issues each individual plans to work on as part of the empathy fatigue process group. Members should be encouraged to begin their check-in statements using feeling-words and good "I" statements so they can take ownership of their current mind, body, or spiritual wellness.

2   After all members have checked in, the group facilitator can begin the group process by asking participants what issues they would like to deal with first, second, third, and so forth. There should be group consensus on what issues need to be addressed within the average 90-minute group session.

3   Participants are encouraged to initiate the Personal Growth Plan as described earlier in this chapter. Individuals may use this opportunity to share and discuss the obstacles or struggles they may be experiencing in their personal growth.

Phase Two: Working Phase—Mapping Your Path

1   The goal of this phase is to further build a trusting working alliance within the group so that each person feels comfortable enough to disclose personal issues. Groups that work well together in this phase have a high level of trust and will provide support for one another, even through difficult emotional periods.

2   The group facilitator should allow members to ventilate. However, the goals of this phase must be focused on developing a more effective and functional personal and professional life. Group participants should assist others within the group to look for any obstacles that may be in the way of achieving a more effective personal and professional quality of life. The most important aspect of this phase is insight, awareness, and being able to look at participants' unused talents and opportunities.

3   Participants are encouraged to discuss the check-in self-assessment questions (see solution-focus question p. 212) as a means of looking at individual growth and change.

Phase Three: Choosing a Path—Getting Group Closure

1   A primary reason why we do not meet our own expectations in life is that we fail to take responsibility for or follow through on the plans we have made. The PGP was developed as a way to encourage individuals to try and initiate a plan of action and take responsibility for their own personal and professional wellness. The final phase of your process group, in the last several sessions, is to choose a path and cultivate those resources that can support you in accomplishing your goals. Remember that there are many different paths you can take to get you where you are going in life. These paths may not necessarily include the PGP model.

2   Various guided activities should be included in phase three. You as well as others may want to create a goal-opportunity as developed by the PGP model, or verbally make a commitment to others in the group. You may begin by listing resources in your environment that have potential for making a significant impact in your life (e.g., a teacher, mentor, or minister/spiritual person, family members, friends, a particular professional helper or provider of services). You may want to continue to network with others in the group after the termination of the group process. It may be helpful to share specific resources, contacts, or other activities that have helped you accomplish your goal-opportunities as you have documented in your PGP. After you have fully addressed an issue and have gotten closure, choose another item that you may have rank-ordered and begin working on this.

3   Group closure is an important aspect of phase three. Some groups may reach their goals after just a few sessions together,

while others may stay together for several months. Regardless of how many sessions your group has spent together, the facilitator should allow each person to make some final comments about the group process or about someone else in the group. The facilitator may challenge group members with solution-focused questions, for example, if we came in contact with you a few weeks or months from now, what would we see as being different about you (e.g., emotionally, physically, cognitively, spiritually)?

CONCLUDING REMARKS

The experience of empathy fatigue is both similar to and different from other types of mental health conditions that require motivation and change to achieve an optimal level of functioning. Achieving such mind, body, and spiritual wellness can take place individually or in a community of other caring participants. To maximize your potential for achieving personal and professional growth, it may be helpful to use both individual and group exploration.

Extraordinarily stressful and traumatic events harm the minds, bodies, and spirits of professional helpers. World events have created a new paradigm of stress, anxiety, depression, and neurosis among helping professionals. Dealing with issues related to life, death, stress, grief, and loss involves a cost to the mind, body, and spirit. Developing a clearer understanding of the risk factors and prevention strategies associated with empathy fatigue is pivotal in developing self-care strategies for the professional counselor. If professionals are expected to maintain large caseloads of clients that have been through many intense experiences, then the profession needs to strongly encourage self-care practices. Help is on the way if counselor educators, clinical supervisors, professional counseling associations, and the individual's employer can all take responsibility for healing the mind, body, and spirit of the professional helper.

References

Ader, R. (1990). *Psychoneuroimmunology* (2nd ed.). San Diego, CA: Academic Press.

Adler, A. (1931). *What life should mean to you.* New York: Little-Brown.

Alberts, M., Vercoulen, J.H.M.M., & Bleijenberg, G. (2001). Assessment of fatigue: The application of the subjective feeling of fatigue in different research studies. In A.J.J.M. Vingerhoets (Ed.), *Assessment in behavioral medicine* (pp. 301–328). Hove, UK: Brunner-Routledge.

Allen, H. A., Stebnicki, M. A., & Torkelson Lynch, R. (1995). Training clinical supervisors in rehabilitation: A conceptual model for training doctoral-level supervisors. *Rehabilitation Counseling Bulletin, 38*(4), 307–317.

American Counseling Association [ACA]. (2003). *ACA Taskforce on Counselor Wellness and Impairment.* Retrieved March 3, 2006, from http://www.counseling.org/wellness_taskforce/index.htm

American Counseling Association. (2005). *ACA code of ethics.* Retrieved December 2, 2007, from http://www.alabamacounseling.org/pdf/ACA2005CodeofEthics.pdf

American Diabetes Association [ADA]. (2000). Type 2 diabetes in children: Consensus conference. *Diabetes Care, 23,* 381–389.

American Medical Association [AMA]. (2004). *Report on the Council of Judicial and Ethical Affairs: Discipline of impaired physicians.* Retrieved November 17, 2007, from http://www.ama-assn.org/ama1/pub/upload/mm/369/2i04.pdf

American Nurses Association [ANA]. (2007). *Impaired nurses resource center.* Retrieved November 17, 2007, from http://nursingworld.org/MainMenuCategories/ThePract iceofProfessionalNursing/workplace/ImpairedNurse.aspx

American Psychiatric Association. (2000). *Diagnostic and statistical manual of mental disorders* (4th ed., text revision). Washington, DC: Author.

American Psychological Association [APA]. (2007). *Advancing colleague assistance in professional psychology.* Retrieved November 17, 2007, from http://www.apa.org/practice/ACCA_Monograph.pdf

Arokiasamy, C. R. (1994). *What happens if I say "Damn you God?"* Carbondale, IL: Avanti.

Assagioli, R. (1965). *Pyschosynthesis.* New York: Viking Press.

Baker, E. K. (2003). *Caring for ourselves: A therapist's guide to personal and professional well-being.* Washington, DC: American Psychological Association.

Baranowsky, A. B. (2002). The silencing response in clinical practice: On the road to dialogue. In C. R. Figley (Ed.), *Treating compassion fatigue* (pp. 155–170). New York: Brunner-Routledge.

Bar-On, R., & Parker, J. D. (2000). *The handbook of emotional intelligence: Theory, development, assessment, and application at home, school, and in the workplace.* San Francisco: Jossey-Bass.

Barone, D. F., Hutchings, P. S., Kimmel, H. J., Traub, H. L., Cooper, J. T., & Marshall, C. M. (2005). Increasing empathic accuracy through practice and feedback in a clinical interviewing course. *Journal of Social and Clinical Psychology, 24*(2), 156–171.

Barrett-Lennard, G. T. (1962). Dimensions of therapist response as causal factors in therapeutic change. *Psychological Monographs, 76,* 43.

Barrett-Lennard, G. T. (1981). The empathy cycle: Refinement of a nuclear concept. *Journal of Counseling Psychology, 26*(2), 91–100.

Batson, C. D., Fultz, J., & Schoenrade, P. A. (1987). Distress and empathy: Two qualitatively distinct vicarious emotions with different motivational consequences. *Journal of Personality, 55*(1), 19–39.

Batson, C. D., Sympson, S. C., Hindman, J. L., Decruz, P., Matthew Todd, R., Weeks, J. L., et al. (1996). "I've been there, too": Effect on empathy of prior experience with a need. *Personality Social Psychology Bulletin, 22,* 474–482.

Bauza, V. (2007, October 21). Breaking hospital language barriers: Interpreters help patient, doctors discuss healthcare. *The Chicago Tribune,* C12.

Beck, A. T., Ward, C., Mendelson, M., Mock, M., & Erbaugh, J. (1961). An inventory for measuring depression. *Archives of General Psychiatry, 4,* 561–571.

Berger, R. M. (2006). Prayer: It does a body good. *Sojourners Magazine, 35*(2), 17.

Bergin, A. E. (1988). Three contributions of a spiritual perspective to counseling, psychotherapy, and behavior change. *Counseling and Values, 33,* 21–31.

Bernard, J. M. (1997). The discrimination model. In C. E. Watkins (Ed.), *Handbook of psychotherapy supervision* (2nd ed., pp. 310–327). Boston: Allyn and Bacon.

Bernard, J. M., & Goodyear, R. K. (2004). *Fundamentals of clinical supervision* (3rd ed.). Boston: Pearson.

Bishop, D. R., Avila-Juarbe, E., & Thumme, B. (2003). Recognizing spirituality as an important factor in counselor supervision. *Counseling and Values, 48*(1), 34–46.

Blocher, D. (1983). Toward a cognitive developmental approach to counseling supervision. *Counseling Psychologist, 11,* 27–34.

Borders, L. D., & Leddick, G. R. (1987). *Handbook of counseling supervision.* Alexandria, VA: Association for Counselor Education and Supervision.

Brennan, B. A. (1987). *Hands of light: A guide to healing through the human energy field.* New York: Bantam Books.

Brothers, L. (1989). A biological perspective on empathy. *American Journal of Psychiatry, 146*(1), 1–16.

Business Wire. (2004, August 17). Besides English how many languages are spoken in Chicago? Retrieved February 23, 2008, from http://findarticles.com/p/articles/mi_m0EIN/is_2004_August_17/ai_n6163662

Byrd, R. (1988). Positive therapeutic effects of intercessory prayer in a coronary care unit population. *Southern Medical Journal, 81*(7), 826–829.

Campbell, J. (1971). *The portable Jung.* New York: Penguin Books.

Canales, M. K. (2004). Taking care of self: Health care decision making of American Indian women. *Healthcare for Women International, 25,* 411–435.

Carkhuff, R. (1969). *Helping and human relations: A primer for lay and professional helpers* (Vol. 1). New York: Holt.

Cashwell, C. S., & Young, J. S. (2004). Spirituality in counselor training: A content analysis of syllabi from introductory spirituality courses. *Counseling and Values, 48*(2), 96–109.

Castaneda, C. (1968). *The teachings of Don Juan: A Yaqui way of knowledge.* Berkeley: University of California Press.

Chalder, T., Berelowitz, G., Pawlikowska, T., Watts, L., Wessely, S., Wright, D., et al. (1993). Development of a fatigue scale. *Journal of Psychosomatic Research, 37,* 147–153.

Chandler, C. K., Miner-Holden, J., & Kolander, C. N. (1992). Counseling for spiritual wellness: Theory and practice. *Journal of Counseling & Development, 71,* 168–175.

Chopra, D. (1995). *The way of the wizard: Twenty spiritual lessons for creating the life you want.* New York: Harmony Books.

Commission on Rehabilitation Counselor Certification (CRCC). (2001). *Code of professional ethics for rehabilitation counselors.* Retrieved December 2, 2001, from http://www.crccertification.com/downloads/30code/A-code/code_effective_0102_updated_format_0105_REV_307I.pdf

Connolly, K. M. (2005). Wellness counseling in business and industry. In J. E. Meyers & T. J. Sweeney (Eds.), *Counseling for wellness: Theory, research, and practice* (pp. 253–260). Alexandria, VA: American Counseling Association.

Corey, M. S., & Corey, G. (1998). *Becoming a helper* (3rd ed.). Pacific Grove, CA: Brookes/Cole.

Corey, M. S., & Corey, G. (2003). *Becoming a helper* (4th ed.). Pacific Grove, CA: Brookes/Cole.

Coulehan, J. (1980). Navajo Indian medicine: Implications for healing. *Journal of Family Practice, 10,* 55–61.

Courtois, C. (1988). *Healing the incest wound: Adult survivors in therapy.* New York: Norton.

Cousins, N. (1979). *Anatomy of an illness.* New York: W. W. Norton.

Csikszentmihalyi, M., & Nakamura, J. (2002). The concept of flow. In C. R. Snyder and S. J. Lopez (Eds.), *Handbook of positive psychology.* New York: Oxford University Press.

Dalai Lama. (1999). *Ethics for the new millennium.* New York: Riverhead Books/Penguin Putnam.

Danieli, Y. (1996). Who takes care of the caregiver? In R. J. Apfel & B. Simon (Eds.), *Minefields in their hearts* (pp. 189–205). New Haven, CT: Yale University Press.

Davis, M. H. (1983). Measuring individual differences in empathy: Evidence for a multidimensional approach. *Journal of Personality and Social Psychology, 44*(1), 113–126.

Davis, M. H., Mitchell, K. V., Hall, J. A., Lothert, J., Snapp, T., & Meyer, M. (1999). Empathy, expectations, and situational preferences: Personality influences on the decision to participate in volunteer helping behaviors. *Journal of Personality, 67*(3), 469–503.

DeVera, N. (2003). Perspectives on healing foot ulcers by Yaquis with diabetes. *Journal of Transcultural Nursing, 14*(1), 39–47.

DiCarlo, R. E. (1996). Human potential: From Esalen to mainstreet. *HealthWorld.* Retrieved February 27, 2008, from http://www.healthy.net/scr/interview.asp?Id=203

Dlugos, R. F., & Friedlander, M. L. (2001). Passionately committed psychotherapists: A qualitative study of their experiences. *Professional Psychology, 32*(3), 298–304.

Dossey, L. (1993). *Healing words.* San Francisco: HarperSanFrancisco.

Duan, C. (2000). Being empathic: The role of motivation to empathize and the nature of target emotions. *Motivation and Emotion, 24*(1), 29–49.

Duan, C., & Hill, C. E. (1996). The current state of empathy research. *Journal of Counseling Psychology, 43,* 261–274.

Dymond, R. F. (1949). A scale for the measurement of empathic ability. *Journal of Counseling Psychology, 13,* 127–133.

Egan, G. (1998). *The skilled helper: A problem-management approach to helping* (6th ed.). Pacific Grove, CA: Brookes/Cole.

Egan, G. (2002). *The skilled helper* (7th ed.). Pacific Grove, CA: Brooks/Cole.

Eisner, B. (1995). Notes on the mysterious phenomenon of loading. *Advances: The Journal of Mind-Body Health, 11*(2), 55–57.

Eliade, M. (1964). *Shamanism: Archaic techniques of ecstasy.* New York: Pantheon.

Elliott, W. (1996). *Tying rocks to clouds: Meetings and conversations with wise and spiritual people.* New York: Image Books/Doubleday.

Emoto, M. (2004). *The hidden messages in water.* Hillsboro, OR: Beyond Words.

Evans, R. W. (2007). Diagnostic testing for chronic daily headache. *Current Pain and Headache Reports, 11,* 47–52.

Fanning, P. (1994). *Taking control of your life.* Oakland, CA: New Harbinger.

Fanning, P. (1994). *Visualization for change: Using the creative power of your imagination for self-improvement, therapy, healing & pleasure (2nd ed.).* Oakland, CA: New Harbinger.

Feldman Barrett, L., Bliss Moreau, E., Duncan, S. L., Rauch, S. L., & Wright, C. I. (2007). The amygdale and the experience of affect. *Social Cognitive Affect in Neuroscience, 2*(2), 73–83.

Feller, C. P., & Cottone, R. R. (2003). The importance of empathy in the therapeutic alliance. *Journal of Humanistic Counseling, Education, and Development, 42,* 53–60.

Figley, C. R. (1993). Coping with stressors on the home front. *Journal of Social Issues, 49*(4), 51–71.

Figley, C. R. (1995). *Compassion fatigue: Coping with secondary traumatic stress disorder in those who treat the traumatized.* Bristol, PA: Brunner/Mazel.

Figley, C. R. (2002a). Compassion fatigue: Psychotherapists' chronic lack of self care. *Psychotherapy in Practice, 58*(11), 1433–1441.

Figley, C. R. (2002b). *Treating compassion fatigue.* New York: Brunner-Routledge.

Figley, C. R., & Stamm, B. H. (1996). Psychometric review of compassion fatigue self test. In B. H. Stamm (Ed.), *Measurement of stress, trauma, and adaptation.* Lutherville, MD: Sidran Press.

Foundation for Shamanic Studies. (2007). Retrieved October 16, 2007, from http://www.shamanism.org/workshops/announcement.php?aid=1

Fox, M., & Sheldrake, R. (1996). *The physics of angels: Exploring the realm where science and spirit meet.* San Francisco: HarperSanFrancisco.

Frankl, V. E. (1963). *Man's search for meaning.* New York: Pocket Books.

Freeman, S. C. (1993). Client-centered therapy with diverse populations: The universal within the specific. *Journal of Multicultural Counseling and Development, 21*(1), 248–254.

Freudenberger, H. J. (1974). Staff burnout. *Journal of Social Issues, 30*(1), 159–161.

Gelso, C. J., & Hayes, J. A. (1998). *The psychotherapeutic relationship: Theory, research, and practice.* New York: John Wiley & Sons.

Gentile, S., Delaroziere, J. C., Favre, F., Samuc, R., & San Marco, J. L. (2003). Validation of the French "multidimensional fatigue inventory" (MFI 20). *European Journal of Cancer Care, 12,* 58–64.

Goleman, D. (1995). *Emotional intelligence: Why it can matter more than IQ for character, health, and life long achievement.* New York: Bantam Books.

Goleman, D. (2003). *Healing emotions: Conversations with the Dalai Lama on mindfulness, emotions, and health.* Boston: Shambhala.

Goodwin, L. R. (2002). *The button therapy book: A practical psychological self-help book and holistic cognitive counseling manual for mental health professionals.* Victoria, British Columbia, Canada: CA Trafford.

Gould, D. (1990). Empathy: A review of the literature with suggestions for an alternative research strategy. *Journal of Advanced Nursing, 15,* 1167–1174.

Graham, M. (2005). Maat: An African-centered paradigm for psychological and spiritual healing. In R. Moodley & W. West (Eds.), *Integrating traditional healing practices into counseling and psychotherapy* (pp. 210–220). Thousand Oaks, CA: Sage.

Greenberg, L. S., Watson, J. C., Elliott, R., & Bohart, A. C. (2001). Empathy. *Psychotherapy, 38*(4), 380–384.

Greene, B. (1999). *The elegant universe: Superstrings, hidden dimensions, and the quest for the ultimate theory.* New York: W. W. Norton.

Groff, S. (1981). *Beyond the brain.* Albany: State University of New York Press.

Gubi, P. (2002, June). *Practice behind closed doors: Challenging the taboo of prayer in mainstream counseling culture.* Paper presented at the Annual Conference of the Society for Psychotherapy Research (International), Santa Barbara, CA.

Gurman, A. S. (1977). The patient's perception of the therapeutic relationship. In A. S. Gurman & A. E. Razin (Eds.), *Effective psychotherapy: A handbook of research* (pp. 503–543). New York: Pergamon.

Halloran, T. M., & Linton, J. M. (2000). Stress on the job: Self-care resources for counselors. *Journal of Mental Health Counseling, 22*(4), 354–364.

Hamilton Usher, C. (1989). Recognizing cultural bias in counseling theory and practice: The case of Rogers. *Journal of Multicultural Counseling and Development, 17,* 62–71.

Harley, D. A., Stebnicki, M. A., & Rollins, C. W. (2000). Applying empowerment evaluation as a tool for self-improvement and community development with culturally diverse populations. *Journal of Community Development Society, 31*(2), 348–364.

Harner, M. (1990). *The way of the shaman.* San Francisco: HarperSanFrancisco.

Hauck, R. (1994). *Angels: The mysterious messengers.* New York: Ballantine Books.

Hawking, S. (1988). *A brief history of time: From the big bang to black holes.* New York: Bantam Books.

Hayes, J. A., Gelso, C. J., Van Wagoner, S. L., & Diemer, R. A. (1991). Managing countertransference: What the experts think. *Psychological Reports, 69,* 139–148.

Hogan, R. (1969). Development of an empathic scale. *Journal of Counsulting Clinical Psychology, 33,* 307–316.

Holt Hutton, R., & Roscoe, E. M. (1901). *Aspects of religious and scientific thought.* New York: MacMillan.

Honervogt, T. (1998). *The power of Reiki: An ancient hands-on healing technique.* New York: Henry Holt.

Hueting, J. E., & Sarphati, H. R. (1966). Measuring fatigue. *Journal of Applied Psychology, 50*(6), 545–538.

Huther, G. (2006). *The compassionate brain: How empathy creates intelligence.* Boston: Trumpeter.

Ibrahim, F. (1991). Contribution of cultural world view to generic counseling and development. *Journal of Counseling & Development, 70,* 13–19.

Ingerman, S. (1991). *Soul retrieval: Mending the fragmented self.* San Francisco: HarperSanFrancisco.

Institute of Medicine and the National Academy of Sciences (IMNAS). (2004). Healthy People 2010, Leading health indicators: A report by the Institute of Medicine and National Academy of Sciences. Retrieved November 15, 2004, from http://www.healthypeople.gov/document/html/uih/uih_4.htm

Institute of Noetic Sciences [IONS]. (2007). Retrieved October 16, 2007, from www.ions.org

International Center for Reiki Training [ICRT]. (2007). Southfield, MI. Retrieved February 22, 2008, from www.reiki.org

Ivey, A. E., & Ivey, M. B. (1999). *Intentional interviewing and counseling: Facilitating client development in a multicultural society.* Pacific Grove, CA: Brooks/Cole.

Jackson, S. W. (1992). The listening healer in the history of psychological healing. *American Journal of Psychiatry, 149,* 1623–1632.

Jenkins, S. R., & Baird, S. (2002). Secondary traumatic stress and vicarious trauma: A validational study. *Journal of Traumatic Stress, 15*(5), 423–432.

Joinson, C. (1992). Coping and compassion fatigue. *Nursing, 22*(4), 116–122.

Jones, M. N. (2007). [Practice characteristics of professional helpers experiencing burnout and compassion fatigue.] Unpublished raw data.

Jung, C. G. (1973). Psychology and religion: East and west. In W. McGuire & R.F.C. Hull (Eds. and Trans.), *The collected works of C. G. Jung* (Vol. 11, pp. 5–105). Princeton, NJ: Princeton University Press. (Original work published 1937)

Junn, E. N., Morton, K. R., & Yee, I. (1995). The "gibberish" exercise: Facilitating empathetic multicultural awareness. *Journal of Instructional Psychology, 22,* 324–329.

Kabat-Zinn, J. (1990). *Full catastrophe living: Using the wisdom of your body and mind to face stress, pain, and illness.* New York: Dell.

Kabat-Zinn, J. (1994). *Wherever you go, there you are: Mindfulness meditation in everyday life.* New York: Hyperion.

Katz, R. L. (1963). *Empathy: Its nature and uses.* New York: Free Press.

Kelsey, M. (1986). *Transcend: A guide to the spiritual quest.* New York: Crossroads.

Kerr, W. A., & Speroff, B. G. (1954). Validation and evaluation of the empathy test. *Journal of General Psychology, 50,* 369–376.

Knobel, H., Javard Loge, J., Brenne, E., Fayers, P., Jensen Hjermstad, M., & Kaasa, S. (2003). The validity of EORIC QLQ-C30 fatigue scale in advanced cancer patients and cancer survivors. *Palliative Medicine, 17,* 664–672.

Kushner, H. S. (1980). *When bad things happen to good people.* New York: Avon Books.

La Monica, E. L. (1981). Construct validity of an empathy instrument. *Research in Nursing and Health, 4,* 389–400.

Lane, R. D. (2000). Levels of emotional awareness: Neurological, psychological, and social perspectives. In R. Bar-On and J. D. Parker (Eds.), *The handbook of emotional intelligence: Theory, development, assessment, and application at home, school, and in the workplace* (pp. 171–214). San Francisco: Jossey-Bass.

Lawson, G., & Venart, B. (2005). Preventing counselor impairment: Vulnerability, wellness, and resilience. Retrieved July 10, 2007, from http://www.creating-joy.com/taskforce/PDF/ACA_taskforce_vista.pdf

Lazarus, R. S. (1999). *Stress and emotion: A new synthesis.* New York: Springer Publishing.

Lee, C. C., & Richardson, B. L. (1991). *Multicultural issues in counseling: New approaches to diversity.* Alexandria, VA: American Counseling Association.

Linehan, M. M., & Osman, A. (2002). Using reasons for living to connect to American Indian healing traditions. *Journal of Sociology and Social Welfare, 29*(1), 1–6.

Linley, P. A., & Joseph, S. (2007). Therapy work and therapists' positive and negative well-being. *Journal of Social and Clinical Psychology, 26*(3), 385–403.

Littrell, J. M., Lee-Borden, N., & Lorenz, J. A. (1979). A developmental framework for counseling supervision. *Counselor Education and Supervision, 19,* 119–136.

Loganbill, C., Hardy, E., & Delworth, U. (1982). Supervision: A conceptual model. *Counseling Psychologist, 10,* 3–42.

Marci, C. D., Ham, J., Moran, E., & Orr, S. P. (2007). Physiologic correlates of perceived therapist empathy and social-emotional process during psychotherapy. *Journal of Nervous and Mental Disorders, 195,* 103–111.

Maslach, C. (1982). *The burnout: The cost of caring.* Englewood Cliffs, NJ: Prentice-Hall.

Maslach, C. (2003). *Burnout: The cost of caring.* Cambridge, MA: Malor Books.

Maslach, C., & Jackson, S. E. (1981). The measurement of experienced burnout. *Journal of Occupational Behavior, 2,* 99–113.

Maslach, C., & Jackson, S. E. (1986). *Maslach burnout inventory manual* (2nd ed.). Palo Alto, CA: Consulting Psychologists Press.

Maslach, C., & Jackson, S. E. (1996). *The Maslach burnout inventory. Manual* (2nd ed.). Palo Alto, CA: Sage.

Maslow, A. H. (1968). *Toward a psychology of being* (2nd ed.). New York: Van Nostrand Reinhold.

Mayne, T. J., & Bonanno, G. A. (2001). *Emotions: Current issues and future directions.* New York: Guilford Press.

Mayne, T. J., & Ramsey, J. (2001). The structure of emotion: A nonlinear dynamic systems approach. In T. J. Mayne and G. A. Bonanno (Eds.), *Emotions: Current issues and future directions* (pp. 1–37). New York: Guilford Press.

McCann, L., & Pearlman, L. A. (1989). Vicarious traumatization: A framework for understanding the psychological effects of working with victims. *Journal of Traumatic Stress, 3*(1), 131–149.

McCann, L., & Pearlman, L. A. (1990a). *Psychological trauma and the adult survivor: Theory, therapy, and transformation.* New York: Brunner/Mazel.

McCann, L., & Pearlman, L. A. (1990b). Vicarious traumatization: A framework for understanding the psychological effects of working with victims. *Journal of Traumatic Stress, 3*(1), 131–149.

McCormick, R. M. (1997). Healing through interdependence: The role of connecting in First Nations healing practices. *Canadian Journal of Counselling, 31*(3), 172–184.

McKenna, J. J. (2000). On being at both center and circumference: The role of personal discipline and collective wisdom in the recovery of soul. In M. E. Miller & A. N. West (Eds.), *Spirituality, ethics, and relationship in adulthood: Clinical and theoretical explorations* (pp. 257–282). Madison, CT: Psychsocial Press.

Mehl-Madrona, L. (1997). *Coyote medicine: Lessons from Native American healing.* New York: Fireside/Simon & Schuster.

Merton, T. (1961). *New seeds of contemplation.* New York: New Directions.

Michielsen, H. J., DeVries, J., Van Heck, G. L., Van de Vijver, F.J.R., & Sijtsma, K. (2004). Examination of the dimensionality of fatigue. *European Journal of Psychological Assessment, 20*(1), 39–48.

Mijares, S. G. (2003). *Modern psychology and ancient wisdom: Psychological healing practices from the world's religious traditions.* Binghamton, NY: The Haworth Integrative Healing Press.

Miller, G. (2003). *Incorporating spirituality in counseling and psychotherapy: Theory and technique.* Hoboken, NJ: John Wiley & Sons.

Miller, G. (2005, September). Spirituality and psychotherapy. Symposium conducted at the annual meeting of the Licensed Professional Counseling Association of North Carolina (LPCANC). Greensboro, NC.

Miller, G. D., & Baldwin, D. C. (1987). Implications of the wounded-healer paradigm for the use of the self in therapy. In M. Baldwin & V. Satir (Eds.), *The use of self in therapy* (pp. 130–151). New York: Haworth Press.

Miller, L. (1998). Our own medicine: Traumatized psychotherapists and the stresses of doing therapy. *Psychotherapy, 25*(2),137–146.

Mitchell, K. K. (1994). *Reiki: A torch in daylight.* St. Charles, IL: Mind Rivers.

Moodley, R. (2005). Shamanic performances: Healing through magic and the supernatural. In R. Moodley & W. West (Eds.), *Integrating traditional healing practices into counseling and psychotherapy* (pp. 2–14). Thousand Oaks, CA: Sage.

Moodley, R. & West, W. (2005). *Integrating traditional healing practices into counseling and psychotherapy.* Thousand Oaks, CA: Sage.

Moody, R. (2005, November). Life after life. Symposium conducted at the annual meeting of the Professional Association of Rehabilitation Counselors (PARC). East Carolina University, Greenville, NC.

Moore, T. (1996). *The re-enchantment of everyday life.* New York: Harper Perennial.

Myers, J. E., & Sweeney, T. J. (2004). The indivisible self: An evidence-based model of wellness. *Journal of Individual Psychology, 60,* 234–244.

Myers, J. E., & Sweeney, T. J. (2005). *Counseling for wellness: Theory, research, and practice.* Alexandria, VA: American Counseling Association.

Myers, J. E., Sweeney, T. J., & Witmer, J. M. (2000). The wheel of wellness counseling for wellness: A holistic model for treatment planning. *Journal of Counseling & Development, 78,* 251–266.

Naisbitt, J. (1984). *Megatrends: Ten new directions transforming our lives.* New York: Warner Books.

National Board for Certified Counselors (NBCC). (2007). National Board for Certified Counselors Code of Ethics for Supervisors. Retrieved October 3, 2007, from http://www.nbcc.org/extras/pdfs/ethics/nbcc-codeofethics.pdf

National Library of Medicine, National Institutes of Health. (2007). Retrieved October 21, 2007, from http://www.nlm.nih.gov/hmd/greek/greek_asclepius.html

Native Languages of the Americas. (2007). Retrieved May 6, 2007, from http://www.native-languages.org/help.htm

Newsome, S., Chambers Christopher, J., Dahlen, P., & Christopher, S. (2006). Teaching counselors self-care through mindfulness practices. *Teachers College Record, 108*(9), 1881–1900.

Nezlek, J. B., Feist, G. J., Wilson, C., & Plesko, R. M. (2001). Day-to-day variability in empathy as a function of daily events and mood. *Journal of Research in Personality, 35*, 401–423.

Nouwen, H.J.M. (1972). *The wounded healer.* New York: Image Books/Doubleday.

O'Halloran, T. M., & Linton, J. M. (2000). Stress on the job: Self-care resources for counselors. *Journal of Mental Health Counseling, 22*, 354–365.

Orlinsky, D. E., & Ronnestad, M. H. (2005). *How therapists develop: A study of therapeutic work and professional growth.* Washington, DC: American Psychological Association.

Oschman, J. L. (2002). Science and the human energy field. *Reiki News Magazine, 1*(3), 1–8.

Pargament, K. L., & Zinnbauer, B. J. (2000). Working with the sacred: Four approaches to religious and spiritual issues in counseling. *Journal of Counseling and Development, 78*, 162–171.

Parson, E. R. (1993). Ethnotherapeutic empathy (EthE): II: Techniques in interpersonal cognition and vicarious experience across cultures. *Journal of Contemporary Psychotherapy, 23*, 171–182.

Patterson, C. H. (1984). Empathy, warmth, and genuineness: A review of reviews. *Psychotherapy, 21*, 431–438.

Pearlman, L. A., & MacIan, P. S. (1995). Vicarious traumatization: An empirical study of the effects of trauma work on trauma therapists. *Professional Psychology: Research and Practice, 26*(6), 558–565.

Pearlman, L. A., & Saakvitne, K. W. (1995). Treating therapists with vicarious traumatization and secondary traumatic stress disorders. In C. R. Figley (Ed.), *Compassion fatigue: Coping with secondary traumatic stress disorder in those who treat the traumatized* (pp. 150–177). Bristol, PA: Brunner/Mazel.

Peck, M. S. (1993). *Further along the road less traveled: The unending journey toward spiritual growth.* New York: Simon & Schuster.

Pedersen, P. (2000). *A handbook for developing multicultural awareness* (3rd ed.). Alexandria, VA: American Counseling Association.

Pert, C. B., Dreher, H. E., & Ruff, M. R. (2005). The psychosomatic network: Foundations of mind-body medicine. In M. Schlitz, T. Amorok, and M. Micozzi (Eds.), *Consciousness and healing: Integral approaches to mind-body medicine* (pp. 61–78). St. Louis, MO: Elsevier, Churchill, & Livingstone.

Pines, A., & Aronson, E. (1988). *Career burnout: Causes and cures.* New York: Free Press.

Pirsig, R. (1976). *Zen and the art of motorcycle maintenance.* New York: Bantam.

Polanski, P. J. (2003). Spirituality and supervision. *Counseling and Values, 47*(2), 131–141.

Ponterotto, J. G., & Bensesch, K. F. (1988). An organizational framework for understanding the role of culture in counseling. *Journal of Counseling & Development, 66*, 237–241.

Prince, M. I., & Jones, D.E.J. (2001). Measuring fatigue in medically unwell and distressed patients. *Current Opinion in Psychiatry, 14*(6), 585–590.

Prochaska, J. O., & DiClemente, C. C. (1982) Transtheoretical therapy: Toward a more integrative model of change. *Psychotherapy: Theory, Research and Practice, 19*, 276–288.

Prochaska J. O., DiClemente, C. C., & Norcross, J. C. (1992). In search of how people change. *American Psychologist, 47*, 1102–11044.

Rae Jenkins, S., & Baird, S. (2002). Secondary traumatic stress and vicarious trauma: A validational study. *Journal of Traumatic Stress, 15*(5), 423–432.

Rand, W. L. (2005). *The Reiki touch: Develop your skills to heal yourself and others.* Boulder, CO: Sounds True.

Rando, T. A. (1984). *Grief, death and dying: Clinical interventions for caregivers.* Champaign, IL: Research Press.

Reeve, M. E. (2000). Concept of illness and treatment practice in a Caboclo community of the Lower Amazon. *Medical Anthropology Quarterly, 14*(1), 96–108.

Ridley, C. R. (1995). *Overcoming unintentional racism in counseling and therapy: A practitioner's guide to intentional intervention.* Thousand Oaks, CA: Sage.

Ridley, C. R., & Lingle, D. W. (1996). Cultural empathy in multicultural counseling: A multidimensional process model. In P. B. Pederson & J. G. Draguns (Eds.), *Counseling across cultures* (4th ed, pp. 21–46). Thousand Oaks, CA: Sage.

Ridley, C. R., Mendoza, D. W., & Kanitz, B. E. (1994). Multicultural training: Reexamination, operationalization, and integration. *The Counseling Psychologist, 22,* 227–289.

Robinson, D. (2005). Way of the Shaman. *Foundation for Shamanic Studies.* Retrieved February 28, 2008, from http://www.shamanism.org/workshops/calendar.php?Wkshp_ID=10

Rogers, C. R. (1951). *Client-centered therapy: Its current practice, implications, and theory.* Boston: Houghton Mifflin.

Rogers, C. R. (1957). The necessary and sufficient conditions of therapeutic personality change. *Journal of Consulting Psychology, 21,* 95–103.

Rogers, C. R. (1959). A theory of therapy, personality, and interpersonal relationships as developed in the client-centered framework. In S. Koch (Ed.), *Psychology: The study of a science. Vol. 3. Formulations of the person and the social context* (pp. 184–256). New York: McGraw-Hill.

Rogers, C. R. (1961). *On becoming a person.* Cambridge, MA: Riverside Press.

Rogers, C. R. (1980). *A way of being.* Boston, MA: Houghton Mifflin.

Russell, R. K., Crimmings, A. M., & Lent, R. W. (1984). Counselor training and supervision: Theory and research. In S. D. Brown & R. W. Lent (Eds.), *Handbook of counseling psychology* (pp. 625–681). New York: John Wiley.

Salston, M., & Figley, C. R. (2003). Secondary traumatic stress effects of working with survivors of criminal victimization. *Journal of Traumatic Stress, 16*(2), 167–174.

Sapolsky, R. M. (1998). *Why zebras don't get ulcers: An updated guide to stress, stress-related diseases, and coping.* New York: W. H. Freeman.

Schaper, D., & Camp, C. A. (2004). *Labyrinths from the outside in: Walking to spiritual insight—A beginner's guide.* Woodstock, VT: Skylight Paths.

Schauben, L. J., & Frazier, P. (1995). Vicarious trauma: The effects on female counselors of working with sexual violence survivors. *Psychology of Women Quarterly, 19,* 49–64.

Schwartz, C. E. (1994). Introduction: Old methodological challenges and new mind-body links in psychoneuroimmunology. *Advances: Journal of Mind-Body Health, 10*(4), 4–7.

Schwid, S. R., Covington, M., Segal, B. M., & Goodman, A. D. (2002). Fatigue in multiple sclerosis: Current understanding and future directions. *Journal of Rehabilitation Research and Development, 39*(2), 211–224.

Scotland, E. (1969). Exploratory studies of empathy. In L. Berkowitz (Ed.), *Advances in experimental social psychology* (Vol. 4, pp. 271–314). New York: Academic Press.

Scott, N. E., & Borodovsky, L. G. (1990). Effective use of cultural role taking. *Professional Psychology: Research and Practice, 21*(3), 167–170.

Seaward, B. L. (1997). *Stand like mountain flow like water: Reflections on stress and human spirituality.* Deerfield Beach, FL: Health Communications.

Seaward, B. L. (2006). *Essentials of managing stress.* Boston: Jones & Bartlett.

Seibert, A. (2005). *The resiliency advantage: Master change, thrive under pressure, and bounce back from setbacks.* San Francisco: Berrett-Koehler.

Selye, H. (1976). *The stress of life.* New York: McGraw-Hill.

Shafranske, E. P., & Malony, H. N. (1996). Religion and the clinical practice of psychology: The case for inclusion. In E. P. Shafranske (Ed.), *Religion and the clinical practice of psychology.* Washington, DC: American Psychological Association.

Shapiro, S. L., Warren Brown, K., & Biegel, G. M. (2007). Teaching self-care to caregivers: Effects of mindfulness-based stress reduction on the mental health of therapists in training. *Training and Education in Professional Psychology, 1,* 105–115.

Shealy, N., & Myss, C. (1990). *The creation of health.* Walpole, NH: Stillpoint Press.

Siegel, B. S. (1990). *Peace, love, and healing.* New York: Harper & Row.

Simonton, O. C. (1978). *Getting well again.* New York: Bantam Books.

Skovholt, T. A., Gries, T. L. & Hanson, M. R. (2001). Career counseling for longevity: Self-care and burnout prevention strategies for counselor resilience. *Journal of Career Development 27*(3), 167–176.

Skovholt, T. M., Tabitha, L., & Hanson, M. R. (2001). Career counseling for longevity: Self-care and burnout prevention strategies for counselor resilience. *Journal of Career Development, 27*(3), 167–175.

Skovholt, T. M., & Ronnestad, M. H. (1995). *The evolving professional self: Stages and themes in therapist and counselor development.* New York: John Wiley & Sons.

Sollod, R. N. (2005). Spiritual and healing approaches in psychotherapeutic practice. In R. Moodley & W. West (Eds.), *Integrating traditional healing practices into counseling and psychotherapy* (pp. 270–281). Thousand Oaks, CA: Sage.

Stamm, B. H. (1995) *Compassion fatigue: Coping with secondary traumatic stress disorder in those who treat the traumatized.* New York: Brunner-Routledge.

Stamm, B. H. (2005). *The Professional Quality of Life Scale: Compassion satisfaction, burnout and compassion fatigue/secondary trauma scales.* Institute of Rural Health, Idaho State University. Retrieved February 27, 2007, from http://www.isu.edu/'bhstamm. A collaborative publication with Sidran Press, www.sidran.org

Stebnicki, M. A., Allen, H. A., & Janikowski, T. P. (1997). Development of an instrument to assess perceived helpfulness of clinical supervisory behaviors among rehabilitation post-practicum supervisees. *Rehabilitation Education, 11*(4), 307–322.

Stebnicki, M. A. (1998). Clinical supervision in rehabilitation counseling. *Rehabilitation Education, 12*(2), 137–159.

Stebnicki, M. A. (1999, April). *Grief reactions among rehabilitation professionals: Dealing effectively with empathy fatigue.* Paper presented at the NRCA/ARCA Alliance Annual Training Conference, Dallas, TX.

Stebnicki, M. A. (2000). Stress and grief reactions among rehabilitation professionals: Dealing effectively with empathy fatigue. *Journal of Rehabilitation, 6*(1), 23–29.

Stebnicki, M. A. (2001). Psychosocial response to extraordinary stressful and traumatic life events: Principles and practices for rehabilitation counselors. *New Directions in Rehabilitation, 12*(6), 57–71.

Stebnicki, M. A. (2006). Integrating spirituality in rehabilitation counselor supervision. *Rehabilitation Education, 20*(2), 137–159.

Stebnicki, M. A. (2007a). Empathy fatigue: Healing the mind, body, and spirit of professional counselors. *Journal of Psychiatric Rehabilitation, 10*(4), 317–338.

Stebnicki, M. A. (2007b). Integrating spirituality in rehabilitation counseling. *Rehabilitation Education, 20*(2), 115–132.

Stebnicki, M. A. (2007c). *What is adolescent mental health? Helping disconnected and at-risk youth to become whole.* Lewiston, NY: Edwin Mellen Press.

Stein, K. D., Jacobsen, P. B., Blanchard, C. M., & Thors, C. (2004). Further validation of the multidimensional fatigue symptom inventory—short form. *Journal of Pain and Symptom Management, 27*(1), 14–23.

Stoltenberg, C. (1981). Approaching supervision from a developmental perspective: The counselor-complexity model. *Journal of Counseling Psychologists, 28,* 59–65.

Stoltenberg, C. D., & Delworth, U. (1988). Developmental models of supervision: It is development?—A response to Holloway. *Professional Psychology: Research and Practice, 19*(2), 134–137.

Sue, D. W. (1996). Ethical issues in multicultural counseling. In B. Herlihy & G. Corey (Eds.), *ACA ethical standards casebook* (5th ed., pp. 193–200). Alexandria, VA: American Counseling Association.

Sue, D. W., & Sue, D. (1990). *Counseling the culturally different* (2nd ed.). New York: Wiley & Sons.

Sweeney, T. J., & Myers, J. E. (2005). Optimizing human development: A new paradigm for helping. In A. Ivey, M. B. Ivey, J. E. Myers, & T. J. Sweeney (Eds.), *Developing strategies for helpers* (2nd ed., pp. 39–68). Amherst, MA: Microtraining.

Tafoya, T., & Kouris, N. (2003). Dancing the circle: Native American concepts of healing. In S. G. Mijares (Ed.), *Modern psychology and ancient wisdom: Psychological healing practices from the world's religious traditions* (pp. 125–146). New York: Haworth Integrative Healing Press.

Tillich, P. (1952). *The courage to be.* New Haven, CT: Yale University Press.

Trippany, R. L., White Kress, V. E., & Allen Wilcoxon, S. (2004). Preventing vicarious trauma: What counselors should know when working with trauma survivors. *Journal of Counseling & Development, 82,* 31–37.

Truax, C. B. (1963). Effective ingredients in psychotherapy: An approach to unraveling the patient-therapist interaction. *Journal of Counseling Psychology, 10,* 256–263.

Truax, C. B. (1967). A scale for rating of accurate empathy. In C. R. Rogers, E. T. Gendlin, D. J. Kiesler, & C. B. Truax (Eds.), *The therapeutic relationship and its impact: A study of psychotherapy and schizophrenics* (pp. 555–568). Madison: University of Wisconsin Press.

Truax, C. B., & Carkhuff, R. R. (1967). *Towards effective counseling and psychotherapy.* Chicago: Aldine-Atherton.

Updegraff, J. A., & Taylor, S. E. (2000). From vulnerability to growth: Positive and negative effects of stressful life events. In T. H. Harvey and E. Miller (Eds.), *Loss and trauma.* Philadelphia: Brunner-Routledge.

U.S. Census Bureau. (2000, January). *National population projections by race, Hispanic origin, and nativity.* Retrieved February 18, 2007, from http://www.census.gov/population/www/projections/natsum-T5.html

Vash, C. L. (1994). *Personality and adversity: Psychospiritual aspects of rehabilitation.* New York: Springer Publishing.

Vash, C. L., & Crewe, N. M. (2004). *Psychology and disability* (2nd ed.). New York: Springer Publishing.

Walsh, R., & Vaughn, F. (1993). *Paths beyond ego: A transpersonal vision.* New York: Putnam.

Wang, Y., Davidson, M. M., Yakushko, O. F., Bielstein Savoy, H., Tan, J. A., & Bleier, J. K. (2003). The scale of ethnocultural empathy: Development, validation, and reliability. *Journal of Counseling Psychology, 50*(2), 221–234.

Weil, A. (1995). *Spontaneous healing.* New York: Ballantine Publishing Group.

Weil, A. (2005). *Healthy aging: A lifelong guide to your physical and spiritual well-being.* New York: Alfred A. Knopf.

Weiss, L. (2004). *Therapist's guide to self-care.* New York: Brunner-Routledge.

West, W. S. (1997). Integrating psychotherapy and healing. *British Journal of Guidance and Counseling, 25,* 291–312.

West, W. S. (2003). The culture of psychotherapy supervision. *Counselling Psychotherapy Research, 3,* 123–126.

West, W. S. (2005). Crossing the line between talking therapies and spiritual healing. In R. Moodley & W. West (Eds.), *Integrating traditional healing practices into counseling and psychotherapy* (pp. 38–49). Thousand Oaks, CA: Sage.

Wester-Anderson, J. (1994). *Joan Wester Anderson on angels.* In R. Hauck (Ed.), *Angels: The mysterious messengers* (pp. 3–33). New York: Ballantine Books.

WHOQOL. (1998). Development of the World Health Organization WHOQOL-BREF Quality of Life Assessment. *Psychological Medicine, 28,* 551–558.

Wilber, K. (1996). *A brief history of everything.* Boston: Shambhala.

Wilber, K. (2006). *Integral spirituality: A startling new role for religion in the modern and postmodern world.* Boston: Shambhala.

Wilson, J. P. (2001). An overview of clinical considerations and principles in the treatment of PTSD. In J. P. Wilson, M. J. Friedman, and J. D. Lindy (Eds.), *Treating psychological trauma and PTSD* (pp. 59–93). New York: Guilford Press.

Witmer, J. M., & Granello, P. F. (2005). Wellness in counselor education and supervision. In J. E. Meyers & T. J. Sweeney (Eds.), *Counseling for wellness: Theory, research, and practice* (pp. 261–271). Alexandria, VA: American Counseling Association.

Witmer, J. M., & Sweeney, T. J., (1992). A holistic model for wellness and prevention over the lifespan. *Journal of Counseling & Development, 71,* 140–148.

Witmer, J. M., Sweeney, T. J., & Myers, J. E. (1998). *The wheel of wellness.* Greensboro, NC: Authors.

Worldwide Productions. (2007). Retrieved October 28, 2007, from http://www.timeofthe sixthsun.com/index.php?option=com_frontpage&Itemid=1

Worrall, A. A., & Worrall, O. N. (1970). *Explore your psychic world.* New York: Harper & Row.

Worthington, E. L., Jr. (1987). Changes in supervision as counselors and supervisors gain experience: A review. *Professional Psychology: Research and Practice, 18,* 189–208.

Worthington, E. L., Jr. (1988). Understanding the values of religious clients: A model and its application to counseling. *Journal of Counseling Psychology, 35*(2), 166–174.

Young, M. (1998). *Learning the art of helping.* Upper Saddle River, NJ: Prentice Hall.

Appendix: Special Resource List for Self-Care

American Counseling Association. (2003). *ACA Taskforce on Counselor Wellness and Impairment*. Retrieved March 3, 2006, from http://www.counseling.org/wellness_taskforce/index.htm

Brennan, B. A. (1987). *Hands of light: A guide to healing through the human energy field*. New York: Bantam Books.

Davis, M., Robbins Eshelman, E., & McKay, M. (1995). *The relaxation and stress reduction workbook* (4th ed.). Oakland, CA: New Harbinger.

Fanning, P. (1994). *Taking control of your life*. Oakland, CA: New Harbinger.

Figley, C. R. (2002). *Treating compassion fatigue*. New York: Brunner-Routledge.

Fox, M., & Sheldrake, R. (1996). *The physics of angels: Exploring the realm where science and spirit meet*. San Francisco: HarperSanFrancisco.

Goodwin, L. R. (2002). *The button therapy book: A practical psychological self-help book and holistic cognitive counseling manual for mental health professionals*. Victoria, British Columbia, Canada: CA Trafford.

Harner, M. (1990). *The way of the shaman*. San Francisco: HarperSanFrancisco.

Hauck, R. (1994). *Angels: The mysterious messengers*. New York: Ballantine Books.

Ingerman, S. (1991). *Soul retrieval: Mending the fragmented self*. San Francisco: HarperSanFrancisco.

International Center for Reiki Training, (2007). Southfield, MI, Retrieved from http://www.reiki.org

Kabat-Zinn, J. (1990). *Full catastrophe living: Using the wisdom of your body and mind to face stress, pain, and illness*. New York: Dell.

Kabat-Zinn, J. (1994). *Wherever you go, there you are: Mindfulness meditation in everyday life*. New York: Hyperion.

Kelsey, M. (1986). *Transcend: A guide to the spiritual quest*. New York: Crossroads.

LeShun, L. (1974). *A self-discovery guide of how to meditate*. Boston: Bantam.

Maslach, C. (2003). *Burnout: The cost of caring*. Cambridge, MA: Malor Books.

McKay, M., Davis, M., & Fanning, P. (1997). *Thoughts and feelings: Taking control of your moods and your life*. Oakland, CA: New Harbinger.

Mehl-Madrona, L. (1997). *Coyote medicine: Lessons from Native American healing*. New York: Fireside/Simon & Schuster.

Merton, T. (1961). *New seeds of contemplation*. New York: New Directions.

Miller, G. (2003). *Incorporating spirituality in counseling and psychotherapy: Theory and technique*. Hoboken, NJ: John Wiley & Sons.

Mitchell, K. K. (1994). *Reiki: A torch in daylight*. St. Charles, IL: Mind Rivers.

Monaghan, P., & Diereck, E. G. (1999). *Meditation: The complete guide.* Navato, CA: New World Library.

Moodley, R., & West, W. (2005). *Integrating traditional healing practices into counseling and psychotherapy.* Thousand Oaks, CA: Sage.

Myers, J. E., & Sweeney, T. J. (2005). *Counseling for wellness: Theory, research, and practice.* Alexandria, VA: American Counseling Association.

Schaper, D., & Camp, C. A. (2004). *Labyrinths from the outside in: Walking to spiritual insight—A beginner's guide.* Woodstock, VT: Skylight Paths.

Seaward, B. L. (1997). *Stand like mountain, flow like water.* Deerfield Beach, FL: Health Communications.

Seaward, B. L. (2006). *Essentials of managing stress.* Sudbury, MA: Jones and Bartlett.

Weiss, L. (2004). *Therapist's guide to self-care.* New York: Brunner-Routledge.

Index

SPRINGER / PUBLISHING COMPANY

Grief Counseling and Grief Therapy

A Handbook for the Mental Health Practitioner, Third Edition

J. William Worden

"Worden ... has again provided mental health professionals with a superb guide describing specific principles and procedures that may be helpful in working with bereaved clients undergoing normal or abnormal grief reactions .... an extremely practical book and an invaluable resource."

—*Contemporary Psychology*

In this updated and revised third edition of his classic text, Dr. Worden presents his most recent thinking on bereavement drawn from extensive research, clinical work, and the best of the new literature. Readers will find new information on special types of losses—including children's violent deaths, grief and the elderly, and anticipatory grief—as well as refinements to his basic model for mourning. It now not only includes the four "tasks of mourning" but also seven "mediators of mourning." In addition, a series of vignettes, the best of the first and second editions, plus several new to this edition, bring bereavement issues to life.

Table of Contents

- Preface
- Introduction
- Attachment, Loss, and the Experience of Grief
- Understanding the Mourning Process
- Grief Counseling: Facilitating Uncomplicated Grief
- Abnormal Grief Reactions: Complicated Mourning

- Grief Therapy: Resolving Complicated Mourning
- Grieving Special Types of Losses
- Grief and Family Systems
- The Counselor's Own Grief
- Training for Grief Counseling
- Bibliography
- Index

2001 · 244 pp · Hardcover · 978-0-8261-4162-0

11 West 42nd Street, New York, NY 10036-8002 • Fax: 212-941-7842
Order Toll-Free: 877-687-7476 • Order Online: www.springerpub.com

Healing the Heart of Trauma and Dissociation with EMDR and Ego State Therapy

Carol Forgash, LCSW, BCD
Margaret Copeley, MEd, Editors

"This book pioneers the integration of EMDR with ego state techniques and opens new and exciting vistas for the practitioners of each."

—From the Foreword by **John G. Watkins**, PhD, founder of ego state therapy

**HEALING
THE HEART OF
TRAUMA AND
DISSOCIATION**
with **EMDR** and
Ego State Therapy

Editors   Carol Forgash
Margaret Copeley

The powerful benefits of EMDR in treating PTSD have been solidly validated. In this groundbreaking new work nine master clinicians show how complex PTSD involving dissociation and other challenging diagnoses can be treated safely and effectively. They stress the careful preparation of clients for EMDR and the inclusion of ego state therapy to target the dissociated ego states that arise in response to severe and prolonged trauma.

Special Features

• Key aspects of this new approach to EMDR

• The first definitive look at the use of EMDR to treat dissociation and the dissociative disorders

• Opens a window into the psyches of clients whose healing depends on their therapists' enlistment of integrative interventions

• Provides practical applications for a full range of mental health prac-titioners: psychiatrists, psychologists, social workers, nurses, and counselors

• Clearly outlines the phased treatment that extends the EMDR preparation phase to create safety and stability for complex trauma clients

• Provides cutting edge information for graduate students in the mental health fields

2007 · 384 pp · Hardcover · 978-0-8261-4696-0

**11 West 42nd Street, New York, NY 10036-8002 • Fax: 212-941-7842
Order Toll-Free: 877-687-7476 • Order Online: www.springerpub.com**